The Military Family

THE GUILFORD FAMILY THERAPY SERIES
Alan S. Gurman, Editor

THE MILITARY FAMILY

Dynamics and Treatment

Edited by
FLORENCE W. KASLOW
*Florida Couples and Family Institute
and Duke University*

and

RICHARD I. RIDENOUR
Naval Hospital, San Diego

Foreword by Francis J. Braceland

THE GUILFORD PRESS
New York   London

LIBRARY OF CONGRESS CATALOGING IN PUBLICATION DATA

Main entry under title:

The military family.

(The Guilford family therapy series)
Bibliography: p.
Includes index.
1. Military dependents—Medical care—United States—
Addresses, essays, lectures. 2. Soldiers—United States—
Family relationships—Addresses, essays, lectures.
3. United States—Armed Forces—Medical Care—Addresses,
essays, lectures. 4. Family medicine—United States—
Addresses, essays, lectures. 5. Family social work—
United States—Addresses, essays, lectures. 6. Family
psychotherapy—United States—Addresses, essays, lectures.
I. Kaslow, Florence Whiteman. II. Ridenour, Richard I.
III. Series.
UB403.M55   1984   362.8'2   84-4583
ISBN 0-89862-055-4

Contributors

DAVID T. ARMITAGE, MD, JD, Colonel, Medical Corps, U.S. Army, and Chief, Department of Psychiatry and Neurology, Dwight David Eisenhower Army Medical Center, Fort Gordon, Georgia

JOHN ELDERKIN BELL, EdD, Associate Professor Emeritus, Department of Psychiatry and Behavioral Sciences, Stanford University, Stanford, California; Lecturer, Department of Psychiatry, School of Medicine, University of California, San Francisco, California; Adjunct Professor, Reader, San Francisco Theological Seminary, San Anselmo, California; and formerly, Psychologist, Veterans Administration Hospital, Palo Alto, California

JOHN E. CHURCHILL, MSW, CSW-ACP, Chief of Hypnotherapy, Adult Outpatient Mental Health, Wilford Hall U.S. Air Force Medical Center, Lackland Air Force Base, Texas; and Assistant Practicum Professor, Our Lady of the Lake University, San Antonio, Texas

PATRICIA W. CRIGLER, PhD, Commander, Medical Service Corps, U.S. Navy, and Director, Substance Abuse Department, Naval Hospital, San Diego, California

MELANIE C. EYRE, BA, Budget Specialist, Navy Family Support Program, Washington, D.C.

EDNA J. HUNTER, PhD, Director, Family Research Center, United States International University, San Diego, California

FLORENCE W. KASLOW, PhD, Private practice, West Palm Beach, Florida; Director, Florida Couples and Family Institute, West Palm Beach, Florida; and Adjunct Professor of Medical Psychology, Department of Psychiatry, Duke University, Durham, North Carolina

DAVID V. KEITH, MD, Department of Psychiatry, Park Nicollet Medical Center, Minneapolis, Minnesota

RUTH ANN O'KEEFE, EdD, Director and founder, Navy Family Support Program, Washington, D.C.

RICHARD I. RIDENOUR, MD, Captain, Medical Corps, U.S. Navy, and Psychiatrist and Director, Residency Training Program in Psychiatry, Department of Psychiatry, Naval Hospital, San Diego, California

ALEX R. RODRIGUEZ, MD, Commander, Medical Corps, U.S. Navy, and Medical Director, Civilian Health and Medical Program of the Uniformed Services (CHAMPUS), Department of Defense, Aurora, Colorado

MARIO R. SCHWABE, MD, Captain, U.S. Navy, and Chairman, Department of Psychiatry, National Naval Medical Center, Bethesda, Maryland

DAVID L. SMITH, EdD, Deputy Director, Navy Family Support Program, Washington, D.C.

ROBERT E. STRANGE, MD, Captain, Medical Corps, U.S. Navy, Retired, and Director, Northern Virginia Mental Health Institute, Falls Church, Virginia

CARL A. WHITAKER, MD, Professor Emeritus, Department of Psychiatry, University of Wisconsin Medical School, Clinical Sciences Center, Madison, Wisconsin

THEODORE G. WILLIAMS, MD, Captain, Medical Corps, U.S. Navy, and Chief, Alcohol Rehabilitation Service, Naval Regional Medical Center, Long Beach, California

Foreword

I am honored by being asked to write the foreword to this timely and interesting work, and though the honor pleases me, the responsibility concerns me for I fear not being able to do the book justice. So much has happened and is happening in Naval and military medical practice since I was released from active duty as head of the NP Section and Special Assistant to the Surgeon General nearly 40 years ago that commenting on advances as important as those described herein gives me pause.

The volume is truly a compendium on the professional care of military families and of the various problems they encounter in the service as well as those they bring in with them. Earlier on most of these problems had to be neglected due to the exigencies of building up and preparation for war, years of combat, and then the gigantic task of demobilization. The medical corps had an essential part to play in all phases of this venture, and I fear that families and their problems were neglected or referred to the too few chaplains and the all too few social workers who were part of the military at the time.

While thinking about the contents of this volume I came across two items which accentuated for me the timeliness of its appearance. The first was word that the Navy Bureau of Medicine and Surgery (BuMed), which we served in wartime and thereafter, had been redesignated "Naval Medical Command, Washington, D.C." and "*that it will have a much needed emphasis on health promotion.*" This last mentioned occurrence surely is a major step in the right direction!

The second item was a newspaper article entitled, "They Search for Anchors" with the subtitle, "Submariners' Wives Learn to Call Their Homes Their Ships." The article dealt poignantly with the long absences of husbands and fathers who, in the line of duty, had shipped silently out to sea, usually on missions which would last for months, and who would be incommunicado most of that time. Sometimes these families need help and, fortunately, now it is attainable.

Though this book is written primarily for professional therapists working with military families, it is bound to appeal to a much wider group for it treats problems comparable to those encountered daily in civilian life. It will have to be tailored for those in civilian life, because the great force of government will not exert the same influence, and families will not have that security to fall back upon.

The editors have done a first-class job, both in the selection of material to be discussed and in the quality and knowledge of the contributors. Ridenour, from his viewpoint as a Navy Captain and an educator, carefully differentiates the problems and dilemmas encountered between military and civilian life. As a Navy officer he has had it impressed upon him that duty comes first. He knows the regular occurrence of household relocations and the concurrent disruptions of friendship and family. He is cognizant of the need to adapt family conditions to the rigid requirements of military life.

Some families have trouble adapting in civilian life; some never do. When a family member then enters military service the situation often becomes even more complicated and the necessity of giving high priority to the treatment of family problems becomes obvious.

Kaslow literally takes the neophyte by the hand as she discusses the training and supervision of mental health professionals in their efforts to understand and treat military families. Obviously expert in therapeutic matters, she notes that given the rapidity with which orders to ship out may be received, clinicians will need to be adept at crisis intervention and brief therapy with military families beset by emotional problems. Both Kaslow and Ridenour correctly insist that therapists who work in a military setting should know well their own emotional perspectives and their place in the problem situation they will encounter.

Kaslow summarizes the whole treatment effort well as she writes, "One final thought: The family is still the most basic institution in our society, and therapists are among those who can help revitalize and enrich family living so that it becomes more satisfying for the members as a group and for each person individually. For our country to continue to flourish, military families, like their civilian counterparts, need to have at their beck and call the best service we can offer them."

There is no doubt but that the medical services have made considerable progress in family care and have come an incredibly long way in the recognition and treatment of problems of wives and children of military personnel. In the military, child abuse, spouse abuse, and the problems of single parents seem to receive more rapid and focused attention than in civilian agencies. Part of this, of course, is due to the unified nature of the military services, along with its "esprit de corps," while comparable situations in civilian life are less easily identified and treatment is harder to mandate. Fortunately, this too is changing, and there is less denial of the extent and seriousness of these social and familial problems.

One particularly encouraging aspect of the efforts to help military families is that they are apparently receiving support and encouragement from officers of "the line." As Rodriguez notes, "After having been ignored, tolerated, and reacted to negatively for so long, it is apparent that to be a military family can now be viewed as a positive identity."

Because of the nature and requirements of the services, military families, are frequently disrupted by moves between military and civilian areas. At times they may even be viewed as minority groups—outsiders, if you will—and may experience pressures due to this factor alone. Fortunately, the Department of Defense now listens to the problems and tries to meet the requirements they pose. It is safe to say that this volume will command even more attention from the services in the future, and it is even possible that it will be required reading for all dealing with military personnel.

Among military children there are special problems brought on by separation from a parent, frequent moves, changes of schools, loss of friends, transcultural experiences, isolation, and sometimes child neglect and child abuse as well as parental alcoholism. In the face of all of this, plus the absence of distant fathers and the presence of resentful mothers, many Oedipal-stage boys naturally can become depressed, yet this is little different from what is found in the civilian population. In fact, as this book points out, there are special strengths in many military families who are able to tolerate the stresses of military life in healthy fashion, and the boys weather this developmental task well. Rodriguez, in his chapter on children in military families, notes that because of the closeness of family ties, children of the military compare favorably with their civilian peers and though there are some maladjustments, the children as a rule tend to be resourceful and self-reliant, for experience has taught them that they are their own best advocates.

On the subject of incest, Crigler found that 80–85% of women treated for alcoholism reported having been sexually abused in childhood, some of them by fathers, stepfathers, elder brothers, other relatives, or family friends. Often the victims had suppressed these happenings and they only came to light while the alcoholic was under treatment. Some of these women became seriously depressed, others became psychopathic, and all had low self-esteem and were fearful of the information about the abuse leaking out. Should this occur in military life, the family is in double jeopardy and all members need attention and therapy to keep the family reasonably intact—the passage of time will not make this situation go away. This problem is also coming to light in civilian life now more than ever before.

Ridenour states, "America continues, it seems, a love–hate–tolerance cycle with its Armed Forces. While the nation persists in evaluating the necessity, worth, place, and design of its military services, those who comprise this force and their loved ones are doing some assessing themselves." This is a pregnant statement, as is proven by the great distress of the service members who fought in Vietnam and who were ignored or insulted upon their return home. It also applies to the students in colleges who are in the ROTC. A few years ago these young men were mocked and insulted and even called "baby killers." Fortunately, attitudes toward military service personnel are much better now, even respectful, and one hopes that detractors will carefully reassess their criticisms.

As Schwabe and Kaslow note in their consideration of violence in the military family, the military established a Child Advocacy Center in 1978 to help turbulent families and to prevent child abuse. Later, in 1979, spouses who were subject to abuse and/or sexual assault were included. This is certainly an excellent step forward and the military is to be commended for it.

It is in the attention to, and excellent handling of, the military individual or family addicted to alcohol or substance abuse that the military services, and the Navy in particular, have attracted the most public attention (so much so that a number of prominent government family members have appealed to Navy centers for help, and to one center in particular).

Alcoholism and drug abuse pervade all segments of American society and in this volume Williams carefully considers both of these problems. At times, and in some quarters, these illnesses reach epidemic proportions. Apparently no family is immune—some individuals begin the use of the drugs to avoid stress or rejection and then continue using them to help cope with life's problems. Clubs become the hub of social life in the military and in many of them alcohol flows freely.

The problem of alcoholism in both enlisted ranks and among older officers is recognized by the services. Williams speaks of the "military family syndrome" as being highlighted by separation, transiency, and interrupted parenting. As in civilian life, some families are better off when the father is away and the wife is the clear head of the household. It is upon the father's return that difficulties may develop. After a short honeymoon reunion, questions of leadership arise, a power battle ensues, and therapeutic assistance may be needed. Williams states that treating drug abusers apart from the family is an exercise in futility. If the problem is left alone the family may self-destruct—suicide or even homicide might eventuate. Thus, a copatient (usually a spouse) is involved in treatment also.

In view of what seems to be the increasingly litigious nature of our present culture, I was quite interested in Armitage's chapter on legal issues in military families. I am glad to note that these families have help near at hand. Frequently in civilian life it is unaffordable.

I could go on and highlight each chapter, but space does not permit a satisfactory discussion of them here. A foreword is like a military spy plane: It simply tells one what is there. It is up to the readers to ferret out the situations of interest to them.

In this excellent book it becomes obvious that the military is cognizant of the advances in the treatment in family problems, and that it is moving rapidly to utilize the best approaches and extend its offerings through the recent establishment of Family Service Centers. The Navy in which I served was indeed a bastion of single men, for most men who were married and had children were excused from the draft. This was a plus for all concerned, for we could not then have handled the problems discussed here. The present military has its own challenges: an all volunteer force, and the wide sweep of individuals that that encompasses; more women service members; more single-parent families. All of this necessitates concern for "the military family," discussed so articulately in the pages of this volume.

In sum, the book is particularly well done. It is complete and it "covers the waterfront." I recommend it highly and I congratulate those who conceived of it and all who helped carry the idea to fruition.

FRANCIS J. BRACELAND, MD
Rear Admiral, MC, USNR, Retired
Scholar-in-Residence, St. Joseph College
Editor Emeritus, *American Journal of Psychiatry*

Preface

Strange as it may seem, until the last decade there was little discussion about the military family and a paucity of references to it in the literature. Those involved with the military were divided into two categories, "active duty" personnel and "dependents."

In *The Right Stuff*, Tom Wolfe portrays the "machismo" expectations of, by, and for men in the armed services. (See Chapter 7 for an elaboration on this point). The mission comes first! The role of the spouse and children was, and in many ways still is, to support the husband's commitment; he is the celebrated warrior and their unconditional faith in what he is doing must be assumable. Duty, honor, and country are priority values and patriotism is a central tenet in the family's personal belief system and the military community's shared ideology. Traditionally, a draftee is expected to uphold this code and all that it implies; career officers seek out service in the armed forces because this life-style represents the values they believe in most. Women who chose to marry them have been thought to agree, implicitly or explicitly, knowledgeably or naively, to become part of the service way of life that revolves around and flows from the man's military obligations and relationships.

Today, with the advent of a predominantly volunteer military, significant others are no longer called "dependents." They are "beneficiaries." Increasing numbers of single and married women have enlisted, making the multifaceted tapestry of the military even more complex and giving a different blend to the child-caring and wife-as-spouse-at-home aspects of family life. Another far-reaching change is that, just as in the civilian sector, military couples are also experiencing a spiraling divorce rate. It is no longer uncommon for the husband to get primary child custody—if (1) he has the better benefit package available which covers the children; or (2) he is likely to lead a less mobile life than his wife and be more frequently physically on the premises to provide parenting. Laws concerning divorced wives' right to a military exhusband's retirement funds have been in a state of flux, with ramifications for substantial changes in the financial world of the exspouse.

In our separate and joint teaching endeavors with mental health personnel in the military we found we needed to be cognizant of these psychosocial, legislative, and economic issues and developments; the similarities and differences between civilian and military families; and the special complexity of lives challenged by frequent separations, relocations, and reunions. All of this had to be interwoven with all of the standard theoretical and clinical material presented in graduate and professional training and beyond to psychiatrists, psychologists, and social workers. This represented a huge task in relatively unexplored terrain.

Given our awareness of the dearth of comprehensive, in-depth literature on this topic, the renewed national attention to the importance of a solid and highly viable military, and the request of Seymour Weingarten, Editor-in-Chief of The Guilford Press, that we write a book providing extensive and analytic coverage of this multidimensional subject, we decided to undertake the challenge and are pleased that it reached fruition. Throughout, the reader will recognize that this volume also emanated from a recognition of the following factors: the confluence of (1) the developments in government policy which led to a predominantly volunteer armed service; (2) the expanding awareness that the support of the servicemember's family of his[1] being and remaining in service is critical to maintaining the necessary numbers; (3) that therefore the well-being and reasonable contentment of the military family is a salient concern of the government; and (4) the tremendous value of the burgeoning field of family theory and therapy which provides the general sociocultural and psychological ethos and backdrop for this book, and its potential for enabling servicemembers to lead more personally satisfying and socially productive lives.

To provide the content and context we deemed essential we decided to invite several leading figures in the field of family therapy as well as numerous respected experts in the several psychotherapeutic professions in the various branches of the military to write chapters. Fortunately, an impressive array of knowledgeable individuals agreed to participate in this unique project. Jointly, we have attempted to cover all of the major family-related topics and problems which confront members of the Armed

1. Except where circumstances require otherwise, the pronoun "he" is used rather than the awkward "he or she" and is not intended to have sexist connotations. Given that the large majority of service personnel are male, this usage was deemed acceptable.

Forces, their significant others, and those in the government who are charged with making decisions regarding military personnel, where and when they are dispatched, and the provision of psychiatric and social services for them.

It is our sincere hope that government policy and planning personnel; medical officers and commanding officers; medical, psychiatric and other mental health staff members and chaplains; those in such offices as the Secretary of the Army, Navy, and the various Surgeon Generals; legislators; as well as the faculties and staff members of various teaching and training programs and treatment facilities will find this informative and illuminating reading. We believe it will be useful in the ongoing search to find new ways to meet the needs of service-families. We urge directors of service connected internships and residency training to incorporate content on family dynamics and treatment into their curricula. It is also our hope that many others in the military community as well as in the civilian sector that provide services will find this volume interesting and enlightening. Another aspiration is that this volume will stimulate more definitive research on the topics addressed herein.

Richard Ridenour would like to thank his three families: (1) his professional family—particularly Drs. Robert Pottash, James Sears, Florence Kaslow, and Carl Whitaker—for encouraging him to be himself and to appreciate and expand the broad horizon which constitutes the world of families; (2) his parents, Martha and Ira Ridenour, who provided him with the love and security which has allowed him to take risks; and (3) his wife, Leslie, whose love, understanding, and support is very deeply appreciated.

Florence Kaslow wishes to express her gratitude to the many people in her personal and professional life whose trust and confidence in her work, albeit at times unorthodox, made it possible to follow the light, sometimes dim and sometimes brilliant, that has beckoned her to pursue family therapy creatively and intensively. Particularly important in her originally being invited to serve as a Consultant to the Navy's Department of Psychiatry Residency Training Program in Family Therapy in 1975 in Philadelphia were Drs. Richard Ridenour, James Sears, and John McGrail; and Dr. Reed Larsen who first asked her to be a Distinguished Visiting Professor at Lackland Air Force Base in 1981. Also, part of her exposure to service connected families was accrued during the many years she served as a Consultant to the Philadelphia VA Mental Health Clinic at the request of Eugene Cohen and Norman Johnson, in the Social Work

Service there. Out of these involvements have evolved many treasured friendships and much of the impetus for this book. To her devoted and caring parents, Rose and Irving Whiteman, who so highly valued education and social justice, to her husband, Solis Kaslow, and their two children, Nadine and Howard, her thanks for teaching her so much about family dynamics, functioning, individuating and sharing, and her abiding love to them for being part of her own special family.

We both appreciate the many families who have entrusted their innermost thoughts and feelings to us in the sanctuary of our offices and in the open lecture halls when we have taught through live demonstration interviews, To them; to all of the authors who so generously gave of their time and expertise to contribute chapters to this book; to our editor, Seymour Weingarten, who gave us great latitude to pursue our own predilections in the preparation of this work; and to our spouses who uncritically understood the time we each needed to invest to get this organized, edited, and written—our sincerest appreciation.

FLORENCE W. KASLOW
RICHARD I. RIDENOUR

Contents

1

The Military, Service Families, and the Therapist

RICHARD I. RIDENOUR

> "I don't know if I love you anymore. I know I need you and I depend upon you for certain things. Yet, sometimes you embarrass me. If I didn't have to worry about you I could do other things I dream of and spend more money on those dreams."
>
> "Well, I don't know if I love you as much either. You're very hard to love at times. You don't seem to understand me and you keep changing your mind about me. You only seem to care or come to me when you're in trouble. I don't know where or how I belong in your life. You don't appreciate me!"

This brief interchange could probably be heard regularly in the office of any mental health professional. It may represent any of a number of intrafamily relationships in conflict. However, it is recounted here to represent metaphorically the current relationship between the United States and its military defense forces. America continues, it seems, a love–hate–tolerance cycle with its Armed Forces. While the nation persists in evaluating the necessity, worth, place, and design of its military services, those who comprise this force and their loved ones are doing some assessing themselves. The marines, the soldiers, the sailors, the air force personnel, and their families are asking many questions today. For example, are they, their problems, their rewards, and their lives as special and/or different as they are often told they are by their government, their military command, and by the civilian community around them? This country's move to an all volunteer force and the increased recognition of the effect of family members' attitudes upon military retention rates

The opinions or assertions contained herein are the private views of the writer and are not to be construed as official or as reflecting views of the Department of the Navy or the Department of Defense.

Richard I. Ridenour. Captain, Medical Corps, U.S. Navy, and Psychiatrist and Director, Residency Training Program in Psychiatry, Department of Psychiatry, Naval Hospital, San Diego, California.

necessitate attention and that answers be found to the questions raised by these issues.

There seems little doubt that the military family presents a somewhat different portrait than does its civilian counterpart. Some unique facets of service life that quickly come to mind are (1) frequent separations and reunions—with many details sometimes secret and the length often contingent upon current world crises situations; (2) regular geographical household relocations—with disruptions of friendships, activities, schooling, employment of other family members, and often with the total cost never completely reimbursed; (3) living life under the dictum that the mission must come first; (4) the need to adapt the family's natural growth and spontaneity to the rigidity, regimentation, and conformity demanded by the job and the nature of the military; (5) the specter of early retirement for the career fighting man in comparison with his civilian counterpart in the same age group; (6) the omnipresent rumors and background threat of loss during a mission by death, injury, or capture; (7) feelings of detachment from the mainstream of nonmilitary life around them, due sometimes to the isolated nature of some duty stations and often owing to the overt or covert discrimination by the surrounding population; (8) the security of knowing that a vast system exists to support them in meeting their needs for survival; (9) the ability to look forward to work that involves travel and adventure in different parts of the world as their association with the military system continues; (10) the knowledge that they may not have to face or completely deal with a difficult situation in one place because they may be leaving there soon; (11) the effect of a certain rank or rate on social pressures, family and individual stresses; and (12) the feeling of some lack of personal control over pay, promotion, and other benefits. The matter of the servicemember's pay and benefits being regularly discussed and debated in the public forum, with the ever present threat of change, has also become a part of the picture of life in today's military. This questioning process has undermined the promise of security used by the government in the past to attract and maintain adequate levels of personnel.

The police officer and his family must constantly deal with the threat of death or injury and there is a continuous struggle over the amount of public funds to be allocated for salaries. Every physician's family knows from waiting for dinners or from last minute changes of plans, that the mission, or in this case, the patient must come first. Many firms, due to the nature of the business world, have in recent decades required frequent job-related relocations for their employees. It is evident, therefore, that large segments of our society deal with one or more of these aforementioned concerns and stresses; however, there may be no other major group that confronts so many or all of them as those in the Armed Forces.

While it appears that these various aspects of a family's enmeshment in the military system can be discussed in great detail individually, it seems more important to generate a conceptual model that delineates the impact of these and other issues upon the unique style and structure of each family involved. Having such a model available becomes particularly crucial when a crisis situation develops involving one of our families and they seek our help. It enables the psychotherapist seeing such a family to view the mix of military related issues and those normal evolutionary matters against an explanatory framework that combines an appreciation for the *military factors* and for *family dynamics.*

Although family systems theory and therapy has now been in existence for about 30 years, the utilization of this approach on a broad scope with military families is relatively new. Yet, this conceptual system and therapeutic methodology has a great deal to contribute in enabling helping professionals, especially mental health professionals, to understand and intervene more effectively in treating military personnel and their families in the 1980s. A family systems theory approach might also be useful in helping the Armed Forces themselves confront and deal successfully with current concerns being expressed by its members and their families. This chapter will attempt to use a family systems perspective in discussing some of the unique features of military life for active duty persons and their families. It is hoped that doing so will increase the versatility, utility, and spontaneity of our responses as helping professionals to our military families in distress.

THE MILITARY AS AN EXTENDED FAMILY NETWORK

Every mental health professional is aware that an evaluation of any couple or family must certainly include an examination of the sparks that started it toward becoming a reality. In looking at a family that is part of the military constituency, not only is it necessary to look at mate selection, but also the therapist must become aware of why that family joined the military, or was formed initially in a military setting, or has remained in such a setting.

Perhaps a young man ran away from home by joining the Navy. He may or may not realize or admit that this was his motivation. Perchance a short time later he met a young girl, from his culture or another, who coincidentally was also running away from her family of origin. Or, conceivably, one or both could have been sent forth by their families to experience and see the world—what I call the Marco Polo effect. No matter, however, because Bowen's theory that persons at the same level of individuation marry gets acted out and indeed they become husband and wife (Bowen, 1978). After a brief honeymoon trip back to their families of origin to show off each other, they begin to fight to see which one of the two constellations their newly formed family will be like (Whitaker & Keith, 1981). Certainly this is not the case just in a military setting. However, the situation in this infant household is now complicated even more by the immediate entrance into the marital picture of a fourth family network, the military family network.

Indeed, the service presents itself as, and in many ways is, an alternate or extended family system. Its work, social and rank structures provide siblings, friends, parents, grandparents, and even "family enemies." It expects loyalty and obedience. It provides services and benefits that leave almost no phase of life untouched as long as the family and its members are compliant with its wishes. This assumed extended family controls income, geographical locations, provides or affects spare-time activities, safety, clothing, shelter, food and medical care, and promises future benefits.

Thus, the newly formed marital dyad having come about possibly as a result of escape from their respective families has perhaps unconsciously run toward becoming part of a third extended family system. By joining this extended family, the couple gives the military much authority over their lives. Odds are heavily in favor of the fact that they have not thought about and/or discussed with each other their immediate or future relationship with this system or its eventual place in their life. Everyone associated with the military will deal repeatedly with these matters of authority and dependence versus independence. The newlyweds might not like being separated by a 6-months-long deployment but they may accept it because of the security of a steady guaranteed income and readily available medical care. They may soon plan to enlarge their family with the addition of a child.

At a time when both of these individuals are dealing with the issue of dependence versus independence in their marital relationship, after having placed the same battle with their own families of origin *on hold* by escaping that scene by joining the service, they must now fight their personal war on a third front. This is the essence of what Bowen calls triangulation (Bowen, 1978). When mental health professionals first come into contact with families in the military setting, these families are often in conflict with either the military or with each other over a matter related to the real or imagined demands of the service family network. Just as some couples triangulate their relationship in a period of crisis by drawing a child into many of their interactions, and others attempt to do this with the therapist who they hope will serve as a buffer or judge, couples in the service may use the military as the third party in their dealings with one another. At these times, they may project blame and responsibility for what occurs in their family upon their commanding officer, other high-ranking authority figures, or upon the larger network, the service itself. Therapists dealing with these families in such times of upheaval must not allow themselves to become allied with such maneuvers.

It is highly likely that the crisis the family has found itself in is related to a marker event in its own evolutionary process or in the normal progression of its life in the service. These include such things as joining or leaving the service, the birth or adoption of a child, a loss, or a separation due to a deployment. When such events occur it is incumbent upon the therapist to refocus the attention of the family upon itself and its part in the unfolding drama and to facilitate their developing strategies for easing these passages and making them worthwhile individuation growth experiences.

THE MUTUAL ADOPTION PROCESS

The previous section has dealt with one set of reasons for joining the military and it may be helpful at this point to look more closely at this particular process. Whitaker has called joining the military, the "military adoption process" (Whitaker, 1982). I would like to add one word and designate it the *mutual* military adoption process—mutual, that is, between the service member (or family) and the military itself. The military member has, knowingly or unknowingly, selected a new extended family, new authority figures, and a new value system. Just as it is certain that few inductees have thought out this process, it appears that the military has never come to grips with what it means to be an adoptive parent. This can be seen clearly in its attempts to deal with those persons who fail or get into trouble. By analogy, when a child is having great difficulty, adoptive parents often need help and support to deal with the resultant disappointment, bewilderment, and/or guilt (Kaplan & Sadock, 1981), and turn to a therapist hoping he or she can "fix the child." When mental health professionals are called on by commands for evaluations of military personnel having problems they often find in this call a similar request to "fix the servicemember—as child," and to alleviate the command's confusion behind the formal referral for assessment. Paying attention to this hidden call can lead to a better working relationship with these commands, and to the identification of problem areas in the military's own complex relationship network. Indeed the referred active duty member may even be the "extended family's" identified patient or scapegoat. Acceptance of this possibility can lead to recognition of administrative problems needing to be dealt with or to other personnel problems such as an alcoholic more senior member of the command who is negatively affecting the identified patient and others. Something akin to this type of extended military family network analysis has been carried on effectively by F. D. Glogower and his colleagues at the Department of Psychiatry, Naval Hospital, San Diego, California, under the name of "shipboard liaison."

Thus, it seems that adoptive parents, nuclear or military, when considering their child's problematic behavior may need to take a good look around their family network. The following quotation raises some fascinating thoughts:

> Adopted children have an increased incidence of mental disorders. These disorders tend to become manifest primarily during adolescence. The identity crisis that erupts normally at that time is typically associated with rebellion and parental rejection. Adopted children may run away from home at that time in search of their natural parents. . . . Overt psychotic reactions may occur. (Kaplan & Sadock, 1981, p. 723)

This correlates well with what military psychiatrists and psychologists have seen for years in their work with young active duty personnel who function like adolescents in adoptive families. They use drugs and alcohol for escape and rebellion; many who have a history of unauthorized absences (UA) become psychiatric patients. Military therapists see psychotic reactions in personnel, especially during their recruit training, who have no previous psychiatric history and whose clinical picture really seems to fit no clear diagnostic category. It is interesting to note how many servicemembers go back to their families of origin and live with or near them while UA/AWOL, and to consider that this is often the very situation they had fled from when they joined the military. Therapists working in active duty settings have discussed among themselves the many patients they see who have experienced emotional and occupational difficulties after returning to duty following a visit home to their family of origin. The family is a pivotal controlling agent in any adolescent's life— "far out of proportion to time spent with them and in spite of physical distance" (Whitaker, 1975, p. 207). Numerous issues surrounding the family of origin play a major role in the lives of adopted persons. Perhaps the military itself should pay more attention to similar issues. Knowing how a servicemember in trouble has dealt with authority figures in his family might be of considerable predictive value in determining what type of problems he will encounter in the military and what might best help to prevent or solve them.

THE QUESTION OF LOYALTY

Conceivably each new service-connected family soon faces a most perplexing question. Which family will this new family embryo by loyal to: its own; the husband's; the wife's; or to the military's? The evolution of this loyalty flux is one of life's regular tasks (Boss & Whitaker, 1979). It is an undeclared war with many battles and never a final peace treaty. It has been recognized by neither the family which has given up its son, daughter, wife, or husband for adoption by the military; nor by the adopting branch of service itself. From the viewpoint of the military's extended family style and demands, the mission takes precedence, and therefore, often the servicemember's relationship with his peers or "adopted siblings" is found to take precedence over that between himself and his spouse, children, or parents. At least this is what is expected to take place. This aspect of life in the armed forces carries with it natural conflicts that are best handled if admitted and respected beforehand. An example of such a problem that was never addressed is inherent in the story of an enlisted sailor who was a valued technician serving the end of a second enlistment period with plans for a career in the Navy. While he was on a prolonged deployment, caused by a world crisis situation, his maternal grandmother, who had raised him, died suddenly. He was unable to return in time for the funeral. He served out the remaining months of his tour with anger and decreasing job performance and left the Navy. He found it intolerable to remain in the service which he felt had caused him to forsake his loyalty to his grand-mother.

DEPENDENCY

Among other concerns, the question of loyalty and allegiance are brought to the surface by this tale. These values are closely tied to dependency in the service setting, a concept often thought of in terms of one person being dependent upon another. Whitaker reflects that "real dependency is the dependency of each member of the couple or the family on the supra unit—the couple or the family" (Whitaker, 1982b). For those in the military, this supraunit might be the military family network or one of the other family systems involved. Active duty men and women are taught to depend on each other as a unit, but there is respect for individual response in a crisis and for shifts in job responsibilities with incapacitation. Healthy families also operate in this fashion, maintaining a sense of the separate identity of each member and at the same time a commitment to the overall unit structure and its goal (Kaslow, 1981a).

Armed Forces personnel are subject to deployments of varying frequency and duration. The nature and length of the typical mission varies according to the branch of service (Doering & Hutzler, 1982). They and their families are advised to depend upon available military family agencies, medical systems, clubs, and other allied organizations or in-dividuals during these times. Many spouses choose to depend heavily on their own extended families of origin during such periods. Single parents seem most comfortable seeking help from relatives. Many families, how-ever, go to great lengths to handle any problems that arise themselves. Recent studies of Air Force families seem to indicate that often ties with friends and work associates tend to be weak with service families and, as a result, these contacts are not a strong source of support. Single-parent families are most likely to consult friends or neighbors during a crisis (Orthner & Bowen, 1982). During these separations, the at-home family may shift mechanisms of internal operation and its members will alter their role and job descriptions. Healthier families in the military system are often recognizable by the freedom and ease with which this is done.

This seems to depend mainly on the home-based spouse's comfort with the comings and goings caused by deployments and the couple's own level of individuation. Deployments may provoke crises and "family arguments." Indeed, the crises may be blamed on another aspect of the larger ecological system and may be evoking memory traces of one's past. This is illustrated by the following brief case:

A 23-year-old woman, the wife of a junior Naval officer deployed for the previous two months, was seen in a Navy Mental Health Clinic for suicidal ideation. She stated emphatically that she wanted to die and needed her husband home. Additional information was that she had a 3-year-old daughter at home and that she also had asked her mother to come and stay with them during her husband's absence. She blamed the Navy for her loneliness and ensuing despair and for the fact that she was so upset that she was becoming fearful she would hurt her daughter. This young woman had no past personal or family history of psychiatric illness or treatment and gave a picture of a normal developmental history for herself. Her mother was called and she arrived accompanied by her granddaughter. In an interview with the three of them together it was rapidly revealed by the grandmother that during a period of job-related separation between her and her husband, years before, she had become despondent and beaten her daughter (the patient) severely on one occasion. She had called her husband, he had returned, changed jobs, and it did not happen again. The identified patient reported no memory of this until reminded and then wept profusely. Following this meeting, the grandmother and her daughter were seen in regular sessions during the deployment period. Both women became initially despondent, but this was resolved rapidly. The husband returned from his tour of duty, having been promoted.

It is thus suggested that therapy with individuals or families at such times of crisis may often need to involve the appropriate refocusing of the actual argument and placement of the conflict in the perspective of *the* appropriate family system. A way must also be found to make the seeking of such help more acceptable to our families and the services themselves and to make it readily available in a nonthreatening manner.

THE EVOLUTION OF THE FAMILY IN A MILITARY SETTING

Individuals and families pass through normal evolutionary stages during their existences. These have been well described by various psychodynamically oriented and family oriented authors. One such useful and simple description of the normal family life cycle is a sociological perspective used by Doering and Hutzler in their Rand Corporation 1982 study entitled *Description of Officers and Enlisted Personnel in the U.S. Armed Forces.* This delineates six stages in the family life cycle: The first begins with the marriage; the second with the birth of the first child; the third stage with the birth of the last child; the fourth stage starts with the permanent departure of a child from home; the fifth or "empty nest" stage debuts with the last child leaving home and lasts until the death of one spouse; and the final stage ends with the death of the remaining spouse. Being a part of the global military family network will add another set of superimposed stages or marker events, not characteristic of all families. These include such transitions as joining the military, the first prolonged separation, and then reunion periods; periodic moves or geographic relocations, especially those away from extended family of origin roots, often beyond the control of the family unit itself and leading sometimes to a group feeling of impotency; periodic culture shock; mandatory shifts in job or career directions for a military member's spouse due to a service related relocation; retirement and/or shift of career goals for the service-member and the associated life changes which occur much earlier than for their civilian peer families. Given these and other factors, and considering the impact of these events or stages in normal military life, it becomes crucial that in working with each service family, the following questions be given attention:

1. Where is this particular family in terms of its own stages of evolutionary development?

a. It is "just married" and in its infancy, exploring and excited about or fearful of the larger world around it?
b. Is it just expanding with its first child born?
c. Is it shifting gears as the children are leaving?
d. Has it recently lost a member or undergone a change in its structure?

2. Where is each member of this family along the evolutionary process of his or her own individuation?

a. Is the level of individuation age appropriate?
b. What are the current dominating emotions in his or her relationship with the own family of origin; is it anger, sadness, happiness, etc.?
c. Is each member using geographical distance to separate from the family of origin?

d. Does the level of individuation of each spouse allow the other to continue to grow and expand his or her own individuation and maturity or does it place demands that constrict or stifle this process? (i) Is the servicemember about to be deployed for an extended period afraid that his spouse will handle the separation very well and therefore decide she doesn't need him? (ii) Does he demand that she will fail in her coping efforts during his absence and/or does he set up the financial and support systems so that she has to fail to cope successfully?

3. Where is the family in terms of its evolution and relationship with the military extended family network?

a. Is it experiencing its first long service-enforced separation?
b. Is it reintegrating following the reunion after such a separation?
c. Where is it regarding transition living? (i) Is the family awaiting orders to move? (ii) Has it just moved? (iii) Is it putting off settling important issues by using an upcoming move as an excuse to procrastinate?
d. Is it early retirement time? (i) Does this precipitate a premature fear of aging and mortality? (ii) What readjustments are posed by reentry into civilian life and the loss of the structure provided by military life? (iii) Philosophy-of-life concerns and differences that may have been present and hidden by child-rearing needs may now come to the fore.
e. What is its general comfort level with and attitude toward the military? Important clues to this are the following: (i) use or nonuse of available natural military support systems, social agencies and service family centers; participation in base clubs, events, schools; establishment of friendships with other service-connected families or avoidance of same; use of service medical facilities and exchanges. (ii) presence of open discussion in the family about military-related issues. (iii) When the spouse and children show awareness of and appreciation for the active duty member's job.

4. What style has it developed to deal with the periodic separation and reunion phenomenon? While the issue of separations and reunions is dealt with in many of the other chapters of this book, it is also important to consider here how each family deals with the absent member. Do they keep him in their thinking appropriately, or do they exclude him? Hill's

(1945) study on family adjustment to the stress of separation showed that those who included the absent member handled reunions without significant distress while those who excluded him found a most serious crisis when he came home. A pattern is sometimes seen in senior and retired military families where the wife and children have come to no longer take the husband into account in the making and executing of plans, as a response to his many absences over the years. This management style met the needs of the family and the absentee member for years. However, later in life when he wants to reenter the system, often the family coalition cannot or will not realign to readmit him.

    5. Is there any special impact upon the family caused by its being in a particular branch of the military? It is important to recognize major differences in the various branches of the Armed Forces of the United States. While the tendency here has been to generalize remarks about service family life for all services, attention must be given when working with particular families to the significant differences that exist between branches of the military. There are variations in the nature of the personnel in each branch, the types of available duty stations, the length and frequency of separations and deployments, the way each group is trained to see itself and the nature of its mission. The following facts are indications of some of these differences (Doering & Hutzler, 1982):

a. The shortest lengths of time in a given location were reported by Marine Corps enlisted personnel and by Navy officers, with the longest by Air Force enlisted personnel and officers.
b. Enlisted men and women in the Marine Corps, on average, tend to be older than enlisted personnel in other services.
c. Air Force men tend to be older than men in other services (enlisted & officer personnel).
d. Navy and Marine Corps personnel tended to spend more time separated from their families than do members of the Army and Air Force. (In the 12 months preceding the study approximately 20% of Naval officers studied were separated 5–8 months from their families as opposed to approximately 7% of Air Force officers and 6% of Army officers studied.)
e. Air Force enlisted personnel plan to spend more years in the military than do personnel of other services. These persons also showed a higher level of satisfaction with service life over the personnel of other branches. Professionals working to help service

families should appreciate the uniqueness of each branch and look for any effect this uniqueness might be having on the family's life at that moment.

6. Is this family a single-parent family? In confronting this emerging trend, the military mirrors the problems of the rest of society today. In 1960 1 out of 10 children under age 18 was living with one parent; in 1978 it was almost 1 out of 5 children; and by 1990 estimates are that it will be 1 out of every 4 children under 18 years of age (Radin, 1981). The service, like the civilian community around it, has had great difficulty adapting to this phenomenon. The various military branches are beginning to review policies regarding assignment, benefits, and other concerns related to this type of family. The recent trend toward more fathers taking over the custodial, physical parenting role in cases of divorce and separation, and the fact that, in terms of numbers, the military remains male dominated, has caused the Armed Forces to grapple with this issue earlier than they might have wished.

7. Does the changing role of women in the military have any effect on the family's current situation?

    a. In 1980, the Department of Defense (DoD) set recruiting goals that included raising the representation of women to approximately 12.5% by 1985 (Doering & Hutzler, 1982).

    b. Recent studies have shown that women who enter the military tend to be older than men when joining and women have tended to remain for shorter periods than men thus far (Doering & Hutzler, 1982).

    c. The fact that increasing numbers of women are entering the service should be considered here because it has great impact on the types of families that will be seen more and more in the military. There will be more service-connected families where both spouses are active duty personnel. Additionally, we must address what is likely to occur when the wife and mother is an active duty member, likely to be deployed with her husband remaining behind as the "dependent."

    d. Recently this issue was highlighted at the Naval Hospital, San Diego, with the arrival of the 1982–1983 medical intern class. An orientation program was presented for them and their spouses which included a review of gynecological services available and a presentation by the Navy Doctors' Wives Club. There was nothing special, however, planned for the male spouses of arriving interns. (Change may come hard, even for the enlightened!)

8. The helping professional should be on the lookout for other factors in the life of the military family that could be having great impact upon it at a time of crisis. These can include: the spouses having different cultural, ethnic, or racial backgrounds; the presence of adopted or foster children; the issue of spouse or child abuse; the presence of alcoholism or other drug abuse; the occurrence of significant physical or mental illness; financial difficulties; and/or employment stresses for the other spouse. (Many of these issues are dealt with elsewhere in this book.) These other life factors further individualize a family and its needs and may intensify its conflicts with a superimposed rigid military system. Cognizance of these influencing factors also aids the therapist in understanding that particular family's responses or set of available coping mechanisms. For example: Compared to U.S. civilian wives, wives in dual-military marriages and Asian-born wives are somewhat more likely to report lower marital satisfaction. Asian wives also express finding it harder to confide in their husbands (Orthner & Bowen, 1982). Such facts may influence these couples' communication patterns and therefore their response to stress.

9. Is the family's crisis being influenced by its position in the military's rate/rank structure?

a. Since many privileges and benefits are affected by the active duty member's rank, this factor can greatly affect the unit's sense of potency to act in any situation involving the service.

b. Stresses upon the family and its individual member can differ with rate or rank. (i) Officers concerned with a career in the military and still moving up are likely to experience more stress in their roles than younger officers not yet career committed or than older officers preparing to retire (Stoddard & Cabanillas, 1976). Their spouses appear to experience similar stresses in like circumstances. (ii) The higher the rank, the greater the career commitment (Orthner & Bowen, 1982).

c. One indication of a healthy working spousal relationship can be the couple's individual recognition and appreciation of how the other deals with these position/rank-related stresses. Do they help each other with this?

d. The feeling that impotency affects the larger military family network, at times exhibited by families of lower enlisted grade personnel, often leads to acting out behavior by the family scapegoat or by the designated needy person in the family. Such is the nature of much so-called depression in military wives. (i) Often a feeling that the system will respond positively will resolve a crisis or cure a "depression." (ii) Sometimes acknowledgment of a sense of impotency or lack of control will begin to reverse the situations.

10. What is that service family's concept of how the military in general sees that family itself—an important factor in whether that group will remain in the armed forces over time (Orthner & Bowen, 1982).

VIEWING THE HELPER IN A MILITARY SETTING

While treating and working with families in the military system, the therapist may be considering the aspects of life in the service previously discussed. It is vital that the professional helper be profoundly aware of where he is in his own life regarding each of these areas and the military in general. It is amazing how difficult this often appears to be and how many therapists working with these families refuse to do so. We agree to look at why this family or that one has joined the military, or at why one young woman married a sailor who will be gone for most of the first year of their marriage and frequently thereafter. Yet, therapists often do not analyze why they are there themselves treating these families or how they feel about them, and why they apply the techniques and styles to help them that they do. They may rationalize about it; they may expound academically upon it, but they may not carefully examine it in the same way that they evaluate the patient(s). There should be room under the microscope of therapy for the affect of the therapist(s) as well as that of the patient(s).

Therapy with service families may free some to leave the military and may help others to become individuated enough to choose to remain a part of the military and its extended family system. It is a strong contention here that the helper must not become a controlling foster parent and try to influence the family's choice while it is making it. He should respect the family members right to make and live out *their* own choices. One goal of therapy should be the recognition of this struggle over choice and the knowledge that the struggle is continuous. Another goal is to establish increasing comfort with the ambiguity of life and choice and to foster a diversity of methods to deal with it.

In treating military families there is often a tendency to utilize that type or style of therapy with which the therapist is most comfortable or that which is in vogue at that moment—for example, structural, psycho-dynamic, experiential, gestalt, supportive, educational, "diaclectic," com-municational, instructional. Perhaps it would be wiser to decide just what is the problem presented, the dynamics of this situation, what the family would like to be accomplished by the treatment, and to utilize the form of therapy that is likely to be most effective in achieving these goals (Kaslow, 1981b). Experienced family therapists working in military settings will openly acknowledge that what these families often want at first is for the military to change in some way. Most clinicians agree that this is probably beyond the scope of the family therapy session. Therapists working with these groups often experience special problems that call for a wide-ranging variety of intervention strategies. Some curves often thrown by the system's "pitcher" at the therapist "catcher" include family members suddenly absent due to deployment; a pervading sense of fear over the impact of any therapy upon the servicemember's career; and rigid time limitations due to work conditions or impending moves (the therapist's or the family's). There are also frustrations experienced by therapists who like to bring in original and extended family members and cannot, due to the often great geographical distances/separations which are common in the military. Therapists working in such an arena are often isolated personally and professionally like the families themselves. These and other such problems often cause the professional helper working in this service environment to feel, realistically, that they must settle for reduced therapeutic goals and that they must do so much more than their col-leagues working with other patient populations. We as therapists must come squarely to grips with these facts and with the feelings in us stirred up by them.

It is exhilarating to search for the ideal. What might be an ideal method to deal with the traditional family in the military setting (two spouses, together with children, one spouse an active duty member) experiencing turmoil? Using Whitaker's (1982) idea of family therapy as a kind of foster parenting and due to personal preference of not being a single foster parent, it is recommended here that the ideal might be a heterosexual cotherapy team, or at the very least, a cotherapist guest or consultant. It is hypothesized that the ideal plan for treating these families in distress should be conceived around the type of family (i.e., dual-career, foreign-born spouse, single-parent, officer vs. enlisted, etc.) (This will be covered later in Chapter 13 on the training of therapists to work with military personnel.)

Finally, those of us, in or out of the military itself, who work with these families are constantly fighting to maintain some equilibrium *between* creation of a spontaneity of action and affect (or freedom of family evolution) and the natural, necessarily rigidly conservative nature of the service extended family network. This seems a constant and difficult struggle. If we can appreciate it in ourselves, we will surely be aware of and value it in "our military families."

REFERENCES

Boss, P. G., & Whitaker, C. Dialogue on separation: Clinicians as educators. *The Family Coordinator*, July 1979, 391–398.

Bowen, M. *Family therapy in clinical practice*. New York: Aronson, 1978.

Doering, Z. D., & Hutzler, W. P. *Description of officers and enlisted personnel in the U.S. armed forces: A reference for military manpower analysis* (R-2851-MRAL). Santa Monica, Calif.: Rand Corporation, 1982.

Hill, R. The retiring father and his family. *Marriage and Family Living*, 1945, *7*, 31–34.

Kaplan, H. I., & Sadock, B. J. *Modern synopsis of comprehensive textbook of psychiatry* (Vol. 3). Baltimore: Williams & Wilkins, 1981.

Kaslow, F. W. Profile of the healthy family. *Interaction*, Spring/Summer 1981, *1*, 1–15. (a)

Kaslow, F. W. A diaclectic approach to family therapy and practice: Selectivity and synthesis. *Journal of Marital and Family Therapy*, July 1981, 345–351. (b)

Orthner, D. K., & Bowen, G. L. *Families in blue: Phase II*. Washington, D.C.: SRA, 1982.

Radin, N. The role of the father in cognitive, academic, and intellectual development. In M. E. Lamb (Ed.), *The role of the father in child development* (2nd ed.). New York: Wiley, 1981.

Stoddard, E. R., & Cabanillas, C. E. The army officer's wife: Social stresses in a complimentary role. In N. Goldman & D. Segal (Eds.), *The social psychology of military service*. Beverly Hills, Calif.: Sage, 1976.

Whitaker, C. The symptomatic adolescent—An AWOL family member. In M. Sugar (Ed.), *The adolescent in group and family therapy*. New York: Brunner/Mazel, 1975.

Whitaker, C. Personal communication, 1982. (b)

Whitaker, C., & Keith, D. Symbolic–experiential family therapy. In A. S. Gurman & D. P. Kniskern (Eds.), *Handbook of family therapy*. New York: Brunner/Mazel, 1981.

2

Legal Issues Encountered in Treating the Military Family

DAVID T. ARMITAGE

Modern America has been described as litigious, a society whose members run to lawyers and go to court to argue even minor disagreements. Awareness of "rights" and the fashionable model of "assertiveness" have engendered impatience as people strive to deal with the complex relationships of an ever changing world. Since disputes can occur in all human relationships, situations arise within the therapeutic context which can lead to legal action. Furthermore, mental health professionals treat patients affected by circumstances involving civil and criminal law. Since members of the Armed Forces and their families experience unique legal problems in addition to those encountered by the civilian community, familiarity with these legal issues has practical value for those who provide care to military families.

The sections which follow address particular issues wherein mental health personnel, the military family, and the law meet.

ISSUES LIKELY TO BE ENCOUNTERED
AT THE BEGINNING OF EVALUATION AND TREATMENT

ELIGIBILITY FOR EVALUATION

It is a criminal offense in violation of U.S. law to extend health services to a nonbeneficiary, except in emergency situations. (An emergency situa-

The opinions or assertions contained herein are the private views of the writer and are not to be construed as official or as reflecting views of the Department of the Army or the Department of Defense.

David T. Armitage. Colonel, Medical Corps, U.S. Army, and Chief, Department of Psychiatry and Neurology, Dwight David Eisenhower Army Medical Center, Fort Gordon, Georgia.

tion is defined as one in which there is imminent threat to the life or well-being of a person.) Prior to initiating an evaluation, staff must verify that the person is eligible for care. In addition, the duration of eligibility should be established to avoid premature termination of care.

NATURE OF THE EVALUATION

Different legal issues arise depending on whether an evaluation is voluntary or involuntary. *An active duty military member has no right to refuse a psychiatric evaluation if the member's commander gives a lawful order for the evaluation.* The assessment may begin unless invasive or potentially dangerous (high-risk compared to low-potential benefit) evaluation procedures are contemplated. For anyone other than active servicemembers, however, an evaluation must be voluntary. An exception exists when limited data from emergency room personnel, police, or direct visualization of a person are suggestive of mental disturbance *and* dangerous behavior. A brief evaluation is in order to determine whether the individual should be *referred* for involuntary hospitalization and more extensive evaluation. "Referred" is emphasized because only an active duty servicemember can be involuntarily admitted to a military facility. Civilians must be managed in accordance with applicable state law. It is critical that procedures for dealing with a noncooperative, seriously disturbed civilian patient, including temporary restraint and transportation to a nonmilitary facility, be established and known by hospital staff, legal officers, and the military police. *By not taking steps to hospitalize a disturbed person, legal action might be instituted against the professional and/or the hospital if the disturbed person or a third party is subsequently injured.*

Although the presence of a person in the emergency room, clinic, or office implies consent to be evaluated, a civilian who does not seem dangerous and refuses to continue the process must be allowed to leave even if mental health personnel believe that the person needs psychiatric treatment. A thorough notation should be entered in the health record. If no health record is available, a memorandum for the record should be made and retained by the clinician. Other staff members who may have been present and know the circumstances should be listed.

Parents may bring their minor children (age of minority differs from state to state) for evaluation and admission to military facilities. Even if the children object, reasonable actions taken by mental health staff, including restraint if required, are allowable, based upon the voluntary approval of the parents or legal guardians.

INFORMED CONSENT

After the initial assessment of a civilian, the clinician may recommend a more extensive evaluation or treatment. Informed consent of the patient is required. Such consent must be *knowledgeable, competent*, and *voluntary*. Every effort must be made to clarify for the patient exactly what is being proposed, the benefits expected, and the risks involved. For example, commencement of psychotherapy may lead to increased anxiety; family therapy may temporarily upset the intermember relationships; and hospitalization could have an impact on future insurance eligibility. The acute and long-term effects of medications need special attention. Risks of *not* following the recommended course of action, plus alternatives to the plan and their risks, must also be discussed. All *possible* risks need not be mentioned to the patient—only those factors which, in the words of the law, might lead a "reasonable person in similarly situated circumstances" to refuse the treatment. Mental health staff often are concerned about the potential antitherapeutic effect (or even flight from therapy) resulting from informing a patient of risks, fearing that persons with mental disorders may have trouble understanding the nuances of "risk–benefit." If, after thorough and careful thought, a clinician concludes that informing the patient of a risk may do more harm than good, he may withhold the information. But the clinician is wise to consult with a colleague and discuss his position with the patient's family, noting the consultation in an official record. It may be possible to discuss the risks of continued treatment with the patient at a later time.

Although there are many sides to the *voluntary* factor in informed consent, courts have held that pressures inherent in the circumstances in which a patient gives consent may vitiate the voluntariness of that consent. It might not be considered voluntary for a hospitalized patient to be told, "Take this medicine voluntarily, or we'll have to give you a shot." Consent is *not* voluntary if obtained by fraud, deceit, or threat.

If a civilian enters treatment voluntarily but then refuses to accept certain aspects of the therapeutic regimen, it is useful to suggest to the patient that a second medical opinion be sought. If the second opinion concurs with the original plan and there are no reasonable alternatives, the circumstances should be documented and the patient informed that treatment cannot be ethically continued without full cooperation. If the patient requests it, referral to another resource is required.

Informed consent to treatment involving military patients should meet the requirements of voluntariness, competency, and knowledge. If a written consent procedure is used, the type of treatment, along with the pertinent risks, benefits, and alternatives, should be written in terminology understandable to the person from whom the consent is being sought. Technical terms may be placed in parentheses for interprofessional communication. A note in the medical record should include what was discussed with the patient, date of discussion, who was present, and the patient's apparent reaction. The individual informing the patient about the treatment must be the person providing the treatment or responsible for directing a team providing care to the patient and must identify himself by name and role. If the patient thinks that the staff member is a psychiatrist, and he is really a member of another profession, the consent may not be valid. It certainly will not be informed!

Although staff in military facilities frequently wish it were not so, the fact is that a competent servicemember may refuse treatment of a non-emergency nature. There are specific regulations covering refusal which should be consulted (AR600—20 October, 1980, Personnel-General: Army Command Policy and Procedure). In an emergency, treatment may be given involuntarily long enough to bring the situation under control. Whatever treatment is used should follow the "least restrictive" lines, and should be terminated if the patient wishes when the emergency no longer exists. Interpreting "emergency" too freely must be avoided.

If the servicemember is believed to be incompetent, a Medical Evaluation Board is conducted. A court-appointed guardian will be necessary to provide consent for treatment if the patient is declared incompetent.

A complicated process is set in motion if a competent servicemember (or guardian of an incompetent) refuses treatment which has a reasonable chance of and is aimed at returning the member to productive military service. Persistent refusal may lead to disciplinary or administrative action. The member or guardian may, at any time, modify a rigid position and consent to treatment. It should be emphasized that active duty personnel have a right to refuse treatment without adverse legal consequences if the treatment would not lead to return to active duty. An explanation of rights, plus encouragement and support, should be offered to the member to join in an appropriate and reasonable treatment plan, but coercion must be assiduously avoided.

ISSUES OF CONFIDENTIALITY AND PRIVILEGED COMMUNICATION

Confidentiality is an ethical or moral issue involving the assumption that verbal or written communications between individuals are private and will not be revealed to third parties unless authorized. Confidentiality of communications in treatment is a duty owed by the professional to the patient, although there are exceptions to the general rule.

It is often believed that confidentiality does not exist in the military setting. This is incorrect. Confidentiality of private communications between mental health personnel and their military patients is essential, both legally and ethically, although limited when a legitimate "need to know" arises. This exception occurs when someone in an official capacity must have information in order to maintain the strength, discipline, and morale of the Armed Forces (common accepted practice). If a service-member is working with highly sensitive security-related material, or in a special job such as nuclear arms, the commander has a need to know whether that person is suffering from substance abuse or a mental disorder. The commander does not need to know intimate details about the sexual life, fantasies, marital disagreements, or family problems of the servicemember, but he may need to know that problems are occurring which may affect the person's performance.

An individual referred by his commander for evaluation of unusual behavior, substance abuse, or homosexuality must be told that the commander has a need and a right to have information resulting from that evaluation. In child abuse situations, a military family may be mandatorily referred for evaluation by a court. Material from that evaluation may be revealed to the court or the court's agent (such as a welfare or family services agency) if the law so provides.

A military person or his family undergoing treatment may acknowledge the commission of a crime. In such a situation the therapist should stop the patient from making any further statements and advise him of his right against self-incrimination. If the patient really desires to continue discussing the criminal activity, he may do so but the therapist could consider it clinically and legally important for the servicemember to consult legal counsel. The therapist should consult with the Judge Advocate General's Office as to his own risk of being charged with committing "misprision of a felony," that is, covering up an illegal act after the fact.

When a servicemember or spouse in therapy reveals a serious intent to harm an identifiable third party, mental health personnel have an ethical (and perhaps a legal) duty to warn the threatened individual (Tarasoff, 1976). Breach of confidentiality in such a situation is justified. Not all of the several jurisdictions which have addressed the issue have followed Tarasoff. An excellent review of this has been conducted recently by Belli (1981–1982, p. 2). It is important to discuss with patients at the outset of evaluation and treatment that if, in the judgment of the evaluator, the patient is potentially dangerous to himself or to others, the evaluator will have to take steps to prevent injury, thereby breaking confidentiality.

The presence of persons in a therapy situation who are not necessary or even related to the therapy, such as students or trainees, either military or civilian, requires prior approval from the patient. This is especially important when asking a psychiatric patient to appear before a medical conference or grand rounds. A patient must not be coerced into such an appearance. Some teaching institutions inform a patient beforehand that admission to their facilities implies consent to being involved in teaching situations. When videotaping therapy sessions for teaching purposes, all parties involved should give informed consent and preferably sign releases authorizing future use of the videotape. Since supervision is involved in all training programs, it is important to tell military families treated by professionals-in-training that the trainee is being supervised by a faculty professional who must hear details of the case. It is often helpful to introduce the supervisor to the patient.

Clinicians should be very cautious about discussing cases in public, such as in the hallway of the hospital, in dining facilities, or in settings not specifically arranged to help the patient or educate trainees. Mental health personnel from their earliest training should learn and conform to the requirement that patient care information (even with names deleted) must not be discussed with their own families, spouses, or friends. This is not only unethical and illegal, but also unwise, because it places the family in an awkward position. In a military setting the therapist's family may know the patient or his family, and see them socially. This caveat extends to secretaries, receptionists, and others who work with mental health clinicians.

Because the military outpatient health record is seen by many clerical people and others not involved with the mental health care of patients, utmost discretion should be used as to what details are placed in these records. The fact that a patient is being seen, the diagnosis, and medications being taken are important to have in a medical record. However, details about the patient's fantasies need not be entered. Regulations authorize the maintenance of detailed psychiatric case files separate from the outpatient medical record, controlled by mental health staff.

Therapists should bear in mind the difference between confidentiality and falsification of data. Some medical personnel have avoided placing a diagnosis of alcoholism in a military member's medical record out of concern that it would end the member's career. Policies regarding administrative management of personnel with substance abuse problems are made in accordance with the needs of the Armed Forces. Military medical authority at the level of the Surgeons General provides input to these policies, and considers recommendations for change offered by clinicians. Whatever changes may or may not take place, falsification of medical diagnoses by commission or omission is illegal and professionally unacceptable. Confidentiality is maintained by insuring that the documents containing the diagnoses are available only to authorized individuals.

Privileged communication is a legal term concerning private writings or comments made between individuals having a special relationship. For trust, confidence, and openness to occur in these relationships, the law grants a special privilege to the communicator—the right to prevent those special communications from being revealed in legal proceedings. The privilege, which belongs to the patient and not to the therapist, varies in extent. In the psychotherapist–patient privilege, there are so many exceptions requiring communications to be revealed that the privilege is severely watered down.

In contrast to confidentiality, privileged communication between servicemembers and health care professionals does not exist in the military setting—with one qualification. When psychiatric evaluations are requested by defense counsel for servicemembers charged with military crimes, a limited privilege exists regarding the information disclosed by the patient to the psychiatrist. Only the results of the evaluation in terms of the presence or absence of a mental disorder and certain legal conclusory statements may be made known to the prosecution. Release of detailed content of the evaluation is controlled by the defense strategy. In all other circumstances communications involving mental health personnel and active duty personnel and their families are not privileged under military and federal law.

Nevertheless, if the servicemember or dependents were involved in legal proceedings in a state court, state law would then apply. Most states have laws allowing privileged communication between physician (psychiatrist) and patient, psychologist and patient, and some between "psychotherapist" and patient. No state grants absolute privilege. Most states require reporting of actual or suspected child abuse and data relevant to commitment of a patient to a mental hospital. Even in these situations one must exercise discretion about what information is necessary to convey.

A servicemember under care of a therapist in a civilian community may not be accorded privileged communication if military interests are at stake. It is important to point this out to a person considering treatment either alone or with family members. Consultation with a Staff Judge Advocate is appropriate.

If the military family is brought into treatment without a clear discussion of the nature and extent of confidentiality and privileged communication, it is questionable whether or not the requirements for informed consent have been met. While a servicemember is involved in evaluation or therapy with his spouse or family, a problem could arise requiring details of the evaluation or treatment to be exposed in military legal proceedings. The spouse might later sue for divorce and child custody in the court of a state having a privileged communication law. To support her case the spouse may wish to enter evidence from the psychotherapy or psychiatric evaluation. The servicemember might claim privilege for those communications. However, if the communications were already revealed and a matter of record in the military court system, relevant parts could be entered in the state court action. Even when there is a state law regarding privileged communication, a spouse is not necessarily precluded from discussing in court what was revealed in the therapy sessions. In a child custody case the court may require data from family therapy to be revealed, deciding that the best interests of the child are controlling.

In all situations where material is communicated to a mental health worker employed by the government, the Privacy Act of 1974 applies. With few exceptions there are serious penalties for revealing information without the consent of the individual concerned. Communications among and between medical personnel responsible for treatment of the military member and his family are permissible if the personnel are essential for treatment. However, releasing information about diagnosis and treatment outside the treatment setting, or to external agencies not authorized to have the information, or to people within the military who do not have a clear-cut need to know, could constitute a violation of the Privacy Act and subject the violator to substantial fine and imprisonment. If permission is given by the servicemember, the information and to whom it is to be released should be agreed upon by patient and therapist.

Release of information to relatives also requires prior permission in most cases. Although a family member may show great concern about the patient, information released by the mental health staff may be used to damage the patient in the future through harassment, argument, or litigation in divorce/child custody proceedings. Nevertheless, there are times when family members must be given information, not only for their own peace of mind, but to effect the meeting of business commitments by the patient. The patient may not be competent to consent to release of information. It is wise in such circumstances to consult the Office of the Judge Advocate for guidance.

The issues of confidentiality and privileged communication are complex, frequently changing, require a mixture of legal knowledge and sound clinical judgment, and prove a challenge to the patience and professional expertise of clinicians working with military families.

MALPRACTICE

The word "malpractice" strikes fear in the hearts of most professionals. Even though federal law places both military and civilian government-employed mental health practitioners in a more secure position relative to personal liability in suits instituted against them for malpractice, legal action has been and continues to be instituted against individual practitioners as well as against the government. The issue of malpractice in military health care systems is unique because of The Federal Tort Claims Act and the Gonzales Bill (Medical Malpractice—Actions against the U.S.), which will be described later.

While the term malpractice actually means bad practice, it has been and is used to describe a variety of ethical, civil, and criminal violations committed by health care professionals in the course of dealing with their patients. The main purpose of malpractice law is to compensate persons who are injured by poor medical practice. Improving mental health care practices and acting as a deterrent to professionals who may be tempted to deliver a lower level of care than generally accepted by the professions are additional objectives.

Most malpractice suits are instituted by patients who feel that they have been harmed in some way in the course of treatment—physical harm, emotional harm, harm to reputation, and harm to civil rights. Civil harms known as torts may result from the actions of mental health staff. Battery is an unlawful and undesired touching or invasion of one individual by another. Unless a patient is unconscious, the unwarranted performance of a physical examination or the drawing of blood, even for a good reason, could constitute a battery. Since certain emotionally or mentally disturbed patients may be behaviorally violent, it is difficult to draw a fine line between appropriate restraint, protection of others, and an illegal battery. Even though a patient may require physical restraint, a battery could arise if the patient were restrained with excessive force. The best approach is to use the least restrictive means for controlling behavior of patients.

False imprisonment is an intentional tort to which mental health personnel are prone. The term intentional refers to a desire to effect a certain outcome, in this case to limit another person's movement or freedom of movement. While an active duty member may be confined to a military medical facility without his permission, failing to obtain consent from a civilian family member for psychiatric hospitalization in a military facility could constitute false imprisonment.

Military mental health personnel may act as petitioners for involuntary commitment to a civilian facility. If a psychiatrist makes an incorrect diagnosis which justifies admission when the correct diagnosis would not warrant admission, a charge of false imprisonment is possible. Statutory requirements for commitment must be followed to avoid false imprisonment.

Since mental health professionals have a duty to keep their patients' confidences, unauthorized breaches of confidentiality are actionable. (See above, "Issues of Confidentiality and Privileged Communication.")

Closely related to breach of confidentiality and, at times, extremely hard to differentiate from it, is the tort of *invasion of privacy*. Invasion of privacy involves *extensive revelations* about a person's private thoughts, behavior, experiences, and history, exemplified by the presence of non-essential personnel during treatment when permission is not received from the patient. Patients have the right to refuse to talk with anyone. They also have the right to prohibit their medical records from being seen by persons other than essential individuals involved in their treatment.

Under certain circumstances, a clinician may be sued for defamation of character, slander, or libel. If the diagnostic process was not carefully performed and a term that could be viewed as pejorative was applied to the patient, such as alcoholic or psychopath or sex deviant, the patient could justifiably sue. Clinicians working with military families should be extremely careful to be precise and cautious in the diagnostic process. This does not imply that diagnoses should be avoided for fear of "labeling," but should be rendered in a diligent, professional manner.

Although certain malpractice situations arise more often within civilian practice, personnel working with the military family should be aware of the tort of *undue influence.* In this tort the therapist takes advantage of the treatment relationship to obtain sexual relations, a place in the patient's will, or expensive gifts. If a therapist were to maneuver a patient into a divorce when the patient did not raise it as an option, the uninvolved spouse could sue on the basis of the professional's interference in the marital relationship. (The patient might later bring suit after becoming unhappy with the professional's care!)

While the previous causes for malpractice involved the intentions of the clinician, negligence concerns conduct alone. A psychiatrist, for example, refers a patient to a psychologist for testing. The *intent* is to help the patient and to gain further data for assessment purposes. But if the psychiatrist fails to check the credentials of the psychologist, his conduct (referral) is negligent if the psychologist should be incompetent.

In general, a patient will have a successful cause of action for negligence against a therapist when certain circumstances are met. First, there must be a relationship with the patient which creates a duty in the professional. The duty is usually evaluation and treatment conducted in a reasonable and careful manner. Second, the duty must be violated by failure to meet reasonable standards of care established by the profession. Third, as a result of failure to meet the standards, the patient is harmed. Fourth, the violation of the standards and the harm must be proximately related. "Proximate cause" is a difficult term to define even for the courts. It is not the same as "related to" or "caused by." For example, a lawsuit charging negligence arose when mental health staff failed to properly supervise a disturbed mental patient. The patient ran away, was struck by a train, and killed. The court found that the train was an intervening proximate cause of death rather than the negligent supervision. Even though the verdict was for the mental health staff, another court might have reached a different conclusion.

Negligence in management of suicidal or homicidal patients can lead to a lawsuit if injury or death eventuates. Fault could lie in negligent assessment of suicidal risk or in negligent supervision of the patient known to be at risk.

Other negligence cases can arise: when poorly qualified attendant personnel are hired to care for inpatients; when medical histories and physical examinations are done hastily; when patients are given improper medication, or no medication at all when it is indicated; when somatic treatments such as electroconvulsive therapy are improperly conducted; when behavioral therapy is not closely monitored; when patients are not informed of dangerous effects of medications such as the chance of heat stroke when working in hot, humid weather and taking phenothiazines.

Frequently overlooked in caring for patients is the requirement that a psychiatrist seek competent consultation when uncertain in diagnosis, when the patient's condition is deteriorating, or when the level of care required for the patient is beyond that which the practitioner is capable of rendering.

Professionals are required to keep abreast of current developments in their field. The psychiatrist involved in diagnosis and treatment of inpatients must insure that physical symptoms and illnesses are diagnosed and treated personally, or that appropriate substitute care is sought. Assuming that every somatic symptom is psychological, failing to perform a proper physical examination, or ignoring a patient's complaints, is not only ethically improper, but could lead to serious consequences for the patient and to a lawsuit for the practitioner.

Nonmedical personnel involved in working with the military family should note that those who presume to diagnose or treat conditions which are medical will be held to the standards of care of a medical practitioner. If they do not meet those standards, they can be sued for malpractice.

Given all the possibilities for malpractice, what protection is available to mental health personnel working with the military family? Should federally employed personnel carry private malpractice insurance? Answers to these questions are contained in two pieces of legislation: Medical Malpractice—Actions against the U.S. (1976), popularly known as the Gonzales Bill; and The Federal Tort Claims Act, passed in 1946 and since amended. The latter made it possible for a person injured because of negligence or wrongful act by a government employee to sue the United States in federal court for damages. Individual federal employees could still be sued in state courts. The Federal Tort Claims Act would *not* cover actions for intentional torts (false imprisonment, assault and battery, false arrest, malicious prosecution, abuse of process, or libel and slander) when medical care was involved. Because the federal government has much more money than an individual practitioner, it was unusual for clinicians to be personally sued. But suits were initiated and staff were insecure and uncertain as to their position.

The Gonzales Bill made suit against the United States the exclusive remedy for any party seeking damages for alleged malpractice on the part of Armed Forces medical personnel. In addition, the law provided coverage for intentional torts. If the practitioner were to be sued individually, the Attorney General is authorized to defend the suit. When The Federal Tort Claims Act does not apply, as in military medical care facilities outside the United States, the Bill authorizes the government to "hold harmless or provide liability insurance for any person described" in the Bill. An oversimplified summary would be that the federal government will enter as the defendant in a lawsuit resulting from an alleged tort caused by a government employee acting within the scope of employment. The key words are "tort," "employee," and "scope." The term *employee* is broadly interpreted and includes physicians, dentists, nurses, pharmacists, and paramedical and other support personnel, including technicians, nursing assistants, and therapists. It also includes bona fide volunteers, such as American Red Cross volunteers, and approved rotating medical students and other trainees. The *scope of employment* for military mental health staff is the same as "in the line of duty." The Attorney General of the United States determines whether or not federally employed mental health workers have acted within the scope of their employment when a malpractice suit arises. If the employee is determined not to have acted within that scope, the employee will not be defended by the federal government.

The Federal Tort Claims Act requires that a claim against the government or against an employee of the government for malpractice must be brought within a 2-year period starting from the time of discovery of the act constituting the malpractice, or from the time when an individual by reasonable diligence should have discovered the act. In cases of death, the period begins at the time of death.

Servicemembers are barred from asserting claims against the U.S. government and its employees for personal injury or death arising incident to service (Feres, 1950).

Although the question has been raised as to whether the protection given federal mental health personnel will foster poor care and irresponsible behavior, there is no evidence that care of patients has deteriorated. Reducing the incidence of malpractice by financially punitive means has not been found effective. If clinicians are truly members of a profession, the ethical commitments to quality patient care, respect for one's work and for one's patients should guide behavior above and beyond fear of financial accountability.

Since the primary aim of malpractice action is to compensate persons for harm resulting from tortious acts, the goal is met by the provisions of The Federal Tort Claims Act and the Gonzales Bill. In the final analysis, intelligent, dedicated, skillful care gives patients the best protection from harm, and mental health personnel the best protection from malpractice suits.

OTHER ISSUES INVOLVING TREATMENT PERSONNEL

PATIENT CARE RESPONSIBILITY

An array of medical and nonmedical professionals provide mental health care to the military family. In a military medical care facility, the final responsibility for quality patient care rests with medical personnel and cannot be delegated. Others involved may have intermediate levels of responsibility which should be clearly understood among care providers and approved by appropriate medical authority.

ENTRIES INTO RECORDS

Medical records, as noted in the section on malpractice, are official documentation of a patient's problems, diagnoses, and treatment, but *not* the repository of ill-conceived, off-hand remarks about the behavior or care rendered by mental health staff. Objective data and professional opinion based on data are all that should be entered. If two or more professionals of equal training and stature are involved in the care of a family and disagree on diagnosis or treatment, a conference should be held and a summary entered in the record. If an honest error is made in diagnosis or management, the circumstances involved and a plan for correction should be placed in the record, including what the patient is told about the error. Accusation and blame have no useful purpose in the record.

However, professionals in charge of treatment are obligated to comment in the record about incorrect data, diagnosis, or treatment contained in the written entries of subordinates. Corrective action taken should be documented. Otherwise, it would appear to a court or jury reading the record that the person in charge approved of the erroneous statements.

"MOONLIGHTING"

Mental health professionals employed by the federal government, including those in the uniformed services, may be permitted to practice their professions outside the work setting under very specific guidelines. Under no circumstances may payment be accepted for providing care to a person who is eligible for military medical care or the Civilian Health and Medical Program of the Uniformed Services (CHAMPUS). Colloquially termed "double-dipping," this brings serious penalities.

ACCEPTING GIFTS FROM PATIENTS

Personnel employed by the federal government may be offered gifts of varied value by their patients. The clinical aspects of offering and accepting gifts should be dealt with in the therapy. The legal issue is clear: According to federal regulations, gifts are *not* to be accepted. Although it may seem harmless to accept a small gift, it is better to thank the purveyor for the thought and defer to the regulation.

WHOM DOES THE THERAPIST SERVE?

Military therapists often raise concerns about serving two masters—the patient and the government. There is a concern that the therapeutic needs of the servicemember and his family may conflict with the requirements of the military. Situations in which conflicts arise have been discussed under "Confidentiality and Privileged Communication." Government-employed clinicians have been hired to provide the best possible care to the military family. Therefore, serving the military family *is* serving the government. When special requirements of military service demand psychiatric evaluation of a member which could lead to loss of military employment, or might lead to a significant change of duty (loss of flight status, nuclear clearance, Top Secret Clearance) the clinician is basically serving the government's interest. This fact, and the limits of confidentiality, should be made clear. If it seems that an unexpected or unusual circumstance creates a conflict of interest between the therapeutic needs of the military family and the interests of the government, such conflict should be made known to the appropriate military medical authority. It is in the government's interest to evaluate the conflict and make all possible efforts to resolve it.

SERIOUS PSYCHIATRIC DISORDERS IN THE SERVICEMEMBER

U.S. law, implemented via military regulations, provides for medically retiring a person who becomes unfit for military duty as a result of psychiatric illness. After thorough evaluation and substantial treatment, three medical officers (a Medical Evaluation Board) review the servicemember's diagnosis, clinical course, and prognosis. Analyzing their findings in the context of regulatory guidelines, the Medical Board states whether the individual is fit for further duty. If the finding is "unfit," the case is referred to a Physical Evaluation Board which reviews the recommendation of the Medical Board, the person's work record, and the degree of disability resulting from the illness, and advises higher military authority as to the most appropriate manner of separation from service (if recommended). If the work record of the member is favorable and his illness is deemed "in the line of duty," he may be recommended for temporary or permanent medical separation with variable benefits. Throughout the entire process, stringent requirements must be followed to insure fairness to the servicemember and to the government. Legal representation, formal rebuttal, and several levels of appeal may be utilized if he disagrees with the findings of the Physical Evaluation Board.

The system is somewhat like workers' compensation, wherein employees are indemnified to various degrees for injuries incurred on the job. The military system provides the member and family important benefits which exceed the usual workers' compensation program. As a result, the military family is somewhat shielded from the potentially calamitous financial impact of a serious psychiatric disorder.

SUBSTANCE ABUSE

Substance abuse is a serious matter to the Armed Forces. Tobacco, marijuana, and alcohol are most frequently abused. Lower on the scale of abuse are sedatives, PCP, amphetamines, and narcotics.

Substance abuse is considered to have an adverse impact upon military discipline and quality of job performance. In July 1983, a policy was implemented, through a Department of the Army message, directing that all officers, warrant officers, and senior enlisted members (grades E6–E9) who are determined to be illegal drug abusers must be processed for separation from the Service. The same policy applies to all second-time drug abusers and all soldiers determined to be drug-dependent. Illegal drugs include marijuana. "Processed for separation" does not mean automatic separation; each case will be reviewed on its own merits. Because of the investment the country has in a trained military member who may be rehabilitatable, a soldier believed to have a substance abuse problem may be referred for evaluation, and entered into a treatment program, if appropriate, without punitive action. Refusal to comply with the program and lack of success in rehabilitation usually result in administrative separation from the Service. Criminal offenses incident to substance abuse are dealt with under the applicable civilian or military law. When a military person abuses *illegal* substances in the civilian community, punishment under military law as well as punishment under civilian law may result. Abuse of illegal substances is viewed as seriously interfering with the goals and mission of the Armed Forces, and thus is service-connected no matter where the abuse occurs.

Non-active-duty members of the military family are not subject to military law but are subject to federal and state laws if drug violations occur in federal or state jurisdictions. However, the servicemember may incur administrative separation from the military if he is unable or unwilling to keep his family from illegal acts which bring discredit upon the military.

MENTAL RETARDATION

Mental retardation in a child may impose great stress on the military family. Serious attention must be given to legal situations encountered in the lives of retarded dependents. Parents of a moderately to profoundly retarded child, after careful diagnosis, prognosis, and family discussion, may wish to place the child in an institution. Problems arise when a mobile military family attempts to secure placement. Private facilities are costly. CHAMPUS will not pay for domiciliary services alone. If the military family is not a legal resident of the state in which the service-member is assigned, that state's resources may be foreclosed. Placement might be available only at great distance in the state of the service-member's legal residence.

Those who assess the child may be asked to assist with direct services when institutionalization or placement in a special class or program is sought. Such services include child and family diagnostic work, psychometric assessment, physical examination, and speech evaluation. Results of the examinations are matched against legal requirements for placement.

Parents often become concerned about the sexual behavior and reproductive potential of a retarded dependent approaching puberty. This concern may lead the parents to request that their retarded dependent be sterilized. The reasons offered include fear that a female child will be taken advantage of and easily seduced, or be unable to properly care for her hygiene needs during menses; or that a male child will lose control of his impulses and commit sexual assault, usually on a younger child. Sterilization is an invasive procedure and usually results in permanent loss of procreative capacity, a capacity considered by the courts to be a basic human right. Consequently, request for sterilization of a minor retarded child is given very strict scrutiny. The court may consider the following points: the clinical condition of the retarded person as to capacity for understanding the nature of procreation and sterilization; the potential emotional impact and adjustment problems engendered either by not performing sterilization or by performing it; the potential ability of the retarded person to care for a child should the event occur; the probability of either pregnancy or violent behavior; the likelihood of a retarded child being born to the person in question (an issue of inherited disorders); and alternative ways other than sterilization for dealing with potential problems. The court will probably not consider convenience issues, such as menstrual hygiene, in the face of the mammoth interference with the rights of privacy and procreation. As part of its deliberations, a wise court will seek help from experts who will be asked to examine the child and the family in light of the questions raised.

When the retarded child reaches maturity, a legal guardian (usually the parents) will often be required. The guardian, however, may not volunteer the retarded ward for sterilization. Nor may the guardian volunteer the ward for mutilative or invasive surgery, or high-risk therapy of any type unless it can be shown (1) that the retarded person is not competent to give an informed consent; (2) that the retarded person stands to gain more than can be lost; (3) that no new medical procedure is on the horizon that might obviate the need for the medical procedure; and (4) that the recommended action is in the best interests of the retarded person. Few state courts will accept jurisdiction for authorizing sterilization of a noninstitutionalized mental incompetent. Procedural safeguards are paramount, which include appointing a *guardian ad litem* (a person especially appointed by the court—may be but need not be an attorney) to look after the ward's rights during the issue being litigated. Even if given clearance by a court, the sterilization procedure may be disallowed in a military facility for policy reasons. Private physicians might resist the surgery for fear of being sued by someone in behalf of the retarded person later in life. Because of the complex legal issues involving sterilization, those working with the family of a retarded dependent should consult the Judge Advocate General's Office for the most recent position of the relevant courts.

Eligibility of a retarded dependent for military medical care will continue beyond the age of 18 if the retarded person is fully dependent upon the servicemember. If the dependent should become a ward of the state, military benefits are lost.

Another issue clinicians should discuss with the family of a retarded dependent is planning for care of the dependent in the event of death of the sponsor. It is critical to raise the question before a retiring servicemember must decide to accept or reject the Survivor's Benefit Plan. Rejection of the Plan means that *no* further pension benefits are paid to surviving family in the event of the retiree's death.

Arrangements should be detailed in the servicemember's will and in the spouse's will. Discussion and consideration of these less than pleasant possibilities can be facilitated by mental health personnel.

THE MILITARY FAMILY IN A FOREIGN COUNTRY

When a military member is assigned outside the United States, family members may accompany him either at his own expense or under government sponsorship. If the family is sponsored, the government will provide housing, medical care, schooling, and other benefits. Although a non-sponsored family may be given medical care on a space-available basis, the family must meet most of its own needs. In both cases dependents are subject to the laws of the host nation, not the laws of the United States. Problems arise when an American living abroad does not understand the importance placed by people of the host nation on certain behaviors, rules, or procedures. Violations become more serious when the violator disputes the importance of the breach of law. Language barriers further complicate understanding of and functioning within a foreign legal system, which may be opposite to that of the United States in basic orientation to guilt and innocence. Legal systems in some foreign countries presume guilt until the charged party can prove innocence, whereas a person is innocent until proven guilty in the United States.

The servicemember stationed abroad may be subject to the laws of the host nation in addition to military law. Status of Forces Agreements may be negotiated between the host nation and the United States providing for management of service personnel who violate host nation laws. Such agreements may allow the military command to take jurisdiction of a member accused of a crime.

Mentally ill servicemembers who are tried and convicted by the host nation could be placed in a hospital for the criminally insane within the host country. The member does not usually benefit from such hospitalization because neither he nor the treatment staff share a common language. American medical staff may be asked to evaluate the incarcerated member for various administrative purposes, but will not be able to provide treatment. In fact, the patient may have been discharged from the military because of his actions and may be a private American citizen. Care would not be authorized from the military in such a case. In certain circumstances, the host country will permit the United States to assume responsibility for a mentally ill but criminally convicted servicemember if he is returned to the United States and not permitted to reenter the host country.

A troubled adolescent member of a military family in a foreign country may act out his conflicts, embarrassing our country. When the military sponsor is unable to contain such behavior, a sponsored family is sent back to the United States. The sponsor, however, may be required to remain in a critical duty position, and the family will be geographically separated. *Nonsponsored* dependents cannot be returned to the United States by a military commander. The foreign nation may declare the problem-maker to be a *persona non grata* and expel him from its territory. Both sponsored and nonsponsored dependents have been and probably will continue to be tried and punished under host nation laws in egregious cases.

Undesirable behavior on the part of an adolescent can have a negative impact on the servicemember's career, since he is viewed as deficient in caring for his family. In a perverse manner, a teenager can "get revenge" on a parent for real or fancied wrongs. Or the teen may have been given erroneous peer group advice that a little misbehavior will serve to return the family stateside to a more comfortable environment—without adverse consequences. Mental health staff, by early intervention, can disabuse the teenager of his misconceptions and facilitate adjustment to the foreign environment.

DIVORCE AND CHILD CUSTODY

The military family faces special problems where divorce and child custody are concerned. Gaining access to the state courts where divorce and custody actions are handled is often difficult because of residency requirements, jurisdiction problems, or financial constraints. In Georgia the person seeking divorce must be a county resident for at least 6 continuous months prior to filing if living in the civilian community, but residency on a military base extends the minimum time to 1 year.

Considerations of property settlement, alimony, and child custody are of special significance to the military family, since after a divorce is final, most nonmilitary divorcees will not be eligible for benefits. A divorced spouse who was married to a servicemember for at least 20 years while he accrued at least 20 years of active duty for retirement purposes; who was divorced after February 1, 1983; and who has not remarried is eligible under the Uniformed Services Former Spouses Protection Act (1983) for military privileges. Medical care is not authorized if the divorced spouse is employed by a firm that provides an employee medical benefit plan. Proper forms must be completed, and a Uniformed Services Identification and Privilege Card obtained. In all other cases, medical care, exchange, and commissary privileges are immediately cut off. Substitutes for these benefits may need to be provided in order to maintain the previous standard of living of the nonmilitary divorcee. Their children, if still supported by the military sponsor, continue to be eligible for military privileges no matter with whom they live.

When divorce is decided upon, the distribution of marital property is determined by the laws of the state in which the action occurs. To appreciate the variations in approach to property distribution faced by military families, consider the following principles applied by different states. First, there is a unity-of-the-person doctrine, wherein the husband takes title to all marital property, and title determines ownership. Second, the title approach may generally rule, but the court can ignore title and distribute some of the property to the wife if she has made an especially outstanding contribution to obtaining that property. Third, certain states look upon marriage as a partnership of equals. When those equals split, the law allows for equal division of all marital property. Fourth, the theory of equitable distribution accounts for the individual contributions of the spouses to the acquisition of their property. The contributions (including money, work, special services other than expected duties) are rated in percentage terms, and the property distributed on that basis. Fifth, some states use various combinations of the other principles. Most states also provide for exceptions to their general rules when adultery, for example, is the ground for divorce. Property settlements, once accomplished, are usually final and not able to be modified in future litigation.

In *McCarty v. McCarty* (1981), the U.S. Supreme Court held that state courts could not treat retirement pay as community property because Congress intended military retirement pay to be the personal entitlement of the retiree. However, the Uniformed Services Former Spouses Protection Act (1983) now allows state courts to treat retirement pay in accordance with their laws regarding division of property, with certain limitations. The spouse, for example, must have been married to the servicemember for at least 10 years, during which the member performed at least 10 years of service creditable toward retirement; and the court issuing the settlement order must have competent jurisdiction over the member. If the correct procedure is followed, settlements will be withheld and paid by the appropriate center managing the retiree's pay. It would appear that cases not meeting the stipulations of the Uniforms Services Former Spouses Protection Act continue to be governed by the decision in *McCarty v. McCarty*.

Child custody problems also confront the military family, both in the form of original custody disputes at the time of divorce, and later when efforts are made to modify prior custody arrangements. The basis of awarding child custody varies from state to state. Even within the same state, reasons for awarding custody differ, based upon the age of the child. If a child is very young, the "tender years doctrine" might be followed in which the child is awarded to the mother *if* she is fit. A child over the age of 14 might be permitted to decide which parent to live with. Custody of children of other ages could be based upon the "best interest of the child" doctrine. In the latter case, the welfare of the child, rather than the rights of the parents, is the main consideration of the court.

As part of the custody decision, a determination will also be made as to who is responsible for providing child support. Often state law requires that the husband support his children, whether or not he has custody. But the courts are becoming more flexible, and may require joint support or support by the mother. If a noncustodial military member is required to support minor children and fails to do so, a levy can be placed against his salary. Retirement pay may be levied against for child support purposes. A court order is required by the provisions of the Social Services Amendments of 1974. For nonmilitary persons who fail to meet their support obligations, the Uniform Reciprocal Enforcement of Support Act (1977) may be applicable, wherein one state can enforce the support decree of another. This act has markedly simplified the troublesome process formerly required to recover nonpaid child support.

The terms of a custody decree are open to modification for a variety of reasons. Usually the court requires that the circumstances of the child's life or conditions set down in the original custody agreement have changed significantly. Allegations of unfitness must be evaluated. One court decided recently (*Bell v. Bell*, 1980) that an unmarried custodial parent living with a member of the opposite sex must relinquish custody of the child to the other parent. This decision follows a presumption that certain parental misconduct is adverse to the child's welfare. Nevertheless, a recent Georgia court made this observation: "While this Court has a sincere concern for the welfare of a child, we likewise must relate that welfare to a parental misconduct and not to the vagaries or vicissitudes that beset every family on its journey through the thickets of life" (*Shover v. Department of Human Resources*, 1980). In addition to immoral behavior and commission of crimes, a serious mental disorder in a custodial parent may require change of custody in the best interest of the child. Frequent absences by the custodial parent have formed the basis of an argument for unfitness as a parent. In several cases involving military families, attorneys attempted to persuade the court to award custody to the nonmilitary member, arguing that the peripatetic nature of military service is against the best interest of the child. If a court were to accept this argument, thousands of military parents would be disqualified from being competent parents. Thus far, no court has accepted the argument. Nevertheless, since interference with the education of the child is one basis for change of custody, it is possible that someone in the future will argue that frequent reassignments of a custodial military member adversely affect the education of the child, and that a custody change should result. Mental health professionals could be asked to testify in such a situation.

Attempts by the noncustodial parent at modifying the custody arrangement are not always polite. The laws of the state granting the original custody decree may conflict with the custody laws of the state in which the child currently resides, creating confusion and handicapping efforts to resolve conflicts. It was hoped that the Uniform Child Custody Jurisdiction Act (1981) would prevent childnapping and nonreturn of a child after visitation with the noncustodial parent. Even with this Act, which has been adopted by most states, problems continue to exist because of poor implementation. Often, a noncustodial parent will use differences in state laws to change the original custody decree and obtain custody of the visiting child. Caught in the middle of these manipulations, the child invariably suffers. If the Act is applied properly, custody rulings cannot be arbitrarily changed without the requested modification being evaluated in light of the original reasons for awarding custody. Nevertheless, geographic separation, lack of adequate resources to hire an attorney, or lack of funds to pay for trips to the states in which litigation is initiated, complicate the active duty person's efforts to regain custody of the child.

If custody is awarded to a military member who does not remarry relatively soon, problems can arise. The availability of that member for duty without a continuing concern about his child's well-being is always in question. Regulations require that a single parent establish a plan providing for care of his child if an unaccompanied overseas assignment is ordered. The problem of single parents in the Armed Forces is being studied further.

Visitation problems often arise after disruption of the military family. A servicemember might divorce, gain custody of a child, and then remarry. If the member is then assigned to an overseas tour of duty with the child and the new spouse, the noncustodial parent might attempt to change the custody by contesting the visitation issue. While the custodial parent has the right to move and, in most cases, to determine the residence of the custodial child, the noncustodial parent also has rights. Visitation arrangements should be carefully considered when military members retain custody of a child. If the nonservicemember is the custodial parent, the servicemember may find it difficult to maintain a relationship with his child. Curtailment of visitation trips because of cost, especially if the noncustodial parent is assigned overseas, can profoundly affect their relationship.

Although the dissolution of a marriage between a servicemember and a nonservicemember has been focused on, it must be remembered that there are military families wherein both parents are active duty military. The problems discussed above, especially visitation and efforts to litigate changes in support or custody, are further complicated when both divorced parents continue on active duty.

Recently, divorce mediation has developed as an alternative or adjunct to the adversarial divorce process. The adversarial approach alone often intensifies disputes over terms of divorce. Mediation seeks to help the parties negotiate an agreement by fostering communication and by persuasion. Although new and controversial, mediation appears to increase client satisfaction, particularly in the area of child support, custody, and visitation (Bahr, 1981; Bendheim & Pickrell, 1980). Mediation may offer the military family an opportunity to arrange terms which are less susceptible to being contested after a divorce.

What recourse does a person stationed overseas have if a spouse leaves with the children and returns stateside with the intention of suing for divorce? What relief is available for the servicemember geographically separated from his family whose spouse moves out of their rented apartment and begins divorce proceedings, with a 2-year lease remaining on the apartment? These and other problems led Congress to enact the Soldiers' and Sailors' Civil Relief Act of 1940 (amended), created to protect the servicemember when, by reason of military service, his ability to fulfill financial and other obligations, or to assert many legal rights, has been compromised. The key feature throughout the provisions of the Act is that military service must *materially* affect the member's particular situation. The mere fact of being in military service does not forestall legal action against a servicemember. There may be circumstances where the servicemember's rights are at issue, such as in a divorce or custody suit. If informed about the suit, he may request a stay in order to secure appropriate legal counsel or obtain leave to attend to the matter. On the other hand, if the member's rights have already been determined or are not at issue, and the military service materially affects his ability to meet an acknowledged financial obligation, he may request a stay in the execution of a judgment. Although there are a number of technical considerations, the member's inability to proceed with litigation of issues or payment of a judgment must be in good faith. Persistent voluntary extensions overseas to avoid legal action would not be tolerated. If the member is unavailable or unable to pay for a short period of time, the court will usually grant the request for a stay. If, however, the court believes that there will be a long unavailability of the servicemember, the court may require that he delay departure for overseas or take leave if overseas, or at least attempt to do so. If leave is denied, the court will usually authorize a stay in proceedings. If the matter before the court deals purely with legal issues rather than with issues of fact, a stay is frequently denied. Stays are also denied in matters contrary to public policy, such as litigation involving child support.

If a servicemember does not appear, either personally or through a legal representative, a default judgment may be entered against him. In a default judgment, the individual who brings the case to court is granted whatever is legally and appropriately requested in the event that the opposing party does not appear. The person bringing suit must certify the military status of the opposing party. If that opposing party is an active duty person, legal counsel must be appointed for him. However, that counsel cannot waive the member's right to reopen the case at a future date and does not count as appearance of the member in court. The attorney is merely appointed to insure that the member's legal rights are protected. At a later time under strict conditions and with carefully defined limitations, the servicemember can request a reopening of a default judgment, if it can be proved that his case was materially prejudiced by military duty, and he has a meritorious or legal defense to the contested issue.

WHERE TO TURN FOR LEGAL ADVICE

For the professional working with the military, legal guidance should be initiated with the Office of the Staff Judge Advocate. In cases where the professional may be at legal issue with the government itself, or if accused of committing an act which clearly exceeded the scope of employment, the professional will be referred to other sources of legal aid in the private sector.

For the military family, a variety of resources may be necessary. A person suspected of or accused of a criminal offense under the Uniform Code of Military Justice (military law) will have counsel appointed for him by the government. He may waive government legal help and pay for private counsel, or may have both military and civilian counsel. In the latter case, he pays only for the civilian counsel. When the criminal offense involves the civilian community rather than a breach of military law, the servicemember may discuss the issue with the military legal office, but in most cases he will not be able to be defended by that office. Private counsel or a public defender will be required. (An attorney would be appointed by the court if circumstances warranted.) Military dependents are not subject to the Uniform Code of Military Justice, and are not eligible for military defense services. They may, however, obtain preliminary guidance and knowledgeable referral to appropriate civilian counsel from the Office of the Staff Judge Advocate.

All members of the military family are eligible to consult legal assistance resources for advice, referral, and certain specific services such as drawing of wills (recommended for all adults), review of sales agreements and leases, analysis of foreclosures, aid in regaining improperly withheld security deposits, advice on handling usurious late fees, and how to make use of the small claims court. A matter of considerable importance which should be brought to the attention of legal assistance involves a collection agency pressuring the servicemember into settling a financial matter by threatening to call or actually calling his commanding officer or senior noncommissioned officer (NCO). If the issue is still in dispute, calling the commanding officer is illegal. The stress experienced by personnel in such situations may be extraordinary and may adversely effect duty performance.

The Armed Forces and the Federal Civil Service are subject to a myriad of regulations which have the force of law. The regulations define both rights and responsibilities in the same vein as do the better known laws. Information about rights and responsibilities applicable to specific circumstances may be obtained from a variety of sources, including the commanding officer, the Equal Opportunity Officer, the Inspector General, and the Staff Judge Advocate.

Unquestionably, military families and the mental health personnel who serve them encounter and are governed by the law in a wide variety of circumstances. By becoming more knowledgeable in how legal matters affect both themselves and their patients, therapists will be rewarded with an increased ability to understand and respond to the clinical needs of the military family.

REFERENCES

Bahr, S. J. Mediation is the answer: Why couples are so positive about this route to divorce. *Family Advocate,* Spring 1981, *3*(4), 32.

Bell v. Bell, 267 S.E. 2d 894 (Ga. 1980).

Belli, M., Sr. Warning of the dangerous patient: A practical approach. *American Journal of Forensic Psychiatry,* 1981–1982, *2*(2), 2.

Bendheim, A., & Pickrell, R. Family disputes mediation: A new service for lawyers and their clients. *Barrister,* Winter 1980, 28.

Federal Tort Claims Act, 23 U.S.C. § 2674 *et seq.* (1976).

Feres v. the United States, 340 U.S. 135 (1950).

McCarty v. McCarty, U.S. Supreme Court No. 80-5 (June 1981).

Medical Malpractice—Actions against the U.S., 10 U.S.C. § 1089 (1976).

Privacy Act of 1974, 5 U.S.C. § 552a (1976).

Shover v. Department of Human Resources, 270 S.E. 2d 464 (Ga. 1980).

Social Services Amendments of 1974, 42 U.S.C. §§ 659–660 (1974), *as amended* by the Social Services Amendments of 1977, 42 U.S.C. §§ 661–662 (Supp. II 1978).

Soldiers' and Sailors' Civil Relief Act of 1940, 50 U.S.C. App. §§ 501–548, 560–590 (1976).

Tarasoff v. Regents of the University of California, 131 Cal. Rptr. 14 (1976).

Uniform Child Custody Jurisdiction Act, Ga. Code Ann. §§ 74-501–525 (1981).

Uniform Reciprocal Enforcement of Support Act, Ill. Rev. Stat. ch. 40, § 1201 *et seq.* (1977).

Uniformed Services Former Spouses Protection Act, PL 97-252 (Sep. 82), now codified in scattered sections of the 10 U.S.C. §§ 1072–1408 (Supp. 1983).

3

Special Treatment Needs of Children of Military Families

ALEX R. RODRIGUEZ

> There is only one child in the world, that child's name is all children.
> —Carl Sandburg

THE SPECIAL CHILD

Military children, like other "special" populations of children, confront special challenges in growing up. By the very nature of their categorization as "military children," an identity is ascribed and acquired which follows these young people into the community and into sequential stages of individual development. As a member of a special category around which a sociocultural lore has developed, the child in a military family must master both unique and common tasks in establishing a sense of self. In this respect, the military child must be able to develop adaptive responses that will allow autonomous development under variable conditions as well as participation in the family and community, both of which are frequently in flux and under stress. Such circumstances are not uncommon in other groups of children who are specially designated by common experiences—such as gifted children or ethnic minority children. This chapter will look at military children from the perspective of what is commonly and anecdotally attributed to them, their families, and com-

The opinions or assertions contained herein are the private views of the writer and are not to be construed as official or as reflecting the views of the Department of the Navy or the Department of Defense.

Alex R. Rodriguez. Commander, Medical Corps, U.S. Navy, and Medical Director, Civilian Health and Medical Program of the Uniformed Services (CHAMPUS), Department of Defense, Aurora, Colorado.

munities; what research-based data have been collected to date that shed light on military child life; and what the current and future needs of these children are for assistance with their special needs.

While each child is unique—physically, psychologically, intellectually, socially, and spiritually—individual characteristics are derived from a number of sources. Thus, any discussion of military children should involve an understanding of the many elements of contemporary civilian and military families and communities which impact on development. While other chapters in this book focus on some of these elements, this chapter will review them in the context of their effects on the military child's biopsychosocial development, particularly in the experience of growing up as an identified military child in a military family and community. In being special, military children primarily gain an identity from an occupational–social spectrum that is subsumed under the special mission of national defense. The multiple human activities involved in this take these children to many civilian and military communities at different chronological and developmental milestones in their lives, with each change necessitating new adaptations. In their successes or failures in these adaptational tasks, military children merit special attention.

THE SPECIAL FAMILY

Military families are regularly confronted with situations that test their capacity for healthy functioning. The traditional and average American family has existed in relatively stable and consistent geographical, socio-cultural, and occupational settings. Although American families now are generally more occupationally mobile than in the past, military families are still disrupted by moves even more frequently than their civilian counterparts (McCubbin, Dahl, & Hunter 1976). Separations are common, as are economic difficulties, alienation from local community institutions, isolation from extended family, and high expectations for conformity to military social norms. Over the years, military families increasingly have moved away from the homogeneous confines of military posts and bases to greater integration into adjacent civilian communities. While this phenomenon has led to opportunities for families to develop a more heterogeneous identity and range of affiliations, it has also confronted them with the task of moving back and forth between military and civilian social systems—with their differing identities, mores, and capacities for integrating the military family. The service connected family can be viewed as a minority institution, and is frequently an outsider in both civilian and military settings, due to its transient nature, which interferes with the community's and the family's own constrained abilities to make it possible for them to live in two communities simultaneously. They must serve as their own medium of communication between these communities, particularly when some of their needs must be met by each. It requires great resourcefulness and flexibility in military families for this to be successful. Success in this dual existence is indicative of the special strengths of some military families—the ones who are likely to have a higher level of future adaptive functioning in multiple settings.

To add to the complexity, the military family is affected by the myriad surging forces in American society. These include a greater breadth in socially determined normative behaviors and attitudes—for people of all ages, sexes, and occupational roles; changes in the primacy of work over leisure as a social value; greater acceptance of changing roles for men and women—particularly in sharing of family tasks, in dual careers, and in independent choice of interests outside the family. All of these have affected the military organization's function and defense policy and planning, by their demonstrated effects on military recruitment and retention. Service families have traditionally been passive to the needs of the military organization; now they are increasingly exercising independent thought in regard to the requisites of military life, and undertaking advocacy roles regarding their needs within the organization. Thus, while the military family has traditionally been stoic and has internalized stressful circumstances, the current trend toward greater family vocalization of the family's needs sometimes indicates a healthier military family and the prospect for a healthier military organization.

The fact that the Department of Defense (DoD) is now listening to ideas for and implementing family programs is also a positive sign—for its appreciation of family needs and for its own effective function. Military managers have begun to recognize the military family as a fundamental part of the military organization, as it is inimically tied to the accomplishment of the defense mission through its interactive and interpersonal ties with the active servicemember and his or her unit. This recognition has largely come about because of various factors, including (1) organizational management theory and research, tying the psychosocial adaptation of the employee to an interlinking of family stability, individual and unit morale, work performance, and retention; (2) increasing technological and skills sophistication in military systems, which makes the organization more dependent on the skills and education of its employees and therefore less apt to consider the employee who has special individual or family needs to be expendable; (3) the all volunteer service, which further restricts the military's options for employee replenishment that would be available under a conscription system; (4) recent American social movements and changes in perspectives on quality of life which have resulted in a more humanistic view of the individual and groups, and an acceptance and advocacy of broader human rights in social systems; and (5) family research, which has shown the strength of the family as a social institution underpinning other social institutions, has demonstrated that healthy families provide productive and cost-beneficial employees, and has documented the many ways that damaged and distressed families can disrupt social units to which they are connected (*Final Report of the White House Commission on Families*, 1981). Through all of this, the military family has emerged as a distinctive type with special needs, strengths, stresses, and problems. Its functioning is innately tied to that of its individual members and that of the communities in which it exists. *After having been ignored, tolerated, and reacted to negatively for so long, it is apparent that to be a military family can now be viewed as a positive identity.*

THE SPECIAL COMMUNITY

The military community is composed of a complex of persons, families and social systems, and has its own unique identity and place in the larger society. Military communities have traditionally been geographically delimited from civilian communities by their compoundlike construction. Within the confines of military installations, service families formerly lived an integrated and sustained existence, at times so apart from the civilian world that there were few reasons for them to venture away from the military "township." The traditional provision of housing, shopping, recreational activities, and schools during the last half-century made the military installation self-contained. The base environment and its people acquired an identity of "otherness" from the larger civilian surroundings. Over time, increased pay, higher costs of providing and maintaining adequate family housing, greater proximity of civilian neighborhoods and conveniences to military installations, and the growing desire of military families to be a part of a more heterogeneous social scene have contributed to military families becoming more a part of civilian communities—both in residence and in participation in its activities. In this sense, the military community now rarely has a separate life of its own. Through the many people who live both inside and outside its boundaries, it is frequently diffused into surrounding civilian settings. This causes it to both lose and gain something, creating some adjustment problems and ameliorating others. The protections and structures that were once built into the closed armed forces community, while generally still present, are but a part of the military family's source of support in most current assignments, particularly in the continental United States. In addition, some installations are removing physical and other barriers that limit access of local civilians to its facilities.

Thus, at a time when American social values and institutions are in a period of developmental flux, military communities in particular are changing in their composition and roles. There are probably few other settings where sociocultural identities are undergoing such sharp modifications. With the current racial and cultural variegation of the military population, there are many opportunities for each family to expand its awareness and involvement with groups beyond its usual experiences. However well some military communities are able to provide for such broadening experiences, the social transitions that ensue may pose a threat to role and identity that triggers a sense of identity diffusion and role loss in some persons in such multicultural and multiethnic settings. This has led to some military communities' becoming a microcosmic extension of the sometimes hostile and divided external world characterized by the defensive group loyalties that color much of the contemporary American "melting pot" society. There is some tendency for ghettoization to occur. When this extends through the family, school, neighborhood, and social groups to the child or adolescent, it may lead to conflicts about social identities, boundaries, and affiliations. The perpetuation of prejudice and narrow group associations threaten a military community's identity, morale, and purpose, and poses a real problem for each child's sense of place in the community. In this light, Escalona (1975) has noted that "even those children not directly affected by social upheaval or instability are seen at serious risk of inadequate ego development when the social reality they perceive diverges sharply from the values they are taught." While some observers view the military community as aswirl in conflict due to its transient and artificially constructed population, its inherently conflictual mission, and its rigid and isolated ways, many others have viewed those in the service community as a relatively preselected population with generally higher adaptive function and a richness of experience. Whatever perspective is adopted, it is generally agreed that these communities constitute special settings populated by people with a unique purpose and challenge. In reviewing the special aspects of life for military children it should be kept in mind that what is known about military families is limited and changing. This realization should lead to a broader and less stereotyped view of them.

THE STRESS OF MILITARY LIFE

WORK STRESS AND FAMILY STRESS

The military family, like all families, functions in a continual state of response to the demands of modern life. Stress for any individual is generated by everyday external and internal stimuli, to which the person is challenged to respond, and in which the degree of biopsychosocial dysfunction is minimized by mental and behavioral coping responses. Stress responses are modulated by not only spontaneous mental mechanisms of defense, such as intellectualization, rationalization, and humor, but also by external support systems. For children, stress is experienced as the levels of perception and vulnerability which are characteristic of developmental periods, and are often closely tied to the stress and adaptation levels of parents and significant others. As parents experience the limits of their own adaptive functioning, the child who partially draws his or her strength from them will concomitantly experience dysfunction and distress.

In an occupationally centered, regimented, and hierarchical organization like the military, there are unique supports and unique problems that emerge as elements in either the adaptive or maladaptive functioning of the active servicemember and fellow employees and family members. Job stress is not unexpected in occupations where competitive and aggressive urges must be channeled into fairly narrow behavioral norms, where job mastery is broken by frequent moves and promotions, and where family life is disrupted by moves, separations, and changes in work schedules. The relation of job stress to role conflict, ambiguity of work modes and responsibilities, boundary conflicts in work settings, overwork or lack of stimulation–challenge, low status, assignment beyond skills or knowledge level, frequent changes in job responsibilities and locale, are all well recognized in the military. When they occur in any organization in which turnover of employees is high, as in the military, then the chances for job stress increase. In addition, stress leading to biopsychosocial developmental disturbances, in both adults and children, will increase with certain life stress events; lack of satisfaction and integration with social, occupational–school, and interpersonal environments; significant losses in goals, self-image, and important persons; and prolonged states of helplessness and hopelessness. These circumstances are common for the military person and family, and provide the situational precursors for dysfunction in any developmental–functional area for the vulnerable person. Reactions to stressful situations are individualized, according to biological vulnerability (e.g., asthma, ulcers, hypertension), social supports (e.g., family, friends, availability of social services), and individual psychological makeup. The family's ability to adequately cope with stressful situations parallels their individual and collective abilities to (1) mesh military rules, procedures, attitudes, and values with their own superego(s); (2) use humor, undoing, sublimation, intellectualization, altruism, creative elaboration, and other higher order mental defense mechanisms; (3) perceive, accept, and integrate insights provided by others that would allow adaptation to difficult circumstances; (4) provide for empathy and open expression and tolerance of feelings and thoughts in family communications; and (5) promote a sense of common identification with social units, and a sense of mutuality, belonging, and caring within the family. Although younger children often do not have as effective coping abilities in their psychological makeup as older children or adults, their functioning does draw on the capabilities of parents and older siblings and these significant adults' abilities to assist the child in his or her age appropriate adaptive responses (e.g., denial, avoidance, play). Older family members who avoid, deny, or isolate as primary means of dealing with stressful situations are at risk for maladaptation. Ultimately, stress and maladaptation in the family operate in a closed cycle with maladaptation in the community and in the work unit. Recognition of these dynamic connections and manifestations of both healthy and disturbed functioning is essential for anyone who works with military personnel and their families, including human service professionals, and military managers and planners.

MILITARY LIFE AND THE FAMILY

Military life is a unique existence, characterized by multiple potentially stressful circumstances. Not all individuals have the psychological flexibility to adapt to novel and difficult situations. Success in previous adaptations to one's home community or previous job does not insure good acclimation to military life. Military communities vary greatly in their composition, level of military regimentation, and mission requirements, degrees of connectedness with civilian life, and social rules and norms. Therefore, families who have successfully adapted to some military settings in the continental United States and/or near family may find themselves under great distress in unfamiliar military and cultural settings. Thus, all military families are continually and potentially vulnerable to changing stressors. Each aspect of change in military family life brings new challenges and requires a delicate accommodation process about which little can be taken for granted. It is imperative that both military leaders and military parents recognize the impact of relocations on children and adolescents, who not uncommonly have difficulty verbalizing their problems with change. This should be of real concern to parents since change in the military is frequent, often unpredictable, on short notice, and imperative. In its impact on the family, change is always a proposition that requires individual and conjoint family adaptation, and the ability to seek assistance when dysfunction occurs. Some families fail to react to problems induced by multiple changes due to pride and a "can do" military attitude; fear of a negative effect on their career if they are identified as having personal problems or not being able to manage family problems; lack of insight that a problem exists; maladaptive psychological defensive reactions to distress or lack of control; and/or lack of available supports or appropriate services. It is important that such situations be more readily anticipated, recognized, and provided for by military leaders and health care–social service providers.

The military has traditionally been a source of refuge and escape: for some, from unsatisfying personal circumstances and economic–occupational constraints; for others, an idealized and orderly way of life where commitment to patriotic and other principles can be lived out; a place of confinement and possible rehabilitation; a setting where aggressive conflicts and fantasies can be expressed; and a milieu where romantic ideals of the self and society, psychological self-maturation into adulthood, and necessary adult skills–knowledge can be sought. Few are ever attracted by a simple desire for "just another job." The institution of the military attracts a polyglot of persons with varying personal and family backgrounds, goals, and capacities. One of the goals of military life is to provide for and direct this diverse group of people toward a common set of objectives, with a common sense of purpose and common means of accomplishing goals. That this form of social engineering is ever successful is somewhat amazing. And that it is achieved with persons who are generally intellectually brighter and psychologically healthier than the civilian counterpart defies the common stereotypical view that the military is composed of misfits and dependent personalities. Preselection by examination, while not capable of totally preventing potentially maladaptive persons from enlisting or being commissioned, does diminish the frequency of that occurrence. The success of the military in accomplishing its mission occurs with some loss of individual and unit effectiveness and achievement of objectives, since they are not always in harmony. This requires a need for give-and-take by the active servicemember, the military organization, and family members, to accommodate to common goals and objectives. To the family's credit, it usually shows great adaptive capacity to difficult demands placed upon it by the military organization's goals. And to the military organization's credit, it has increasingly recognized and provided for such demonstrated needs of families as appropriate housing, schools, social facilities, health care, and social services. However, such provisions have often been limited by budgets or available support personnel, insight into the more subtle psychological factors in military family life, and low responsiveness to individualized and special group needs.

Since children are expected to be compliant and place their needs second to those of the military organization and parents, their needs are often unrecognized and/or neglected. The military child has received low priority in decisions affecting organizational goals. While awareness of and advocacy for children is increasing, the lack of comprehensive child mental health and human services is generally indicative of their low status in many military and civilian communities.

Among the stressful circumstances with which the military family must deal are comparatively low pay, limited housing (availability, quality, privacy, family autonomy), status incongruity (especially for ethnic minorities and women), and frequent moves (Creel, 1981). These constitute difficult situations for lower ranking personnel—who are usually younger, more immature, and include a greater percentage of minorities and those with limited previous occupational and life successes. These at-risk families are rarely sought out on a routine basis for evaluation of needs, assessment of adequacy of adaptation, and preventive assistance, in spite of the fact that they are commonly the families that most need acute interventions for overcoming physical and emotional problems. It seems that crisis intervention and resolution is the common modus operandi of military occupational and community life. This is occurring in families that are affected by broader societal changes in family values regarding sex-role-related family responsibilities for division of labor and in the workaday world. The tendency toward generational adherence to, or relinquishment of, traditional values is played out in most families. Problems occur when the parents are at conflict over differing values and when family values are at odds with the predominant values of the work unit supervisor, local military or civilian community, or others who affect the family's choices. With approximately 50% of families in the United States having both parents working and the increase in dual-career families (Harris, 1981), there is an apparent upsurge in family conflicts related to the demands and values of military life clashing with those of the family, such as the working spouse's reluctance to have a job or career interrupted by a military reassignment. Current instability in the national economy and life-style needs of families provide impetus for both parents to work. As a result, conflicts between parents' work schedules and dissension occasioned by unavailability of a deployed parent and the work schedule of the remaining parent pose problems for all family members. Who is there to meet the children's emotional and other developmental needs? Modern military parents are often faced with making difficult decisions about work and family commitments and their own career aspirations.

Military life—with its attention to regimentation, rules and standards, authoritarian–authoritative modes of discipline, and tight constraints on individual expression—inevitably has an impact on the military family. Military family life can be a caricature of the military unit, as it is affected by the system's broader socializing influences, particularly through parental adoption of military values and through the pervasive expectation for adherence to rules in the military community. A ubiquitous structure, clearly defined social expectations for conduct, and close-quartered opportunities for community camaraderie exist in military communities. To some families these standards and their corollary sanctions may seem intrusive, conflicting with family values, or impeding individual freedom of choice. Rank status in the community is visibly present and manifested by differentials in quality of housing and some social–recreational facilities, although otherwise, military community-life is generally egalitarian in providing services. In such a rank-privileged and oriented social system, this mix of caste formation and egalitarianism may create a dichotomy, particularly for children and adolescents struggling for their identity within the social setting. This difficulty is sometimes exacerbated by parental concerns about child misbehavior which might affect their status in the military and by parental communications about whom it would be safe or acceptable to associate with, especially within the rank hierarchy—particularly that of the officer–enlisted division in social associations. Children are sensitive to this parental anxiety and the anger that follows their breaking community rules; they generally react to these codes of conduct by complying with them, or angrily defying them. In some military communities, particularly those that are isolated or confined and those where rules are strongly enforced, children have little room to make mistakes or test limits of authority in a normal manner, without imperiling family status or the parent's career. This is particularly true when the parents are involved in a struggle for upward social mobility. Wishes for a better socioeconomic and class status cause such parents to integrate the changing power of income with an altering sense of status, charged with constant stimulus for competition and achievement. Promotion and the failure to be promoted in this milieu become issues for the active duty member and family, for their place in the community, and in the effective functioning of the military unit.

These parental sensitivities about group roles, status, and identity become part of military children's repertoire of issues that must be resolved successfully. When the children perceive not only parental anxieties about these issues, but also community conflicts—as manifested by sex and racial–ethnic differences in those acknowledged as high status in the community—then they may be confused about how these conflicts can be resolved. This often leaves the child or adolescent with few choices but to internalize the identity and role conflicts, or act them out behaviorally. This is a common theme in problems brought to child mental health clinics by military families. They are exacerbated by both parental and community inability to provide assistance because the difficulties are not recognized or are minimized; because the parents are not physically present or emotionally available; and when community support systems are inadequate or unresponsive. These children must also resolve the differing feelings about the military mission that many in society hold.

Displays of power and potential for violence, with the containment and moral structuring of aggression, leave many children and their parents struggling with their own impulse controls and moral development. Expressions of such struggles are evident in the larger society but children of warriors such as soldiers and policemen frequently must integrate these value struggles with highly identified cathected love objects. Children who are too often reminded of the power and glory of violent confrontation, such as depicted on television and in the movies, need to be taught other means of expressing aggression and resolving conflict. It is critical that families discuss the innuendoes and contradictions of these issues. While this is done in many families, the issues should also be discussed in schools, churches, organizations such as the Boy Scouts and Girl Scouts, and in other settings that allow for objectivity and social verification, as well as through the local media. If the local civilian community neglects such issues, the military community must address these struggles. (Rodriguez, 1980a, pp. 317–318)

It is ultimately the military leaders—from strategic planners to local commanders—who should assure that such problems are attended to, not only because of concern and responsibility for children and their families in their command, but also because good management would see the cost–benefits of reducing stress and the attendant conflicts which accompany working for the military and living in its communities.

SPECIAL PROBLEMS OF MILITARY CHILDREN

Among the many specific problems with which military children must contend are separations from parents (McCubbin, Dahl, Metres, Hunter, & Plag, 1974; McCubbin et al., 1976; Baker, Cover, Fagen, Fischer, & Janda, 1968; Baker, Fagen, Fischer, Janda, & Cover, 1967; Carlsmith 1973; Cortes & Fleming, 1968; Crumley & Blumenthal, 1973; Hillenbrand, 1976; Longabough, 1973; MacIntosh, 1968; Bey & Lange, 1974; Yeatman, 1981), frequent moves (McKain, 1973; Shaw & Pangman, 1975; Pedersen & Sullivan, 1964; Hunter & Sheldon, 1981; Chaskel, 1974), and retirement (Giffen & McNeil, 1967; Hickman & Hunter, 1981). Special populations of children must adapt to the exigencies of transcultural experiences-overseas assignments (Shaw & Pangman, 1975; Shaw, 1979; Bower, 1967; Werkman, 1979), child abuse and neglect (Comptroller General, 1979), parental alcoholism, posttraumatic (battle) stress disorders of fathers, poverty, single-parent family life (Gosser & Taylor, 1976; Orthner, 1980), and cultural integration problems (Druss, 1965) such as racism and problems experienced by children of racially or ethnically mixed marriages. While some increase in research (Hunter & Nice, 1978; Hunter, Dulk, & Williams, 1980; Croan, Katz, Fischer, & Smith-Osbourne, 1980) on military families and on the special problems of military children has occurred in recent years, it continues to be relatively sparse in volume, and inconclusive in its findings. However, some consistent clinical findings have been generally attributed to the unique circumstances of military family life as it affects children's development (Gonzales, 1970). The culmination of these many difficulties, encountered in the stressful circumstances of military family life, has resulted in some common behavioral-emotional reactions in children, which have been characterized by LeGrone (1978), and challenged by Morrison (1981), as a "military family syndrome." While there is no consensus of such a distinct phenomenon, there is clearly a pattern of predisposition in certain vulnerable families for dysfunction to develop, if the wrong situations occur at the wrong time. While other chapters in this book focus on some of these special problems (child abuse, alcoholism, POW/MIA families, retirement, overseas assignments), two topic areas—separations and moves—require additional discussion in this section, because of their effect on children.

PARENTAL SEPARATIONS

The effects of father absences—temporary and indefinite—on child development and family functioning is one of the areas in which clinicians and researchers have shown the most interest. This is probably due to this being a common experience for many military children. A child's reactions to parental absences vary with the level of preparation of the child for the separation and control over the separation (i.e., knowledge of the length of absence and ability to maintain contact during it); the child's sex and developmental stage; the quality of the relationship between the child and absent and remaining parents; the attitude and coping skill of the at-home parent and other significant persons to provide surrogate parent figures with a positive memory and feeling about the absent parent that maintains the active association of the child with that parent; and the length of the separation. Thus, a not uncommon situation—for example, the unprepared for absence of an emotionally distant father from an Oedipal-stage boy, for an unanticipated length of time, without interim contacts, and where the mother is resentful and depressed—would have a fairly predictable effect on the child. While the prevalence of psychiatric disorders in military children has been variably assessed to be higher or no higher than comparable civilian populations (Gabower, 1960; Lyon & Oldaker, 1967; Cantwell, 1974), most mental health and social service professionals would anecdotally acknowledge the common association of emotional–behavioral problems in children with absentee parents. In addition, return of the absent parent also initiates a period of common stress for both the spouses and the children, as the returning parent attempts to reclaim former roles that others have acquired.

Other situations characterized by absent parents are also worth noting. The absence of active duty mothers from families, while a less usual and relatively recent phenomenon, does occur, although there are no known clinical findings that would indicate this poses problems that are uniquely different from those already noted. There would be expected sex and developmental variations manifested.

Absences of parents for varying periods of time, of course, are not unique to the military. They also occur where the parent must travel in other occupations. While there is limited clinical literature on the effects of such absences in nonmilitary families, it would likely result in similar outcomes. The comparison of childhood emotional and behavioral reactions to parental absences due to occupational requirements has not been correlated to clinical findings related to other parental absences, such as in separation, abandonment, or divorce, but clinical experience would indicate such experiences are not dissimilar in their effect on the child. An excellent literature exists on consequences for children and families where there is father separation due to his being a prisoner of war (POW) or missing in action (MIA) (McCubbin et al., 1974; Hunter, 1981). While this group has received a fair degree of attention and evaluation, the long-term consequences of this experience—particularly for those MIA families where the father's status has not been confirmed—remains to be evaluated. In general, given the norms of family life and human attachments, parental absences are never "normal" and always pose a stress which requires adaptation. The fact that so many persons—both children and adults—presenting with psychological and physical health problems have experienced such losses and absences in their lives make these effects difficult to evaluate, both because loss is almost a ubiquitous experience and often because it occurs in combination with other disruptions. However difficult correlative research might be in this area, it should be universally accepted that such separations will place the family in an "at-risk" status for an indefinite period of time.

MOVES

While the effect of moves, like separations, on children and adolescents is variable, they are among the high stress-producing and potentially disruptive experiences of military family life. Certain children would be considered more vulnerable, based on the general level of parental adaptability and attitude about the move; changes in family habits and parental availability during and following the move; effects on children at certain critical developmental stages where continuity of peer group relationships and growing autonomous functioning away from the family are important; and effects on children with special educational, physical, and psychiatric needs, who would be disrupted by the move, particularly where there might be a lack of equivalent special services at the next place of residence. In general, significant increases in children's emotional and behavioral problems have not been correlated with moves, and the silent manifestations of a family under stress may be difficult to evaluate in terms of individual development and family functioning. When a family feels a loss of control over moves, which results in unexpressed or poorly worked through feelings, problems will generally arise, even if they do not result in referral to a mental health clinic. The inconvenience and economic hardship of moving are well known to all military families, even when they are positive about the move. Of particular note are the extra problems potentially encountered by families who move overseas. The transcultural experience can be stressful for all family members, and requires a more detailed and involved evaluation of the family's capacities for the overseas move than is currently provided. The difficulties in meeting mental health and social service needs of children and adolescents in foreign areas is not only a result of limited professional resources, but also is related to different cultural values which the child must accommodate to family values, the often high availability of illicit drugs, and the frequent lack of recreational–social supports comparable to stateside resources. In summary, no move is without consequences, and all moves are potentially disruptive to individual and family functioning. The military must acknowledge the impact not only of moves on families, but the consequent effects of moved families on military operations.

SPECIAL STRENGTHS OF MILITARY FAMILIES

A commentary is in order about the significant number of military families who are tolerating the stresses of military life in a healthy adaptive fashion, and about what aspects of military life are stabilizing. A well-conceived and carefully conducted study of such families could provide valuable information about what characteristics of biopsychosocial adaptation are most apt to highly predispose a family toward successful functioning in a military community and toward completion of a military career.

Because military community life is somewhat regimented and rule-oriented, it also tends to be relatively predictable, safe, orderly, and well provided for. In fact, some posts and bases are so completely self-contained that it is not uncommon for some families only to leave the immediate environs occasionally. This is probably not any more pathological than the tendency of many people residing in small towns who feel little need to venture out, who are not frustrated by this geographical containment, and who do not manifest any dysfunction as a result. The modern ethics of mobility and exploration are relative values and, when not embraced, do not necessarily indicate maladaption. In such circumstances, many military families lead stable and unremarkable lives and do not warrant negative labels like "passive–dependent."

In contrast to a number of mobile civilian families, most military families have some supports built into moves. In the view of Shaw (1979), "most military installations are similar; the life style changes little from one to another. The father frequently moves to the same job he had at his previous assignment, the family resides in the same type of housing, and the family members meet people who share their values and norms. Military children often exhibit a considerable readiness to accept newly arriving children" (p. 311). In addition, there are some indications that potentially stressful circumstances such as father absence and moves are compensated by conditioned expectations of moves as a social norm, close family ties, and economic and social security (Lyon & Oldaker, 1967). Kenny (1967) has noted that military children, on an average comparison with their civilian peers, are intellectually brighter, exhibit fewer psychological maladjustments, and evidence less juvenile delinquency. While there are some questions about population variables and methodology in this study, the findings are not as surprising when one considers the relatively high incidence of emotional and social dysfunction in the general population and the relative preselection process of military families through examination and training of the active service member. While these studies do not negate the number of problems that military families experience, they do indicate that rates of dysfunction are comparatively lower than might be expected, given the unique demands of military life. This could suggest that military families might utilize the available supports they might be afforded, including a common identity with supportive others; a family and community sense of mission and shared purpose; mutual assistance of family members; and internally mobilized adaptive stress responses that are sharpened by repetitive opportunities for mastery.

Military families, particularly career families, tend to be resourceful and self-reliant, since experience teaches them that they are their own best advocates and providers, and that little should be expected from large bureaucratic organizations. This observation tends to discount the view that military families, conditioned to be compliant and to be responsive only to standard operating procedures, are dependent and passive people. On the contrary, military families are more often conditioned to independent action in a large system that does not always look after their needs. While military families are, in fact, dependent on many aspects of military life—such as work schedules and pay scales—they are frequently creative in exploring their options and are increasingly demonstrating their independence from the military by terminating a career when it interferes with their personal and family life goals. In this respect, they exercise a strength that is not seen in some nonmilitary occupations. In addition, the uniquely positive aspects of military life—expansion of awareness of other people and world communities; participation in, and service to, a special national mission; and shared personal and family pride of accomplishment in a demanding existence—provide a special reward for most military families, including many who experience occasional dysfunctions. In summary, military family life can provide special challenges that require resourcefulness; mastery may be quite rewarding. The strengths of military families should always be assessed along with their problems, and should be utilized in assisting family members through their problem resolution. These allow the military unit to function and accomplish its objectives.

PROVIDING FOR THE SPECIAL NEEDS OF MILITARY CHILDREN

In the 1978 *Report of the President's Commission on Mental Health*, the nation was reminded that children and adolescents are among the most underserved populations requiring mental health services. No mention was made in that report of the approximately 1.6 million children of active service members and .9 million children of retired and deceased military personnel, or of the relatively limited and poorly coordinated services offered to them and their families. There is currently no comprehensive national or military child–adolescent policy, and only limited planning or programming directed toward the military child exists. The limited number of personnel available to administer and provide services for disturbed and troubled children and adolescents is a reflection of their relatively low priority. Like their civilian colleagues, military mental health and social service professionals are maldistributed, overworked, underpaid, and often poorly identified and utilized within the array of health care services. Outwardly, they appear alien to the traditional mental health–social service requirements of the military, which is occupationally and operationally focused. In fact, family members of active duty personnel have often been considered an unwanted burden that interferes with the primary military mission of readiness for war. Thus, it is not surprising that the traditional texts of military psychiatry (Rees, 1945; Solomon, 1944) and the Group for the Advancement of Psychiatry (1960) report on military psychiatry only incidentally mention the significance of children and family members and correlate their mental health needs with interferences in work performance by the servicemember. Of greater concern is that more recent publications that might be expected to provide a more contemporary view are silent on military families. The military psychiatry chapter (Baker, 1975) in the *Comprehensive Textbook of Psychiatry* only mentions the recent literature on POW/MIA families. The annual report of the Surgeon General of the Public Health Service has never mentioned the health or mental health needs of military families, and the 1981 report of the Select Panel for the Promotion of Child Health likewise omitted comment on the health needs of military children and adolescents. This pattern reflects a disturbing tendency when one considers the paucity of DoD and Congressional studies on mental health and social service needs and programs for military children and adolescents. These oversights must be addressed if a truly national assessment of child health status is ever to be made, and if the needs of military children are ever to be recognized and ministered to.

Since military children are often treated in both civilian and military health care systems, they would seem to derive the potential benefits of both. However, while primary pediatric care is generally well provided for, child mental health services and the Civilian Health and Medical Program of the Uniformed Services (CHAMPUS) benefits are limited and unevenly available. Integrated evaluation, referral, and treatment networks among military and civilian health care providers, social services, school systems, and other community-based services have not been broadly or systematically developed. Research and training in direct services for military families are underdeveloped. Military mental health and social services professionals have provided limited advocacy and organization of services, and occupy few positions of leadership within areas of military policy and planning. Many have adhered to the erroneous view that civilian resources are both willing and adequate providers of assistance and that sufficient coordination occurs between military and civilian resources to maximize benefit of these services for military families. Delivery systems should be preventive, family and community-oriented, yet remain primarily crisis-oriented and operationally centered.

In treating the special problems of military children and adolescents, the clinician must be cognizant of not only the unique precipitating stresses related to military family life, but also how to structure clinical services that are specifically addressed to these needs. The clinical and administrative issues raised in this chapter presume that there is nothing inherently different about the military child from other children who have emotional problems that emanate from situational and developmental disruptions (Shaw, 1979). Depressive conditions and characterological–neurotic expressions of stress and disrupted development are similar in clinical presentation to those of children in various other subpopulations; sound treatment requires familiarity with the unique and common elements of the social experience. Thus, the specific treatment needs of military children and adolescents are considered by the author to be less related to any specified treatment modalities than they are to elements of the treatment system. Therapists are encouraged to assume a broader management role that allows for (1) development of early detection and intervention (in primary care, school, and consultative settings in the health care system and community); (2) provision of systematic assessment of local treatment needs, and actual and potential resources; and (3) mobilization of comprehensive services provided by multidisciplinary collaborative service providers. Thus the therapist must not only possess therapeutic skills, but also the ability to provide, design, and manage services for local mental health systems through systematic assessment, training and supervision, and effective coordination.

Despite several hundred military psychiatrists, psychologists, and social workers, comprehensive or coordinated services are a rarity in many military communities. Few professionals are involved beyond direct care in the necessary broader developmental activities of consultation (to local commands, schools, and human services personnel), community liaison work, and network building. They are tied down by the limited scope of their training, local administrative restraints, work-load demands, and lack of resources. Establishing new systems requires time, a solid data base, and management skills that they frequently do not have.

For the occasional professional who does attempt to develop community and family programs, there often has been little direction or support from higher administrative officials. They may experience uncertainty and distrust about administrative decisions which could result in dollar commitments and loss of administrative control. In short, until the more recent advent of various family support activities, military family mental health programs have struggled because there was no unifying policy or planning that adapted programs to local needs. This has resulted in uneven levels and standards of care available for military families.

THE NEEDS: POLICY, RESEARCH, SERVICES, TRAINING

POLICY

As indicated earlier in this chapter, military mental health and social services policy lacks clarity, breadth and depth, and specificity. It is generally not well coordinated with other health and personnel programs. There is limited knowledge of the needs of eligible beneficiaries and a parallel inability to define the real and potential resources in the communities in which military families reside. Modes of assessing standards of services generally are restricted to military hospitals, and cost review is not defined in the broader view of program impact on other health and personnel activities, or on civilian mental health and social services. Only recently have basic comparative analyses been conducted that review cost of military mental health services with CHAMPUS-supported civilian services. However, these analyses lack indices of quality or efficacy of care. In all of this, there is doubt about which programs best meet the goals of the defense mission, and which ones provide the highest level of health and social assurance for military families. The single greatest need is for centralized and coordinated policy and planning. This activity must involve the input of the Veterans Administration (VA) and Department of Health and Human Services (DHHS), as well as state mental health and social services authorities. Such a definition of policy is directly related to the level and effectiveness of advocacy for these services, which can be demonstrated to be required and cost effective. Effective policy development must be the end-product of research, training, and services.

RESEARCH

This book is intended to fill in the gaps about the needs and resources of military families. In order to improve the structure of services, well-designed social research is required to highlight military family dynamics, their effect on military communities, and on correlated individual functioning in occupational and health systems. Research on military organizational behavior in health and social systems is also essential so that patient and provider behaviors in these systems can be better understood, and the systems can be restructured to deliver more effective, cost-efficient services. A research component should be integral to all health and human services delivery systems, and a research attitude integral to all policy formulation.

SERVICES

Direct services should emanate from research findings. While these services should have components of individual crisis care, greater emphasis should be placed on family-centered and preventive interventions. There is an immediate need for more community education and early risk detection programs, school and other community consultative services, and linkages with primary health care providers. These local community coordinated services can be provided without significant increases in budget or personnel through careful management of time and resources, and training and retraining of professionals, support personnel, and volunteers. In my view, the future of mental health service delivery lies in the community mental health movement, particularly when better management practices and interprofessional cooperation are fostered.

Some families move inappropriately through a multiplicity of systems seeking appropriate assistance. This process is costly in dollars and professional time and efforts, because of repetitive contacts and evaluations, and costly to troubled family members in terms of the emotional energy drain and continuing disturbances. CHAMPUS continues to offer expanded benefits and improvements in beneficiary and provider services, but problems in coordinating these benefits with the military direct care system continue.

Despite these problems, there are some recent promising areas of development that require further expansion.

Family Service Centers

The Army, Navy, Marine Corps, and Air Force are currently establishing networks for community-based multiservice family assistance centers. They offer an outstanding opportunity for providing centers that integrate multiple services, such as health promotion and screening, and minor emergency treatment; community education and information assistance; legal services; financial counseling; day care; and psychological and pastoral counseling. These settings offer a place where family needs assessments, education, and research can be provided. Rich opportunities for multidisciplinary collaborative evaluations and services abound in such centralized settings, offering primary support services which can draw on such specialized services of hospitals, state and local child protection services, and local shelters for battered wives and runaway youth. (See Chapter 12 for further discussion of Family Service Centers.)

Day Care

Despite the lack of a national or military policy on day care, there have been some innovative efforts by resourceful alliances of parents, local commands, and social service-mental health providers at some installations. Repeated surveys indicate the priority and benefits of day care services for military families (Orthner, 1980). Such facilities could be an ideal place for child-family assistance, particularly in the identification of children who are at risk physically, emotionally, and intellectually. Some communities have found that their day care centers become a locus for family supports and integration and serve as a community center. The military should adopt a more realistic view of day care as essential for many families and as an integral part of a military benefits program.

School Consultation

The provision of school consultation services should be part of every local command's resource management plan. This can be provided most effectively if the children are concentrated in schools near the installation; however, consultative–referral contacts with local school districts can be arranged to provide for those children attending schools in surrounding civilian communities. Such liaisons provide for the early identification of a child's problems and promote intervention with the school and family. Liaisons should be linked with child–adolescent developmental evaluation services, which should be established by hospital commands to provide comprehensive, multidisciplinary professional assessment and treatment services for children with suspected and established developmental disturbances. I believe these services are among the most salient means of providing for child–family mental health and social service needs, and should be the responsibility of professionals in child and family health and social services (Rodriguez, 1980b).

Systems Development

Limited skills are currently exercised by mental health and social service providers in the development of local health systems. The military should provide for the development, not only of professionals' clinical skills and knowledge, but also for their expanded roles in services delivery. There is a need in every military community for the following: (1) analysis of community mental health and social services needs (through periodic surveys) and resources, in conjunction with established provider–population formulae for professional services staffing; (2) advocacy for resources, provided jointly by professionals and local commands, and utilizing not only budgeted allocations, but also creative resource development (available civilian community services; federal–state–foundation grants; local voluntary coalitions among military units and organizations, churches, service clubs, United Way, etc.); and (3) establishment of local services utilizing volunteers and increased training of semiskilled persons and professionals. Such efforts require organizational skills which are too often lacking at the local level and not perceived by providers or planners. Diminishing resources will lead either to the development of such managerial and coordinating activities, or a crisis in family services.

Research

Military family research is tied to the development of appropriate services, and is one of the most critical current needs in the military health care system. The current increased supports for military family research must continue and be coordinated by a master plan for DoD health care. Greater understanding must be gained about factors that promote healthy individual and family adaptation in and to the military community. At-risk families should be recognized early and their progress monitored systematically. A research attitude in policy planning and service delivery should be among the highest priorities at all levels in the management of the DoD health care and social services systems.

Patient–Client Participation in Treatment Systems

Finally, the military needs to find the means for more active participation of clients in the delivery of community and family services. Providers should be continually seeking ways to stimulate less passivity by recipients of services, and greater autonomous and conjoint resolution of problems and conflicts. An initial step might be the replacement of the term "dependent" in describing beneficiaries. In addition, there may be in existence some successful programs that have utilized patient education about services and benefits, and patient–provider contracts that spell out mutual rights and responsibilities in the service interaction. Such activities can strengthen and clarify the therapeutic and service alliance, and provide for a more informed and involved clientele. Information on innovative programs should be widely disseminated.

TRAINING

Underlying the changes needed in community and family services are the greater tasks of learning and teaching the modes for such changes. Most professional schools and postgraduate training programs are not providing the kinds of experiences that will lead to the development of adequate skills in family and community systems evaluation and development. Where they are provided, there is frequently limited ability to practice those skills—either because the systems are not present that allow such practice or because of other personal practice preferences. Requirements must be increased for postgraduate and continuing education that allow the learning and demonstration of skills in supervision, consultation, community organization, systems management, and community and professional education and training.

The ultimate goal of all policy, research, and services is the development of learning systems that create more effective and sustaining systems of support for the family and the unit. If the professions or health planners–managers are not more responsive to these broader training issues, efforts in the other areas will be greatly minimized by lack of concepts and skills upon which effective services can be developed and delivered.

> If there is anything that we wish to change in the child, we should first examine it and see whether it is not something that could better be changed in ourselves.—Carl Jung

REFERENCES

Baker, S. L. Military psychiatry. In A. M. Freedman, H. I. Kaplan, & B. J. Sadock (Eds.), *Comprehensive textbook of psychiatry* (2nd ed.). Baltimore: Williams & Wilkins, 1975.

Baker, S. S., Cover, L., Fagen, E., Fischer, E., & Janda, E. Impact of father absence: III. Problems of family reintegration following prolonged father absence. *American Journal of Orthopsychiatry*, 1968, *38*, 347. (Abstract)

Baker, S. S., Fagen, E. F., Fischer, E., Janda, E., & Cover, L. Impact of father absence on personality factors of children. *American Journal of Orthopsychiatry*, 1967, *37*, 269. (Abstract)

Bey, D. R., & Lange, J. Waiting wives: Women under stress. *American Journal of Psychiatry*, 1974, *131*, 283–286.

Bower, E. M. American children and families in overseas communities. *American Journal of Orthopsychiatry*, 1967, *37*, 787–796.

Cantwell, D. P. Prevalence of psychiatric disorders in a pediatric clinic for military dependent children. *Journal of Pediatrics*, 1974, *85*, 711–714.

Carlsmith, L. Some personality characteristics of boys separated from their fathers during World War II. *Ethos*, 1973, *1*, 446–477.

Chaskel, R. Effect of mobility on family life. *Social Work*, 1974, *9*, 83–91.

Comptroller General. *Report to the Congress of the U.S.: Military child advocacy programs—victims of neglect* (HRD-79-75). Washington, D.C.: U.S. Accounting Office, May 23, 1979.

Cortes, C. F., & Fleming, E. The effects of father absence in the adjustment of culturally disadvantaged boys. *Journal of Special Education*, 1968, *2*, 413–417.

Creel, S. M. Patient appraisal of current life and social stressors in a military community, *Military Medicine*, 1981, *146*(5), 320–322.

Croan, G. M., Katz, R., Fischer, N., & Smith-Osbourne, A. *Roadmap for Navy family research* (FR 1). Columbia, Md.: Westinghouse Public Applied Systems Division and Office of Naval Research, 1980.

Crumley, F. E., & Blumenthal, R. Children's reactions to temporary loss of the father. *American Journal of Orthopsychiatry*, 1973, *130*, 778–782.

Druss, R. Foreign marriages in the military. *Psychiatric Quarterly*, 1965, *39*, 220–226.

Escalona, S. Children in a warring world. *American Journal of Orthopsychiatry*, 1975, *45*, 765–772.

Final Report of the White House Commission on Families: Listening to America's Families, Washington, D.C.: U.S. Government Printing Office, 1981.

Gabower, G. Behavior problems of children in Navy officers' families. *Social Casework*, 1960, *41*, 177–184.

Giffen, M. B., & McNeil, J. Effect of military retirement on dependents. *Archives of General Psychiatry*, 1967, *17*, 717–722.

Gonzales, V. *Psychiatry and the Army brat*. Springfield, Ill.: Thomas, 1970.

Gosser, R. D., & Taylor, C. M. Role adjustment of single parent fathers with dependent children. *The Family Coordinator*, 1976, *25*, 397–403.

Group for the Advancement of Psychiatry. *Preventive psychiatry in the Armed Forces* (Report No. 47). New York: GAP, 1960.

Harris, L. *Families at work*. General Mills American Family Report, Minneapolis, Minn., 1981.

Hickman, R. A., & Hunter, E. *Military retention and retirement: Reciprocal family-organization effects* (USIU-81-03). San Diego, Calif.: U.S. International University and Office of Naval Research (Code 452), 1981.

Hillenbrand, E. D. Father absence in military families. *The Family Coordinator*, 1976, *25*, 397–403.

Hunter, E. J. *Wartime stress: Family adjustment to loss* (USIU-81-07). San Diego, Calif.: U.S. International University and Office of Naval Research (Code 452), 1981.

Hunter, E. J., Dulk, D., & Williams, J. *The literature on military families: An annotated bibliography* (USFA-TR-80-11). Colorado Springs, Colo.: U.S. Air Force Academy, 1980.

Hunter, E. J., & Hickman, R. *As parents go, so go the children: The adjustment and development of military children* (USIU-81-01). San Diego, Calif.: U.S. International University and Office of Naval Research (Code 452), 1981.

Hunter, E. J., & Nice, S. D. *Children of military families*. Washington, D.C.: U.S. Government Printing Office, 1978.

Hunter, E. J., & Sheldon, R. *Family adjustment to geographic mobility: Military families on the move*, (USIU-80-06), San Diego, Calif.: U.S. International University and Office of Naval Research (Code 452), 1981.

Kenny, J. A. The child in the military community. *Journal of the American Academy of Child Psychiatry*, 1967, *6*, 51–63.

LeGrone, D. M. The military family syndrome. *American Journal of Psychiatry*, 1978, *135*, 1040–1043.

Longabough, R. Mother behavior as a variable moderating the effects of father absence. *Ethos*, 1973, *1*, 456–465.

Lyon, W. B., & Oldaker, L. The child, the school, and the military family. *American Journal of Orthopsychiatry*, 1967, *37*, 269–270.

MacIntosh, H. Separation problems in military wives. *American Journal of Psychiatry*, 1968, *125*, 260–265.

McCubbin, H. I., Dahl, B., & Hunter, E. J. (Eds.). *Families in the military system*. Beverly Hills, Calif.: Sage, 1976.

McCubbin, H. I., Dahl, B., Metres, P., Hunter, E. J., & Plag, J. (Eds.). *Family separation and reunion.* Washington, D.C.: U.S. Government Printing Office, 1974.

McKain, J. L. Relocation in the military: Alienation and family problems. *Journal of Marriage and the Family,* 1973, *35,* 205–209.

Morrison, J. Rethinking the military family syndrome. *American Journal of Psychiatry,* 1981, *138,* 354–357.

Orthner, D. K. *Families in blue.* Greensboro, N.C.: Family Research and Analysis, Inc., and Office of Chief of Chaplains (USAF), 1980.

Pedersen, F. A., & Sullivan, E. Relationship among geographic mobility, parental attitudes and emotional disturbances in children. *American Journal of Orthopsychiatry,* 1964, *34,* 575–580.

Rees, J. R. *The shaping of psychiatry by war.* New York: Norton, 1945.

Report of the President's Commission on Mental Health. Washington, D.C.: U.S. Government Printing Office, 1978.

Rodriguez, A. R. The family in the military community. *Military Medicine,* 1980, *145*(5), 316–319. (a)

Rodriguez, A. R. A community mental health approach to military psychiatry. *Military Medicine,* 1980, *145*(10), 681–685. (b)

Select Panel for the Promotion of Child Health. *Better health for our children: A national strategy.* Washington, D.C.: Department of Health and Human Services (Public Health Service), 1981.

Shaw, J. A. The child in the military community. In J. D. Noshpitz (Ed.), *Basic handbook of child psychiatry.* New York: Basic Books, 1979.

Shaw, J. A., & Pangman, J. Geographical mobility and the military child. *Military Medicine,* 1975, *140*(6), 413–416.

Solomon, H. *Manual of military neuropsychiatry.* Philadelphia: Saunders, 1944.

Werkman, S. The child raised overseas. In J. D. Noshpitz (Ed.), *Basic handbook of child psychiatry.* New York: Basic Books, 1979.

Yeatman, G. W. Paternal separation and the military dependent child. *Military Medicine,* 1981, *146*(5), 320–322.

4

Substance Misuse and Alcoholism in the Military Family

THEODORE G. WILLIAMS

Alcohol and drug use and misuse pervade every segment of American society, reaching epidemic proportions in some sectors. Virtually no person or family is immune from pressure, direct or subtle, to use drugs (including alcohol) as an aid in "coping" with the problems of daily living. Many youths begin their use of drugs for recreational purposes, as an avowed escape from boredom or stress, or as part of the life-style of rebellion or rejection of the "establishment." They may continue their licit or illicit drug use for these same reasons or as a seeming strategy for coping as they move beyond their adolescent years.

In dealing with the family and drug–alcohol misuse, it is important to take into account that the family unit in America is undergoing radical changes due to certain societal trends. Some of these trends, which may be significant vis-à-vis substance abuse (Clayton, 1980) are as follows: a decrease in the marriage rate; an increase in median age at first marriage; an increase in voluntary childlessness; a marked increase in the divorce rate; a decrease in the average duration of first marriages; an increase in single-parent households (especially ones headed by women); an increase in the number of working women who have dependent children; and an increase in the number of nonmarital children. While little is known about the direct correlation between drug use and these social changes which affect marriage, family, parenthood, and children, it is necessary to

The opinions or assertions contained herein are the private views of the writer and are not to be construed as official or as reflecting views of the Department of the Navy or the Department of Defense.

Theodore G. Williams. Captain, Medical Corps, U.S. Navy, and Chief, Alcohol Rehabilitation Service, Naval Regional Medical Center, Long Beach, California.

73

keep in mind that mounting levels of drug use are occurring as we live through these transitions.

Much has been published regarding substance abuse (especially alcoholism), family issues, and treatment of addict families. However, very little research has been done and few articles appear in the literature concerning the military family and substance misuse. I think we need to contrast the idea that family life in the Armed Forces comprises a microcosm of family life in the United States in general with the opposite view that military families are very different from other American families with unique stresses and problems. If we view these as extremes on either end of a spectrum of family life, I believe we will find that most military families fit somewhere between the extremes, depending on many circumstances.

THE MILITARY ENVIRONMENT AND THE FAMILY

The husband/father stationed at a base in an urban or suburban setting in the continental United States may be separated from his family for no more than brief periods. They may live in civilian housing and have a lifestyle little different from that of their civilian neighbors.

On the other hand, the military family living on a small, isolated duty station in a foreign country is likely to be exposed to vastly different stresses and situations which might be conducive to substance use/misuse by family members. These stresses will almost certainly include a feeling of cultural isolation without the customary support systems and recreational outlets available in the United States. In this circumstance the military community turns inward to the military "club" as the hub of social life, where alcoholic beverages are inexpensive and drinking is ritualistic; often heavy drinking is encouraged, and being able to hold one's liquor is admired and expected. The nondrinker will not feel at home at "the club."

Wives of military personnel, particularly in young families, often feel a lack of support (particularly during pregnancy and the infancy of the firstborn child) when separated from parents and other extended family members or friends. As a result they may turn to alcohol, tranquilizers, or sedatives for relief and as a "trusted friend." Male spouses may do the same because they are in a marginal, atypical, minority role.

Teenagers, often angry and rebellious at having been uprooted and separated from their stateside peers, may be exposed to an entirely different (and sometimes lax) drug and alcohol social situation. Overseas, alcohol is often available to youth without age limitations. Hashish and marijuana may be endemic, and various "licit" drugs (amphetamines, sedatives, and pain-killers in combinations unheard of in the United States) are often available in local drugstores, with no prescription required.

Life-styles vary in different branches of the Armed Forces, particularly during peacetime when families are more likely to be stationed with their active servicemember. During peacetime, the Navy and Marine Corps usually require the most frequent and prolonged family separations due to the nature of their deployments. However, some Army and Air Force duty stations are in remote locations and, therefore, those living on base, with or without their families, are quite isolated. During periods of separation from his family, the military man's recreational activities commonly revolve around the use of alcoholic beverages. In fact, many military traditions involve the ritualistic imbibing of alcohol, such as "dining-in" parties and initiations, or the symbolic utilization of alcohol, like "wetting-down" parties or christening a ship with champagne.

DRUG USE BY MILITARY PERSONNEL

The younger servicemember usually utilizes marijuana or other illicit drugs (with or without alcohol) in his repertoire of "recreational" mood-altering drugs. With the military "family man," alcohol remains his "drug of choice." (Holcomb, 1981–1982) This is not to say that "holding your booze" is not also a strong part of the military "macho" image which the young military man strives for. Over half of all active military personnel are under the age of 25 years (approximately 92% male) and the heaviest use of alcohol in military and civilian populations is in the 18–25 age group (Holcomb, 1981–1982). The heaviest use of drugs other than alcohol occurs in this young age group also.

A 1980 anonymous survey of 15,000 active duty military personnel worldwide, conducted for the Department of Defense (DoD) (Burt & Biegel, 1980; Moxley, 1981), documented suspected facts and figures concerning alcohol and drug use. Of those surveyed, 92% reported that they drank some alcohol in the previous year (83% drank within the previous 30 days); 7% reported themselves as alcohol-dependent; 27% reported work impairment directly resulting from alcohol misuse (including drunk on the job) during the previous year (31% in junior enlisted personnel).

Of junior enlisted personnel surveyed, 10% were reported as drug-dependent (drugs other than alcohol); 27% had used some nonmedical drug within the previous 30 days (36% within the past year); nearly all drug users used marijuana or hashish; 19% had used drugs weekly during the past 30 days. Although only 7% of junior enlisted personnel (E1–E5 level) were reported as drug-dependent (drug dependence above E5 was nil), 21% reported work impairment, including 19% reporting "high while working."

This survey shows that the overwhelming majority of nonmedical drug use in the military is occasional, and chiefly by junior enlisted personnel. However, the highest prevalence of drinking alcohol was reported by senior officers, followed by junior officers and junior enlisted personnel, senior enlisted personnel, and warrant officers. Heavy drinking was reported mainly by enlisted personnel. During the previous year 28% of E1–E5s, and about 10% of E6–E9s, reported heavy drinking of beer; 14% of the E1–E5s, and about 5% of E6–E9s, reported heavy drinking of hard liquor; 8% and about 1%, respectively, were comparable figures reported for heavy drinking of wine.

An analysis of this survey of drug and alcohol use in the 18–25 year age group was compared with similar civilian populations (Burt & Biegel, 1980). It showed that there is no general pattern of nonmedical drug use more prevalent for military personnel than civilians. Slightly higher proportions of military personnel than civilians drank during the preceding 30 days and the past year.

THE MILITARY FAMILY SYNDROME

Many mental health professionals who have worked with military families have suggested that the stresses of military life could induce psychiatric illness in military family members. Purported predisposing factors to what has been called the "military family syndrome" are separation, transiency, and differential parenting. Morrison (1981) studied 140 child and adolescent military dependents, and 234 nonmilitary subjects, to assess the validity of this syndrome. He found the two groups to be remarkably similar in psychiatric diagnoses with the exceptions that military dependents were much less likely to have psychosis (1% vs. 8%), and more likely to have an alcoholic father (24% vs. 14%).

When the military family man returns home after a prolonged separation, he may be dependent on alcohol, or another nonmedical drug—although that is much less likely. Some alcoholics in the military can drink cyclically for years, abstaining from drinking or controlling their drinking while with their families, with excessive drinking when away. Eventually most of them lose control of their drinking if the pattern continues.

Some families appear to function more smoothly with an adjustment to frequent prolonged absences of the military husband/father. This is especially true if the husband/father is passive–dependent in personality type with poor leadership and parenting skills. The family may have worked out a reasonably stable "system" of roles and responsibilities in his absence, with the wife/mother as the head of the household. After a brief "honeymoon" period, following his return, confusion of leadership roles may develop with his reluctance to take on responsibilities. As tension mounts he may seek escape through alcohol—usually by spending time away at the military "club" drinking. As his alcohol dependency progresses, family stresses increase and his wife may be understandably unwilling to trust him with family responsibilities which she had heretofore been trying to get him to assume. At this point she may tell a physician, chaplain, psychologist, or social worker: "I've had it with this marriage. He's just like another kid." (She may have four or five children resulting from the earlier sporadic "honeymoons.")

The military family with an obsessive–compulsive husband/father servicemember (usually higher in rank than the passive–dependent type) may also function more harmoniously in his absence, especially if he is an alcoholic. As his disease progresses, his attempts to control his family by running it like a "tight ship" become more erratic and bizarre. For example, in the film *The Great Santini*, the military father (portrayed as a lieutenant colonel, U.S. Marine Corps) lined up his "hogs" (children) at dawn for daily muster.

CONSTANT EMERGENCY LIVING

Probably the greatest cost of alcoholism or drug addiction relates to the disruption and disorganization of the family. For the estimated 10 million alcoholics in the United States, four or five people (usually family members) are seriously affected in a negative way (Kellerman, 1981). After years of living with progressing addiction (defined as psychological and/or physiological dependence on a mind-altering drug, including alcohol), other family members react to the chronic anxieties, stresses, and problems with symptoms similar or identical to those of the addict member.

Reddy (1977), in her booklet *Alcoholism: A Family Illness,* states[1]:

There are certain needs basic for everyone that are usually met in "normal" personal relationships: to love and be loved, to be needed and accepted, to have security and a sense of accomplishment, to feel worthwhile and to have a purpose in life. When alcoholism develops in one of the family, there is little chance of these needs being met. As the alcoholism progresses, needs become more and more unfulfilled. Negative feelings develop and grow and communications break down. Relationships become distorted very slowly and imperceptibly until no one in the family has a healthy personality.

As alcoholism continues its course, the daily stresses and uncertainties experienced by the family members—the *worry, dread, fear* and *anger*—so distort their reasoning powers that most of their reactions are emotional and, often, destructive. The pressure from *constant emergency living* is formidable and a feeling of *doom* hangs over their heads. Generally, there is good cause for *anxiety, apprehension* and *anger* over the continual crises. A period of calm, easy living which might allow for even a little objectivity, is very rare. While the alcoholic is anesthetized from much of the pain of the daily problems, the family members are not. They usually experience the alcoholic's suffering as well as their own. They resent this, but do not know how to avoid it.

Even when uninvolved, the alcoholic still criticizes, challenges and attacks everything that is done or decided by others in the family. Family members feel *defensive, guilty,* and *doubtful* about their attributes and decisions. Feelings of *self-rejection* and *dislike* in both the alcoholic and the family are regularly reinforced. The alcoholic's ability to control the family's feelings and reactions becomes well-developed.

Gradually, *isolation* develops and the alcoholic becomes less and less involved in the daily activities of the family, or in the decisions that have to be made. Activities go on without him—or are curtailed because of his lack of interest. Decisions—even those that concern him—are made by others. The family members tend to sense a growing *brokenness,* a feeling of being *unloved* and *unwanted.*

Most people experience the need to help others. Family members share a strong desire to help the alcoholic, especially in the early stages, and particularly if requests for help are frequent. As with any other illness, however, it is hard for families to be objective. In this illness, because the desire to help becomes complicated with their own personal anxieties and deep involvement in the alcoholic's life, they usually "help" in all the wrong ways. They will try to protect the alcoholic by covering up for him. They will lie for, about, and to him. They will try to control and manage him. They will make threats, but never act on them. They will refuse to discuss the drinking with the alcoholic sober; and yet, insist on

1. Reprinted by permission of Betty Reddy and the Lutheran Center for Substance Abuse, Park Ridge, Illinois.

discussing it when he's drunk! The alcoholic meets every effort with *anger*, *resistance* and *resentment*—and continues to drink! He is effective in using the family members' *anger* and *anxiety* in ways that increase their feelings of *guilt* and *resentment*. The family members also feel increasing *self-hatred, rejection, frustration* and *confusion*. They feel strongly that they should be able to help—but their efforts always seem to be thwarted. *Failure* becomes a constant part of their lives.

Not understanding alcoholism as an illness, they believe the alcoholic could stop drinking if the problems could be resolved, or if he really wanted to stop. Also, it's quite natural that they increasingly focus on the alcoholic's behavior and need for help. This focus contributes to their rationalization that everything would be all right "if only the drinking would stop," and to their denial that anything is wrong with them. Such a viewpoint, coupled with the inability to communicate within the family, intensifies their feelings of being *helpless* and *alone*.

Here, we see the insidious affect on the family of the progressive addiction of one (or more) of its members. All of these intrafamily dynamics may be occurring in the early stages of the progression of the illness which may not be visible to the world outside the family. Typically, the family suffers first, and the most, as the addiction progresses on through the middle and late stages. This progression moves through the alcoholic–addict's increasingly erratic, inappropriate, and bizarre social behavior to financial and legal problems; spiritual isolation and estrangement (lowered moral and ethical standards); medical problems (memory losses, gastrointestinal disturbances, nutritional deficiency diseases, pancreatitis, hepatitis, cirrhosis, etc.); and finally, vocational problems. Generally, by the time the alcoholic–addict's behavior is affecting his job, he is nearing the later stages of the illness. He is losing any semblance of control over his drinking or drug dependency. The chemically dependent person will try to maintain his job performance—often with bursts of frenetic "workaholism"—not only to keep his job (money for alcohol or drugs), but to convince himself and others that he can't be an alcoholic or addict because "I go to work everyday" (never mind the frequent "Monday morning flu").

Also, by this time family members, especially spouses, have colluded consciously or unconsciously, overtly or covertly, with the alcoholic–addict to keep the "family secret" hidden from others. This collusion is necessary to reinforce the family's denial of the problem and to maintain the appearance of normalcy and cohesion to the community. The collusion covers overwhelming fears in family members which are based on negative societal attitudes, stigmata, and stereotypes related to alcohol and drug dependency.

This model of family involvement in a member's addiction exemplifies the male "head of the household" as the addict, and alcohol as the addicting drug. While this is by far the most common situation in military and civilian families, it is by no means the only one. The second most common situation is when the addict is the wife/mother. She may be solely alcohol-dependent (as well as her husband, sometimes), but she is much more likely to be dependent on sedative/tranquilizer/stimulant drugs in pill form than her husband. This "licit" drug dependence ("medications" obtained from physicians) may also involve alcohol continually or sporadically, as sedative drugs are usually cross-tolerant with alcohol and often more convenient to use covertly. The covert nature of addiction in women is important to acknowledge. The strong stigma attached to the woman addict (particularly when she is a wife and mother) has resulted in more secretive drug use patterns which make the identification more difficult and reinforce denial in other family members. Hence, addiction in a woman family member is even more likely to be the "family secret" which often is not acknowledged, even within the family. Military housing areas are often thought of as "fishbowl" living areas, but the sanctuary of a woman's home for isolated drinking is still quite inviolable. There remains a strong stigma against a military wife embarrassing her husband in any way, and thereby negatively affecting his career progression, particularly among officers. It is not uncommon for servicemembers to receive precipitous transfer orders because of a spouse's embarrassing social behavior while intoxicated.

Substance misuse and/or dependency in other military family members generally involves teenagers who are more likely to be abusers of a wide range of drugs, depending on what's currently available or in vogue with their peers. Most teens who use drugs have their "drug of choice," marijuana and alcohol being highest on the list. But, they are likely to be indiscriminate when some chemical is available (even unknown) which is purported to give a "good high" (hallucinogens, PCP, LSD, cocaine, "speed," with various diluting chemicals, many also toxic).

Heroin and narcotic addiction in military *families* is relatively uncommon. An exception is the narcotic-addicted military physician. While the incidence is low, treatment is difficult for several reasons. Perhaps the chief reason is the professionally unethical way the physician appropriates "licit" drugs for his "illicit" use. Also, because the behavior of the physician addicted to narcotics is usually not as bizarre as the alcoholic's, the denial of the patient and his family is even stronger.

There is some evidence to indicate that heroin addiction is more common in the Armed Forces than in civilian life (Burt & Biegel, 1980), but it occurs chiefly in the *unmarried* male youth, generally in certain defined geographical areas, particularly overseas.

ROLES IN THE ADDICT FAMILY

Members of the addict family suffer from a great deal of emotional pain, including feelings of anger, frustration, anxiety, embarrassment, humiliation, isolation, rejection, depression, estrangement, guilt, and low self-esteem. Added to this emotional trauma is a high incidence of neglect, verbal and physical abuse, and incest. All of this results in a breakdown of communication and trust with emotional distancing taking place as the existence of love in the family is questioned.

The family's response to this overwhelming situation is what many call the "family illness" of alcoholism (or other chemical addiction). In defense, the family system readjusts in an attempt to bring about balance or stability. In this readjustment family members take on basic roles. Wegscheider (1981) says, "In ten years of working with alcoholic families, I have watched the same five basic roles being played out in virtually every family. I have labeled them the Enabler, the Hero, the Scapegoat, the Lost Child, and the Mascot" (p. 84). Each family member chooses, subconsciously, the role which, for one reason or another, causes him the least amount of personal stress. This role becomes survival behavior for the individual and at the same time it provides a benefit for the family.

The Enabler is usually the person closest to the addict—the spouse or parent. She is the one most depended upon by the chemically dependent person, and so gradually takes on more and more responsibility with increased repression of feelings of anger, fear, hurt, and guilt. Unable to tell anyone about the "family secret," she may be given tranquilizers by her physician who is unaware of the stresses underlying her complaints of anxiety, depression, insomnia, or psychosomatic disorders. The Enabler's role in the family is to provide responsibility.

The eldest child in the family often becomes the family Hero. He begins to feel responsible for the family pain and tries hard to make things better by becoming a compulsive overachiever. Because of the disease's progression he loses ground and feels consistently inadequate. His feelings of inadequacy, confusion, anger, pain, and loneliness are hidden by his obvious success which provides self-worth for the family. Later, when his perfectionism and "workaholism" fail to cover his feelings of inadequacy and guilt, he may become seriously depressed.

Middle children are more likely to become Scapegoats or Lost Children. The Scapegoat doesn't want to work as hard as the Hero to get attention, prove himself worthy, and hide feelings of hurt, fear, loneliness, and rejection. He withdraws and looks for feelings of belonging outside the family. He aligns himself with other similar children often involved in asocial or antisocial behavior (drug use, running away, delinquency, promiscuity). The Scapegoat provides distraction for the family.

The Lost Child, much the opposite of the Scapegoat, seeks to hide his loneliness, hurt, and confusion by being alone and keeping quietly busy. He is quiet, aloof, shy, independent, and sometimes overweight. He is not given much attention, positive or negative, and because he is one child the family does not have to worry about, his role is to offer the family relief.

The youngest child is often the family Mascot. He learns to get attention and approval by being cute and funny, using charm and humor to survive and cover pained feelings. He provides the family escape through fun and humor. This child may be labeled "hyperactive" and put on a tranquilizer or sedative drug.

According to Wegscheider (1981), "Because of the self-delusion and the compulsive nature of these behavior patterns, the family member takes this behavior into every other relationship. The defense system and repressed feelings become a primary problem for each family member" (p. 88). Because these behaviors are compulsive and destructive they are expensive: Each family member pays a price to survive!

Role reversals also occur frequently in addict families. The most common example is the teenager (usually the eldest child and family Hero) who takes on the parental role of the addict–parent of the same sex (e.g., the teenage daughter of an alcoholic mother may take on household and child-rearing duties). A memorable example in my clinical practice occurred in the family of an alcoholic senior enlisted man who was undergoing alcoholism rehabilitation. Therapeutic contact with his family revealed that his wife had had extensive psychiatric treatment (with several hospital admissions for apparent schizophrenia), was on maintenance antipsychotic medication, and sometimes drank wine excessively. The eldest child was a 14-year-old boy who had taken on the role of the family "parent." He assumed responsibility for his 13-year-old retarded brother (bused daily to a special school) an 9-year-old sister. He did most of the family grocery shopping, cooking, and housekeeping, had a newspaper delivery route, was an "all-A" student and Eagle Scout, played a musical instrument, and somehow found time to have a girl friend. This superachieving family Hero proved to be the family member most resistant to family therapy, seemingly unable (fear of trusting his father's recovery) or unwilling to give up his position of power and control in the family.

BREAKING INTO THE SYSTEM

Only in the past few years have persons working in the treatment of chemical dependency acknowledged the importance of family therapy in this field. Coleman and Davis (1978) state, "The role of the family in supporting the use of drugs by one of its members is a critical issue currently being addressed by a growing number of people" (p. 21). Dell Orto (1974) states that the original reason for instituting group therapy for drug abusers and their families was "the realization that treating drug abusers apart from their families was an exercise in futility." Currently, it is generally believed by workers in this field that without intervention into the family system and treatment of family members the chances of successful recovery of the addict and survival of the family as a unit are much diminished.

We have looked at some of the principal ways family dynamics become altered in addict families. As distorted and unhealthy as addict families can become, one must remember that the family is a system which has achieved some balance. Left to continue on its path the addict family will usually self-destruct eventually. Divorce may ensue, and/or children will leave home as soon as possible (or prematurely). Tensions and pressures can lead to severe violence, even to a homicidal or suicidal extreme.

Usually, family members have little understanding of their interdependent behavior and believe that abstinence in the addict member will (magically) make everything all right. A common response to a plea to involve an addict's spouse in treatment is as follows: "It's his drinking that's the problem, doctor. Just get him to stop and everything will be all right." This unrealistic view is due partly to the strong denial of the family member's own pain and distorted behavior. Additionally, when the family member is able to recognize his own pain and emotional fragility, he often carries strong fears of dealing with multiple negative feelings—a fear and resentment of changing himself while mistrusting the positive changes which may occur in the recovering addict member. In short, family members are often paralyzed by their ambivalence.

Intervention into the family system must be done carefully due to the disturbance in family balance which will result. Sometimes, when the pressures and pain from his drinking or drug dependency become overwhelming, the addict member will seek help on his own. Usually, by this time, family members have long wished for help. In many cases professionals and paraprofessionals who work with military families may be in a position to assist in an intervention with an addict family.

This chapter does not attempt to educate the reader in making the diagnosis of alcoholism or other addiction. There are excellent resources for this purpose. However, there are signs and symptoms that often develop in members of the addict family (other than the chemically dependent member) which, when observed by the alert health care provider, therapist, counselor, chaplain, supervisor, schoolteacher or friend, might serve as "road signs" to lead to the cause of dysfunction in the family. These visible signs of family distress may include complaints of nonspecific anxiety (desiring tranquilizers for relief); insomnia, headaches, back pain, ulcer symptoms, depression, too frequent visits to a medical clinic (often with psychosomatic illnesses); school and behavior problems in children, such as inattentiveness, poor grades, fights, "hyperactivity," truancy (if mother's the drinker, the child may want to stay home to take care of her, or to protect her if she's being abused by the drinking father), bedwetting, or delinquency; poor hygiene or poorly explained frequent bruises noticed in schoolchildren; drug or alcohol abuse; shoplifting; and financial mismanagement.

If we consider the addict as the sickest member of the family, then I think we can rightfully look at him as the primary target for intervention if we are to enter this system and help the family become healthier. The sooner an intervention takes place in the downward progression of an addiction, the more damage can be avoided. However, an intervention is generally more likely to be successful if the addict has suffered considerable emotional pain secondary to his drinking or drug misuse. Often, his denial blocks his awareness of his own emotional pain as well as the pain of those persons closest to him. The strength of the addict's denial of his chemical dependency is awesome. In my opinion it is the most baffling feature of the illness, the feature which makes it most difficult for others to understand the addict's predicament. He will cling to this denial until his demise, permitting his illness to progress, allowing him to avoid seeing his powerlessness over it. His denial permits him to ignore the family problems, as well as mounting financial, legal, and health problems.

Generally, his job is affected last. Although he may miss an occasional morning or day of work due to intoxication or hangovers, he will overcompensate on the job to prove to himself and others that his drinking or drug use is not out of control. As a rule, the chemically dependent person will not ask for help until he has lost almost everything (and/or everyone) of value in his life and he is overwhelmed by the emotional pain associated with his realization of his losses. It is no longer believed that the chemically dependent person must "hit bottom" before help can be effective. Obviously, if he is to avoid reaching that point, intervention must be accomplished earlier. But, which person in the addict's life has the courage to initiate the intervention?

The addict will not seek help toward recovery as long as his needs are being met within the family. In most instances, a change in the family is required before a change in the addict can take place. For family members to do nothing means they will continue to be exploited by the addict and to react in passive, destructive ways. For a family member to take a new, creative approach usually requires help from someone who understands the delicacy of the situation and is practiced in the techniques of intervention. The "helper" may be anyone in the health care professions, a chaplain or minister, a boss or supervisor, an employee assistance counselor, or someone working in the field of treatment for alcoholism or other addictions. Wegscheider (1981) says:

> The family member who issues the first call for help (the intervener) is one who is still in touch with some of his own feelings and cares enough about himself and the rest of the family to take a risk. Make no mistake, seeking help for an alcoholic without his knowledge or consent does seem like a terrible risk. If they are not afraid of his anger, which they usually are, they at least feel that they are being disloyal to him and betraying family secrets. (p. 152)

The most likely intervener is the Enabler, who, as we have seen, has taken responsibility for most everything in the family. Other family members, friends, or employers may also act as the intervener. In the military, someone higher in the chain of command may intervene as off-duty behavior is more likely to come to their attention than in civilian life where an employer usually must wait for the addict's behavior to directly affect his job performance. In the Armed Forces, the addict's commanding officer has the authority to intervene if the servicemember's behavior is in any way reflecting negatively on the service. In fact, the commanding officer may be negligent if he fails to intervene.

The professional or paraprofessional who leads the intervention will carefully prepare all members of the intervention team, usually over a period of time with several meetings before confronting the addict. The intervention team should consist of any persons available who are important in the addict's life. If possible, all family members should participate, unless certain members are very reluctant. A team might also include a family physician, minister, employer or supervisor, attorney, or close relatives or friends. The team leader must get to know the team members to learn the extent of each member's involvement in the family illness. The team leader will usually need to educate the team members about the addictive process to assure that they understand how the addict cannot help himself. They must be truly assured that *only their willingness to risk a confrontation will get him to the treatment he needs.* This goal of treatment needs to be clear to everyone on the team. Sometimes family members are so stuck in their own denial and delusion that they may require counseling or psychotherapy before they gain the courage to go through with a confrontation of the addict.

When the team leader feels that members are psychologically prepared, he should direct all members to make a written list of specific instances when the addict's behavior caused problems for someone. Each list will likely be quite different; due to poor communication in the addict family, many incidents will not be common knowledge. The statements on the lists should be as objective as possible, expressed without hostility or blaming which would make the addict defensive. Most alcoholics–addicts have experienced lecturing, scolding, and judging by people in their lives. They have low self-esteem and do not need another person telling them how badly they have failed. In this type of confrontation, one must not raise the addict's anxiety level too much. *The team must provide sensitive delivery of the truth to the addict about the nature and consequences of his drinking or drug use.* The team must try to establish a trusting relationship with the addict through kindness, gentleness, and compassion, with underlying firmness and realism. *Addicted persons should be told that they are not responsible for becoming chemically dependent, but they are responsible for doing something about it.*

The most important factor in the intervention is that the addict is most likely to respond to the emotional impact of the expression of love and genuine concern by those persons most intimately involved in his life. Reasoning or arguing with him will do no good because of his strong defenses; "cornering" him will likely cause him to run. He must be reached on an emotional level.

Team members must practice reading their lists so that they feel as comfortable and confident as possible. An extemporaneous presentation should be avoided, as any evidence of hesitation or ambivalence in the team members will be exploited by the addict in an attempt to undermine the confrontation. Again, the goal of the intervention must be clear to all participants. As expressed by Johnson (1980): "The goal of intervention, through the presentation of this material, is to have the alcoholic see and accept enough reality so that, however grudgingly, the need for help can be accepted" (p. 57). The goal is usually that the addict accept treatment without delay (he may change his mind with even the briefest delay). In this case arrangements for treatment should be made prior to the confrontation, trusting that the confrontation will be successful.

Sometimes the addict will refuse to accept treatment, but will state that he has "seen the light" and vows to stop drinking on his own (and he really means it!). This oversimplification of his chemical dependency is largely due to his denial. If he is adamant in his vow and refusal, it is recommended that a promise to enter treatment at a later date be extracted from him if he returns to any drinking or drug use.

This family intervention process may not be necessary in the military if the servicemember's commanding officer is willing to order him into treatment at a military facility. It may fall to one of the "helpers" to convince the commanding officer of this need.

It is strongly advised that family members get treatment for themselves whether the addict accepts treatment or not. Without help for family members, the family illness will continue on its debilitating course. If the addict accepts treatment, then it is vital that family members become involved in the treatment process for themselves and to learn what his recovery is all about so they can understand the changes in him and the adjustments which the family will need to make. Too often, family members do not receive treatment and the treated addict returns to the disturbed family system which attempts to regain balance by pulling the addict member back to his previous addict behavior, thereby sabotaging his recovery.

Sometimes family members cannot or will not cooperate to conduct an intervention, or the intervention may fail. I cannot overemphasize that family members should never think of the situation as hopeless. Getting help for themselves (even as the addict continues to drink or use drugs) can be enough to upset the unhealthy "balance" of the family system and may lead to eventual recovery for the addict.

WHAT HELP IS AVAILABLE?

In military and civilian systems that provide services for substance abusers and their families, one generally finds help available at different "levels." These levels are loosely categorized as (I) alcohol and drug abuse education; (II) outpatient counseling programs; and (III) residential treatment programs. Historically, counseling and treatment programs for alcohol misuse and drug problems have been separate. In recent years it has become more common to find polysubstance abuse in the younger segment of the population. As a result, most programs at all three levels accept patients with alcohol or drug problems, or both. An exception occurs with narcotic addicts who are often treated in centers restricted to that addiction.

The question is, who needs what level of help?

Persons who have brought attention to themselves by way of alcohol or drug-related "problem" behavior (drunk driving arrests, public intoxication, drug possession, other social, medical or job problems), but, after proper screening, have not been diagnosed as chemically dependent, would most appropriately be referred to an alcohol and/or drug abuse education program. Many such programs are modeled after the national Alcohol Safety Action Program. Such a program is given in a classroom format over a relatively short period of time, usually comprising 30–40 hours of lectures, films, and group discussions.

Persons who have experienced more serious ongoing alcohol and/or drug-related problems, and are diagnosed as psychologically "dependent" on a mind-altering chemical, but not physically addicted or in need of medical detoxification, may be referred to an outpatient counseling program. This type of program can be tailored to the patient's schedule and needs. Such a program might include a few to several weekly meetings of individual interviews, group therapy, educational sessions, meeting of Alcoholics Anonymous (AA), and family or couples therapy sessions. The most intensive form of outpatient counseling is day treatment (or a modified hospital program) where the patient spends all day in a structured rehabilitation program at the counseling center, clinic, or hospital, and returns to his home at night. Such a program may last several weeks or may be a step between full residential treatment and a less intensive aftercare program. Caution is advised in referring alcoholics and heavily dependent drug users who are resistant to treatment to outpatient programs as first-line treatment. Part-time involvement of such patients may not be intensive enough to break through their denial (and other defenses) and they may comply with the program, "looking good" superficially, but gaining little more than temporary abstinence.

Residential, or inpatient treatment (or rehabilitation) may be advisable for any psychologically or physiologically dependent alcoholic or drug addict, but is particularly indicated immediately following medically supervised hospital detoxification (usually 4–10 days in duration, depending on the drugs involved). Any addict who is resistant to treatment, and therefore in strong denial of his illness, can best be treated in the full-time involvement of a structured inpatient program. Most such residential programs are 3–6 weeks in duration, with the exception of narcotics addiction and adolescent residential treatment programs which are often 90–120 days in duration.

Aftercare is a vital component of outpatient or inpatient treatment. It usually consists of ongoing meetings at the treatment center at frequent intervals over a period of several months following rehabilitation. Aftercare sessions are generally group-oriented, but may include individual sessions, family sessions, and marital counseling.

Halfway houses are residential facilities, usually without active treatment capability, which provide a supportive living milieu for rehabilitees who are not yet ready to return to the full responsibilities of independent living.

Reputable alcoholism–drug addiction treatment programs generally have similar goals of treatment, although methods of treatment may differ. The goals of recovery from addiction, as treated at the Navy's Long Beach Alcohol Rehabilitation Service, include a development of, or return to, a healthy and rewarding life-style without any use of mind-altering chemicals. This usually requires giving up the false sense of control, grandiosity, and dishonesty of the addict and learning new coping skills, turning from isolation and mistrust to a healthy, trusting involvement with other persons in recovery. Methods and techniques used to accomplish these objectives within treatment include heavy emphasis on group counseling (with confrontation, catharsis, and trust-building), individual counseling, education sessions, assertiveness and relaxation training, psychodrama, nutrition counseling, and physical conditioning. Some programs stress behavioral therapy methods, including aversive conditioning. It is the belief at Long Beach that abstinence must remain the ongoing paramount goal, as a truly addicted person cannot return to "controlled" use of his drug of choice (including alcohol) or related chemicals. Further, unless the addicted individual can learn to feel better about himself and his life without using mind-altering chemicals than he did while using them, his chances for recovery are slim.

Alcoholics Anonymous, the self-help group which has grown steadily over almost 50 years, is an important part of most treatment programs. Indeed, involvement in AA alone has resulted in ongoing sobriety for many alcoholics. AA, with its *Twelve Steps* to recovery and its *Twelve Traditions*, provides a structured guide to serene sobriety through a program of regular involvement and identification with other recovering alcoholics, sponsorship, honesty, mutual support, and relinquishing a false sense of personal control to a "higher power" (as interpreted individually). AA meetings take place all over the world and can be located through the AA area office in most communities (listed in telephone book white pages). The ubiquitous nature of AA makes it particularly valuable as a support system for recovering military personnel. Narcotics Anonymous groups are proliferating, and in some locales "Pot-Smokers Anonymous" groups are forming.

Earlier in this chapter the importance of treatment for family members was discussed. Most residential treatment centers (military or civilian) and many counseling centers have the capacity to help family members who have alcohol or drug problems, or who are involved with a chemically dependent active servicemember. This is usually accomplished in conjunction with treatment of the addict member. Outpatient counseling may also be available in lieu of residential treatment. Such treatment should be tailored to the family's needs with family group therapy, couples counseling, teen and child individual and group counseling being the modalities usually available.

Al-Anon, an anonymous, AA-based self-support group for family members and other significant individuals in an alcoholic–addict's life, has proven to be an invaluable resource for such persons, whether or not the addict accepts help for himself. The disruption to the unhealthy addict family system brought about by changes made by nonaddict members can sometimes result in eventual acceptance of help by the addict member. The purposes of Al-Anon (Al-Anon Family Groups, 1972) are the following:

1. To help solve problems due to alcoholism in the home.
2. To share experience, strength and hope with others in similar circumstances.
3. To improve our own emotional health and spiritual growth.
4. To provide a more wholesome environment for the whole family including the alcoholic, drunk or sober. (p. 4)

Alateen, modeled after Al-Anon, is a similar support group for teenagers in addict families. Some Alatot groups have been formed for preteen children also.

The location of Al-Anon, Alateen, and Alatot groups may be found by calling Al-Anon Family Group offices listed in telephone book white pages. Members of families of persons addicted to drugs other than alcohol are welcome at meetings of these organizations.

HELP WITHIN THE MILITARY SYSTEM

The Department of Defense probably has the world's largest employee assistance program. The DoD Alcohol and Drug Abuse Prevention Program has about 3600 staff and professional personnel who direct the program and deliver full-time services to active duty service members, civilian employees, and their family members, with an overall budget in 1980 of $84 million. Approximately 79,000 people in the DoD, identified as having various degrees of substance abuse problems, received some form of treatment and rehabilitation in 1980. Alcohol abuse represented over 60% of the caseload (Moxley, 1981). At last count there were approximately 420 counseling centers and 54 residential treatment centers for substance abuse problems in the DoD system.

In addition to medical and psychiatric evaluation and treatment available to military personnel and their dependents at medical centers of the U.S. Navy, Army, and Air Force the following specialized services are available within the DoD Alcohol and Drug Abuse Prevention Program (A&DAPP):

NAVY

Historically, the DoD A&DAPP began with a small AA meeting, formed to help sailors on the Naval Station at Long Beach, California, in 1965. This service of recovering alcoholics helping drinking alcoholics gradually evolved and expanded to include outpatient counseling, then residential rehabilitation. Eventually, it moved to the Long Beach Naval Regional Medical Center and became the Alcohol Rehabilitation Service which has earned an international reputation for high-quality treatment. Currently, the Navy has numerous facilities providing services at the three levels mentioned above. At Level I, the Navy has established approximately 24 Naval Safety Action Programs (NASAP) at various bases for alcohol abuse education. Additionally, a rapidly expanding Drug Safety Action Program (NDSAP) has recently been established. Drunk drivers and military personnel exhibiting behavior problems associated with alcohol or drug abuse are most appropriately referred to these programs. Interested family members and other persons are generally welcomed at these courses on a space-available basis. At Level II, the Navy has established Counseling and Assistance Centers (CAAC) at almost every base and aboard several of the larger ships. They provide screening and evaluation services for alcohol and drug problems in military personnel, outpatient counseling (limited at some centers), and follow-up services for personnel completing residential rehabilitation programs. Counseling for family members is usually limited due to lack of staff members trained to work with families. The strength of the Navy's Alcohol Prevention Program lies in its emphasis on residential rehabilitation (Level III). Large (80–120 beds) Alcohol Rehabilitation Centers are located at Norfolk, Virginia; Jacksonville, Florida; and San Diego, California. Approximately 22 Alcohol Rehabilitation Services (15–60 beds) are located at Naval Regional Medical Centers in the continental United States and abroad. Most of these facilities have family treatment capability and strongly encourage family involvement when military personnel are undergoing rehabilitation. The Navy emphasizes education of Medical Department personnel in identification, intervention, and treatment of addictive diseases. The Navy Drug Rehabilitation Center (NDRC), San Diego, California (180 beds), is a residential facility for the treatment of military personnel who are addicted chiefly to drugs other than alcohol. The NDRC family treatment capability is limited. On the grounds of the National Naval

Medical Center, Bethesda, Maryland, is located the Tri-Service Alcohol Rehabilitation Facility, a residential treatment facility conjointly staffed by Army, Navy, and Air Force personnel.

MARINE CORPS

Having no medical department of its own, the Marine Corps depends chiefly on the Navy to meet its medical needs. Personnel needing residential treatment (Level III) are usually referred to Navy centers. The Marine Corps provides Level I and II services through Battalion or Wing Counseling Centers on most stations. Generally, they provide services only for active duty personnel, but will refer dependents to local civilian treatment resources.

ARMY

The Army's Alcohol and Drug Abuse Prevention and Control Program is largely a decentralized program. Established on most Army bases are Community Counseling Centers which provide Level I and II services for Army personnel. They provide crisis intervention and referral services for family members on a space-available basis. The Army's policy is that family members are serviced within the capability of existing resources. Community (civilian) resources are utilized to the maximum extent possible (80% funded by CHAMPUS, the federal medical insurance program for dependents of military personnel). Although the Army has not emphasized residential (Level III) treatment, they have established several alcoholism treatment centers in Germany, one in Korea, and one in El Paso, Texas.

AIR FORCE

Services under the Air Force Drug and Alcohol Abuse Control Program are provided chiefly through Social Actions Offices located on every Air Force base. Level I and II services are provided for active duty personnel and evaluations for substance abuse problems in military dependents.

Every Air Force base also has a Mental Health Clinic, often associated with an Air Force hospital. Staff personnel at these clinics also work with substance abuse problems. Outpatient treatment may be available for family members at either Social Actions Centers or Mental Health Clinics, depending on staff capabilities. The Air Force has 10 Alcoholism Rehabilitation Centers (12–40 beds each) providing residential treatment for active duty members. Seven centers are located in the continental United States, plus one each in England, Germany, and the Philippines. All ARCs are required to have family programs. The Air Force has a well-organized system through Social Actions Offices for follow-on monitoring of personnel after completion of rehabilitation.

COAST GUARD

The Coast Guard has designated servicemembers as alcohol and drug abuse resource personnel at district headquarters and other shore commands. Their duties generally extend to matters of education, crisis intervention, and referral for active service members. Public Health Service and Navy facilities are generally used for Level II and III services. The Coast Guard provides some service members to work as alcohol and drug abuse counselors at a few Navy treatment facilities.

This has been only a brief overview of facilities within the DoD A&DAPP. Services may vary at local levels, chiefly due to fluctuations in staffing. In general, effective family counseling and treatment programs for addict families can be found at residential (Level III) alcoholism treatment facilities, rarely in outpatient programs.

FATHER TO SON

One of the most tragic aspects of alcoholism and other drug addiction is the perpetuation of the illness in families. Although statistics vary, it is well accepted that over 50% of alcoholics have an alcoholic parent. The damage to other family members is only beginning to be addressed. An emerging area of treatment is with the adult children of alcoholics. Many of these adults themselves became alcoholics and/or were incest victims as children in alcoholic families who have repressed the trauma for many years. As the stigma decreases, enlightened mental health professionals are able to offer more help with these problems, and self-help groups such as Incest Survivors Anonymous are forming.

The following is an anonymous verbatim quotation written by a senior enlisted man while undergoing treatment for alcoholism in a Navy residential rehabilitation program. Every word is authentic and the story is very typical, vividly illustrating the trauma in an alcoholic family from the perspective of a developing child and adolescent.

While I was growing up, my father was a heavy drinker for as long as I can remember. My mother drank on occasion, but not very much. My father's alcoholism was an embarrassment to me. None of my friends ever came over to our house because my father was always drinking. The only people who ever came to our house were his drinking buddies and their families.

His big hangup when drinking was what a failure and good-for-nothing I was. He was active in sports when he was young and his thoughts were, "Here's a football, be a star." I don't ever remember him trying to teach me anything. He was too busy going to bars or working. I always thought I was a failure in his eyes at anything I tried. When he was drunk it was always my fault. He always related this to my mother and I thought he was trying to turn her against me. My mother was afraid of him when he was drinking. She always agreed with him and made excuses for him. I always felt whatever I did wasn't good enough because he wanted more.

When my parents would argue, the whole neighborhood would know. Just about every family on the block considered me and my sisters as their second set of kids. They always reminded us of this when we were around them. I never felt comfortable at anyone's house, so I just moved from one to another when my parents argued.

As for physical and verbal abuse, I remember a lot of backhands and belts. He called me everything possible, no matter who was around. Everyone always felt sorry for me because of my dad. I couldn't handle it. I lost respect for him and any authority, around 11 or 12. In my head, I never would let him whip me again. When he tried, he would send me to my room. I would be in the door and out the window before he got there. He then took it out on my mother and sisters. I don't remember him ever using anything but a belt on my sisters. Only once did my mother show signs of physical abuse. I have seen her pushed and shoved a lot. He usually threw things or broke windows. When I came home, if he was sober, he would put me on restriction for awhile and nothing was ever discussed. I always ran from him after I was about 13.

One day, when I was about 14 or 15, I was at work and my mother called and said to walk home. I knew something was wrong. I walked home and found them arguing. He was acting crazy and screaming he was going to kill himself. He went to the bathroom and got a razor. Me and my mom got it away from him. He denied it the next day. He cried about it, and that was the first time I had ever seen him show any emotion. Not too long after that, I was in trouble for something, and came home and he was drinking. He started in on me and I told him I didn't want to live here any more. He just said it was his house. I got a set of his car keys and took his car and drove to S.F. and went to his aunt's house. I stayed for 4 or 5 months. He flew up the next day and got his car, and never said anything to me. He called me and wanted me to come home and finish school. He said he would slow down his drinking. This lasted until I was about 16, and I was always in trouble for something, and he started drinking again. I wasn't going to graduate and this was a big thing to him. I was drinking on the weekends and I kept thinking, "Just like him." I was totally fed up with him and nothing seemed to go right for me. I left one day and hitch-hiked to Arkansas to stay at an uncle's house. I stayed there until I was about 17. I called him up one day and asked him to sign for me to go in the Navy. He said not until I came home. I went home and tried to talk to him. This failed due to both our stubbornness and my feelings about him. He wouldn't sign, kept on drinking, and I kept on getting in trouble by drinking. I waited it out and joined the Navy on my 18th birthday (an honorable, masculine occupation offering a steady paycheck, a chance to "be a man" and "see the world;" tattoos followed shortly).

I don't ever remember my mother or father telling me they loved me or were proud of me. My father has never shown any physical love. He never even so much as put his arm around me. He still hasn't to this day. My mother always gives it the "We love you" now. My mother and father still are hesitant when it comes to being close.

Can anyone doubt that alcoholism is a family illness?

CONCLUSION

I have covered aspects of substance misuse and dependency which I feel are most critical and practical in understanding and working with military families. I think it is clear that alcohol and drug problems in military families are quite similar to those of civilian families; but there are some unique stresses, situations, and regulations which impact upon military families. Some of these regulations make intervention into a substance misuse–dependency problem with an active servicemember simpler. However, this is not the case with the family members. Because I believe that intervention into the "family secret" is the most difficult aspect of this problem, a practical strategy of intervention has been covered in detail. It is my hope that this information will aid and inspire persons working with families to "muster up" the courage to help addict families break out of their unhealthy systems into a healthy life of recovery.

REFERENCES

Al-Anon Family Groups. *Alcoholism: The family disease.* New York: Al-Anon Family Group Headquarters, 1972.

Burt, M. R., & Biegel, M. M. *Worldwide survey of nonmedical drug use and alcohol use among military personnel: 1980.* Bethesda, Md.: Burt Associates, 1980.

Clayton, R. C. The family–drug abuse relationship. In B. G. Ellis (Ed.), *Drug abuse from the family perspective.* Rockville, Md.: National Institute on Drug Abuse, 1980.

Coleman, S. B., & Davis, D. I. Family therapy and drug abuse: A national survey. *Family Process,* 1978, *17,* 21–29.

Dell Orto, A. The role and resources of the family during the drug rehabilitation process. *Journal of Psychedelic Drugs,* 1974, *6,* 435–445.

Holcomb, J. F. Alcohol and the armed forces. *Alcohol Health and Research World,* 1981/82, *6* (2) 2–17.

Johnson, V. E. *I'll quit tomorrow.* San Francisco: Harper & Row, 1980.

Kellerman, J. *AA: A family affair.* Center City, Minn.: Hazelden Educational Services, 1980.

Morrison, J. Rethinking the military family syndrome. *American Journal of Psychiatry,* 1981, *138* (3), 354–357.

Moxley, J. H., III. Department of defense. *Military Medicine,* 1981, *146,* 626–630.

Reddy, B. *Alcoholism: A family illness.* Park Ridge, Ill.: Lutheran General Hospital, 1977.

Wegscheider, S. *Another chance: Hope and health for the alcoholic family.* Palo Alto, Calif.: Science & Behavior Books, 1981.

5

Incest in the Military Family

PATRICIA W. CRIGLER

"The family that lays together, stays together," and "Incest is something you do, not something you talk about," are both clear insights into the dynamics of the incest taboo and how it is broken numerous times by people in our country. According to a report from the National Center on Child Abuse and Neglect (1980), one out of every five children is a victim of incest each day. Breaking this statistic down further, the report shows that one girl out of three and one boy out of seven have this experience foisted upon them.

INCEST DEFINED

What exactly is incest? The National Center on Child Abuse and Neglect uses the term "intrafamily sexual abuse" for incest and defines that as abuse "which is perpetrated on a child by a member of that child's family group." It includes not only sexual intercourse, but also any act designed to stimulate a child sexually, or to use a child for the sexual stimulation either of the perpetrator or of another person (National Center, 1980). For the purpose of this chapter, incest is defined as "any act having to require secrecy concerning sexual contact between family members, including not just intercourse, but masturbation, hand–genital or oral–genital activity, sexual fondling, exhibition, and even sexual proposition-

The opinions or assertions contained herein are the private views of the writer and are not to be construed as official or as reflecting views of the Department of the Navy or the Department of Defense.

Patricia W. Crigler. Commander, Medical Service Corps, U.S. Navy, and Director, Substance Abuse Department, Naval Hospital, San Diego, California.

ing." It does not include unconscious sexual gestures which are generally discernible from conscious maneuvers for sexual pleasure on the part of the offending adult.

Incest is often described as the "ultimate taboo," the one taboo that should never be broken, but, as we have clearly seen from the statistics mentioned above, incest does indeed take place. It occurs much more frequently than even the statistics would indicate. It is commonly acknowledged by mental health professionals that incest is one of the least reported of actual crimes against persons. Once the "secret" is broken, the ramifications to the family unit are so widespread that many victims and uninvolved, yet aware, adults will not report the activity to a responsible agency. Even those children who tell someone what has happened are often hushed up, given no support, and sometimes even threatened by the very person whom they originally looked upon to stop the incest. Therefore, we must assume that the incidence of incest is much higher than our reports and statistics would indicate. Indeed, it is "something you do, not something you talk about."

CONSPIRACY OF SILENCE

Why is it that incest isn't talked about more? Most people in our culture are at least in verbal agreement that incest is a behavior to be avoided. We tend to think that all persons who engage in this activity are poor, illiterate, or seriously disturbed. Yet, there are numerous cases on file of physicians, clergymen, lawyers, high-ranking military officers, accountants, bankers, psychotherapists, politicians, and police officers as well as men and women on the welfare rolls who perpetrate this crime. Unfortunately, incest is a painful experience for numerous children every day, children who come from all walks of life and social groupings (*Long Beach, Calif., Press-Telegram*, 1981). There is an actual taboo against talking about incest. Many people engage in magical thinking: "If we don't speak of it, maybe it will go away!" Unfortunately, this is not so. Therapeutically and preventively, the reverse is true. The more the issue is raised, the "secret" broken, and the subject brought to the full light of public scrutiny, the less likely it is to occur or to reoccur. One of the best deterrents to continued incest is the exposure of the behavior outside the family unit (Brinbaum, 1980).

Finally, our individualistic tradition often impedes the reporting of such cases to appropriate protective agencies. There is an unwritten rule in this country that says what happens in the family is sacred, should stay in the family, and is not for public knowledge. People who are entrusted with the protection of children, such as physicians, ministers, and mental health professionals, often hesitate to report abuse. This reluctance is surprising, given the fact that these people, in some states, risk losing their licenses for not reporting such malignant family behaviors. This reluctance is no less true within military circles where it is widely believed that such family matters should be of no concern to commanding officers or even fellow shipmates. Many career-oriented military people fear that such public knowledge would obstruct, if not terminate, their careers. And, in reality, there is some basis of fact for this assumption. However, at least in the Navy, there have been policy changes which allow such information to surface without impeding or terminating careers. The emphasis is on treatment for the family, not always just punishment for the offender.

What can be done to alleviate the pressure to suppress such information and to allow treatment of the whole family, as well as of the individuals who are directly involved? Recently, there has been a positive trend toward the acknowledgment of child abuse as a major problem in our society. As attitudes have changed, laws have been rewritten to protect children both more formally and more successfully from physical child abuse. If we can place incest, the sexual exploitation of children, in the same general category with physical child abuse, then we will have taken away some of the power of the "conspiracy of silence" and possibly can reach more children at an earlier state of their experience. Awareness, information, and attitudinal changes are all effective change agents.

PROFILE OF THE INCESTUOUS FAMILY

Let us turn to an exploration of what a typical incestuous family looks like and, in particular, how an incestuous family in the military presents itself.

Outward appearances of such a family can be very deceiving. Many incestuously involved families look like model families to the outside observer. The family seems to be closely knit, with members playing a supportive role with one another. There may be much affectionate touching by the parents of the children. However, with a closer look, one sees that certain children are often touched, while the other children are either ignored or are assigned more than their fair share of the family's chores.

According to Rita and Blair Justice in their book *The Broken Taboo* (1979), the following is a profile of a typical incestuous family: It is a middle-class unit with two adults having some college education, if not a degree. The couple has been married for over 10 years with the father in business; he has made frequent job changes. (This may equate in the military family to many duty stations as well as service hopping from one branch of the Armed Forces to another.) The father is usually in his late 30s with the mother slightly younger and not working outside the home. The family has three children and the oldest daughter is approaching puberty.

The typical incestuous military family is lower middle-class with little to no college education, married for a shorter time than its civilian counterpart, with younger children. The wife may or may not work, a factor often dependent on the local job market where the family is stationed.

A further look at the family reveals that there are rigid family rules and role relationships. The concept of androgyny is almost unheard of; sex-stereotypical roles and rules are strictly and traditionally assigned and adhered to at all times. The father typically rules the house either with an iron hand or passively with innuendoes, such as implying that if outsiders find out what is going on, he will be sent to jail, thereby splitting up the family. These families do not adapt well to change because their problem-solving skills are few and unreliable. This weakness in the family unit is particularly significant to military families who are destined to move every 3 to 4 years, if not more often.

Communication is poor because of the low self-esteem that is a by-product of the conscious or unconscious awareness of the occurrence of incest. Denial of the incest on the part of all family members is strong and is usually a significant coping mechanism. There is one unwritten and all-pervasive rule in the family, and that is, "We don't talk about what Daddy and _____ do. It will break up the family."

The incestuous family has a confused communication system containing many double messages and much nonverbal communication. Both body and facial language are very powerful in these families. This behavior is obvious when family interviews are conducted to uncover the depth of the incest problem. The nonverbal messages are somewhat vague to the outside observer but are extremely intimidating to family members. Parental glances allude to previous negative reactions the children have experienced when the parents have not been pleased with the children's behavior, such as when they discuss problems with "strangers."

The only consistent message is that the incestuous relationship or activity must never, under any circumstances, be directly acknowledged or addressed. It is this conspiracy of silence that keeps the children dependent on the very vehicle, the family unit, that is creating an unhealthy environment. Each member, not just the ones actively engaged in the incest, has a vested interest in keeping the family intact because, as terrible as the environment is, it is usually the only place family members feel they belong. This phenomenon is particularly true of military families who frequently are relocated and who have often strained or broken their extended family ties. They feel they cannot rely upon neighbors, fellow workers, military physicians, or even schoolmates for fear that the incest information will be turned over to military superiors, resulting in the offender being summarily separated from the service. This action can be a real threat when the servicemember's skills are oriented toward only military type jobs, such as gunner's mate, tank driver, combat soldier, or underwater demolition expert. The closed family is kept bonded together, prohibiting anyone from intruding and discovering the "social travesty." This tight control binds each person closer and allows for little contact or growth with others outside the family. The external world is perceived as being evil and wanting to tear away the involved members, leaving the remaining members with little economic support or no intact family structure to face the perceived hostile world. This cycle alienates the members still further from society. It has a particularly devastating effect on the incest victim, who already feels isolated and deprived of her birthright of a loving home with protective, supportive parents. With the perception that the world is a hostile place ready to rend the family apart, and with the unit also being unable to answer most of the victim's needs, it is easy to understand how the victims and their families sink deeper and deeper into the pathological morass that incest brings to all affected by it (Gottlieb, 1980).

How then does it happen that incest begins in families who look "wholesome" to the outside world? There are several dynamics that converge to allow incest to occur. This chapter will present the most common constellation that seems to involve families.

The frequent geographical moves and the social isolation that military families may experience play a strong role in socially fragmenting the family from the rest of society. Additionally, the nomadic military life interrupts close ties with grandparents and other relatives who might lend stability and provide a safe source of protection for the victim when she asks for help in breaking the secret in the family. One might assume mothers would be a natural source of assistance to the children, but ironically, they are often the last source of help for the victim.

FAMILY DYNAMICS

For illustrative purposes, a typical incestuous family will be described with the father as the perpetrator; the mother in the home, but psychologically absent; the oldest daughter as the victim; and two younger siblings—a younger daughter, who may be the next victim, and a younger brother, who may be an *understudy* for the father and learning the father's pathological ways.

This type of family sets itself into an incestuous pattern long before the actual physical incest begins. Typically, the mother and father have begun to pull apart from each other, each seeking psychological and sometimes physical solace from others in the family. The very fabric of the marriage begins to shred as the two adults begin to make new connections to answer their dependency and comfort needs. If the dependency needs of the father are great and his discomfort with adult women, including his wife, is also high, he may turn to the eldest daughter to receive attention and affection. At first, the wife may be surprised and displeased that he has turned his attention away from her and toward their daughter. However, if she too is in need of peace and quiet, wishing to share some of the burdens of raising the family as well as tending to the needs of her husband, she may grow to welcome the daughter's oftentimes self-appointed task of "keeping Daddy happy." This shift in roles may take place consciously, but most often it occurs unconsciously and within the psychologically acceptable limits of keeping the family intact. This gradual abandonment of the wife and the transfer of sexual interest to the daughter may result in economic deprivation because the father may be discharged from the service should his behavior become known. The fear of being abandoned when at a distant duty station where no relatives are close and the neighbors seem hostile and isolated themselves, perhaps hiding their own family secrets, is a very real one in such families who have poor coping skills to begin with. Also at issue is the possibility of criminal proceedings in the civilian and/or military sector. Families have a very difficult time disclosing a secret for fear of being responsible for sending the offender to jail. Despite anger, hatred, or confusion over the act(s), the need for belonging to one's family unit often prevents reporting. Although often referred to as "loyalty," it may be more truly a need for a sense of identity or a dependent need for the parents' attention and support that keeps the victim from reporting the parent(s).

EARLY DEVELOPMENTAL PATTERN

There seem to be two distinctly different developmental patterns of incest. One pattern begins when the victim is very young. Initially, there is manual manipulation of the child in her bath or when Daddy puts her to bed. There is a gradual expansion of these sexual contacts to include making the child observe Daddy's penis, manipulate it, engage in fellatio, and then finally, at about puberty, intercourse is likely to be attempted by the father. What starts off as a "love game to play with Daddy" turns serious as the child begins to mature into a young woman. This type of incest can go on for many years, with the average range being from about age 2 to about 14, when the daughter begins to be sexually interested in boys her own age. This switch in attention often enrages the father and one of two reactions occurs. He may become overtly jealous of the daughter's boyfriends and try to chase them off by intimidation and/or forbid the daughter to date until a much older age. The other reaction is to abandon the older daughter and to turn his attention to the next youngest daughter. Many older daughters say that they continued to engage in the incest after they believed they could have stopped, erroneously thinking they were protecting their younger sisters from their fathers (Brinbaum, 1980).

LATER DEVELOPMENTAL PATTERN

The other pattern starts at a much later age as the young girl begins to develop secondary sex characteristics. As her body begins to fill out, so do the latent fantasies of the father. He will suddenly "see" his daughter for the "first time." This pattern appears to be particularly prevalent among men who have been deployed for long periods of time and come home to find that their "baby girl" has begun to look like a younger version of their wife, to whom they were at least initially sexually attracted. And while this pattern begins much later in the child's life, it typically lasts from a few weeks up to 2 to 3 years before disclosure occurs or intervening variables stop the exploitation (Finkelhor, 1979).

Having taken a look at the two prototypical incestuous families and how the developmental patterns of such units evolve, the following is a description of the major triad in these families: the father, mother, and daughter.

TYPES OF FATHERS

In their study on incest, the Justices (1979) describe four types of men who engage in incest. These personalities are the symbiotic, psychopathic-sociopathic, pedophiliac, and the "other" type who engages in incest either as a part of his subculture or because he is psychotic.

SYMBIOTIC

The symbiotic personality is an individual who was emotionally deprived as a child himself. He grew up in a family that was cold and did not meet his strong needs for closeness, nor give him a sense of belonging in a warm, loving environment. He did not learn how to satisfy his needs for affection in a nonsexual way and has no idea how to establish a relationship other than in activities involving sex. He cannot usually verbalize his needs but they are strong, and when his marriage no longer gratifies these needs, he thrashes about, eagerly looking for someone to help him fulfill his deep needs. His own daughter, an unthreatening, vulnerable, loving child, becomes the recipient and target of these cravings for affection and warmth which he presents in a sexual fashion. He knows no other way to express these needs.

This type of personality has several subtypes. Some men try to bully others; some try to be persuasive; while still others are shy and try to play on sympathy and misguided loyalty to get their desires met. Another type is the one who uses alcohol and then, following loss of control due to drinking, attempts to fulfill his dependency needs through sex. The Justices call these types the tyrant, the rationalizer, the introvert, and the alcoholic.

A further look at each is warranted as we try to understand the dynamics behind these behaviors.

Tyrant

The tyrant probably is the most typical type found among the military population. He is authoritarian. When he speaks, he appears to be the epitome of a Marine Corps drill instructor or the captain of a ship. He rules, he orders, he demands, and either he receives absolute loyalty and obedience or the consequences will be grave. He brooks no opposition and often uses threats of force or actual physical abuse to have his way inside his family. To his family he is a tyrant, but to his military superiors he may only look like a "good trooper" or a "man with discipline." His family lives in fear of his anger and retribution should they upset him. He is a patriarch and looks at his family as his belongings who must obey him, follow him from one duty station to another, and who are totally subject to his whims. Often, these whims include sex from his daughters. The military macho myth is prevalent in this type. Sex may be the only way such a man has of being close to another human being. He believes that to admit to needs for affection and closeness would be tantamount to admitting weakness. Such an admission would be too damaging to his ego structure, which is built on asserting power and aggression. But this type will allow himself to be close to his daughter if he sees her as weak and vulnerable enough to be dominated completely. With her, he may express some tenderness and affection without fear of appearing weak. However, he usually chooses to express most of his affectional needs in sexual terms. These men are also the most likely to become enraged when they see their daughters becoming sexually interested in their own male peers. The father can become quite violent and engage in persecutory behaviors, such as following his daughter out on a date, verbally questioning her, following the date, and even examining her clothes for signs of sexual activity. His basic distrust of people is so strong that he can never let his guard down sufficiently to develop a truly tender relationship with anyone. In his view, the daughter's dating has only underlined the feeling that no one is to be trusted, that to rule with the iron fist is safest.

Rationalizer

The rationalizer is the subtype who uses his intelligence to obfuscate the issue of incest and to explain it away as a "duty," that a father has to initiate his daughter into sex in the "right way" so that she will know what she's doing and will be able to please her husband. This type follows the developmental pattern of the man who comes home from overseas, finds his daughter to be maturing attractively, and conjures up the excuse of doing his "fatherly duty" by introducing her to sexual activity. He can present a public image of the perfect father who teaches Sunday school, is a model officer and gentleman, and coaches Little League baseball when not out on maneuvers serving his country. He can compartmentalize his life so well that he sees no harm being done to his daughter as he "educates" her to the sexual ways of the world. Quite often, the daughter is mesmerized into also thinking in this compartmentalized fashion until she discusses her father's "educational practices" with outsiders and finds them to be viewed not as education, but as incest.

Introvert

The other subtype that often fits the military mold is the introvert, who spends much time with his family and appears from the outside to be a "good husband and father." Many men in this category present as being strong and protective toward their families. Their wives complement this picture by appearing to be highly dependent upon their husbands. This pattern leads to a very isolated family, the exact form many military families take as they move from duty station to duty station. These men often are social isolates, even from fellow squad members. They usually go home immediately after work and seem to get all their needs met within the family unit. Their wives, however, are not always psychologically so homebound, and will often join afternoon clubs or team sports groups, or engage in civic affairs, often leaving the husband alone with the children. The wife seems to feel the emotional isolation in the home and attempts to expand her world beyond those borders. She often does not work because the family's frequent relocations have given her a poor job record. The couple becomes more and more estranged, and the husband, in his desperate attempt to fulfill all of his needs within the family, reaches out to the daughter to take the place of his psychologically absent wife.

He distrusts the outside world, seeks comfort from within the family, feels unable to ventilate his anger to fellow workers, and, if he is in the military, knows he cannot talk back to superiors. The family becomes a haven from the pressures of the outside world where he can do whatever he pleases with whomever he pleases. He thinks that since he works to support them and suffers the outside world for them, that they should comfort him, however he most desires. He believes his house should be his castle, his fortress.

Often, the retired military man fits into this category. He stays at home due to nonavailability of appropriate jobs or because an illness or a war-related chronic condition has resulted in his medical retirement. The wife will often enter the work world at this point and the husband finds himself at home with the children. He needs comfort and seeks it from his daughter. This situation may seem circumstantial, but the symbiotic personality has to be present for the incest to occur.

Alcoholic

Alcohol abuse and physical and sexual child abuse have long been linked together (Crigler & Pattinson, 1982). One of the characteristics of un-recovered alcoholics is that they have a strong dependency need. The awareness of this psychological condition grates upon many men and they attempt to hide their discomfort by seeking solace in the bottle, thereby perpetuating the problem. Another manifestation of this dependency is to rely on family members to comfort them, to meet their strong needs for affection, and to assuage their fear of abandonment. Often, when returning home from drinking, they will be met at the door by their wife or children who then cook for them or help them into bed. As the wife grows tired of attending to her drunken husband, the oldest daughter often takes over the role of providing him with care and comfort. She begins to believe that she alone can help him with his drinking. In her attempt to be helpful, role slippage occurs; that is, the daughter takes on the role of being a wife, caretaker, and comforter. In his inebriated state, it is easy for the father to view the daughter as the primary love and sex object. She appears to be the perfect and available target for his advances once alcohol has diminished his hesitation to act upon his sexual urges. Both the alcoholic father and the victimized girl attempt to excuse the behavior by blaming the drinking. This pattern of drinking, acting out, feeling guilty, and then drinking more to diminish the guilt may continue for years if someone does not intervene. As drinking in military circles is a socially acceptable activity, these alcohol-related scenes of incest are certainly not unknown to the military community.

PSYCHOPATHIC–SOCIOPATHIC

The psychopathic and the sociopathic personalities are vastly different from the symbiotic personality types we have just explored. This type of incestuous father is interested in novelty, excitement, and stimulation. He has no guilt associated with his incestuous behaviors. He feels deprived and love-starved from his own abysmal childhood and uses sex to satisfy these needs, turning wherever he can to find it, including using his own children, often the boys as well as the girls. This man can be brutal—physically abusive as well as sexually abusive—and yet he can have a charm about him that makes him sometimes seem like a rationalizer: "I don't like to do this but you need to know how to please a man." However, unlike the symbiotic rationalizer, he has no tender feelings for his family. He believes no one is worth trusting or loving. He forms no emotional attachments, but moves from one sexual outlet to another. There appears to be little evidence that the military has more of this type of incestuous father than the general population, with the possible exception of certain special clandestine units that might appeal psychologically to these psychopathic–sociopathic types. However, members of these combat units exhibit a significant amount of physical child and spouse abuse behavior (Crigler & Pattinson, 1982).

PEDOPHILIAC

The pedophiliac differs from the other men of this study in that he is attracted to his daughter when she is very young and physically immature, before her body begins to take on secondary sex characteristics. He is so immature and inadequate that a young child is apparently the only human being he is attracted to and not intimidated by. If married, he cannot usually maintain a sexual relationship with his wife as he believes her to be too mature and overpowering. Many pedophiliacs do not marry so there are little data on these individuals. However, those who do marry follow the early incestuous developmental pattern previously mentioned.

Most sexual activity tends to be limited to kissing, fondling, and some masturbatory behavior. When the child does mature and the secondary sex characteristics develop, the pedophiliac will turn to another small child to answer his sexual/affectional needs. While it may be assumed that the military has pedophiliacs within its ranks, no data exist concerning their prevalence. The number is expected to be no greater, and possibly even less, than the general population.

PSYCHOTIC–CULTURE-PERMISSIVE

The final types of incestuous fathers we will examine are the psychotic and the culture-permissive men.

Psychotic

The psychotic incestuous father comes from a very limited group within the military as the world of the Armed Forces is no place for an individual experiencing schizophrenia or a thought disorder. Whereas it is believed that between 2 and 3% of the population is psychotic, there are relatively few severely psychotic people in the military since they are treated and released if they become too disturbed.

Culture-Permissive

The "other" type of incestuous father is the one whose subculture sanctions incest as a way of life. These fathers learn as young boys that this behavior is acceptable and they pass this attitude on to their own sons. This attitude and behavior is allegedly found in the Appalachian and Ozark Mountains and in the wilderness areas of Utah. If these individuals join the military, they must agree to observe the general rules of the Uniform Code of Military Justice (UCMJ) which states that incest will not be sanctioned or tolerated. Despite their personal beliefs, they must obey the UCMJ or be treated as violators of that code. As these individuals seldom leave the confines of their geographical subculture, it is believed that there are few individuals in the Armed Forces that fit this description of an incestuous father.

In sum, it should be noted that none of these types is totally separate from the others and that overlap occurs between the genre described. The important point is that men who practice incest are seeking to have either their needs for comfort and affection or their desires for excitement and stimulation answered in sexual ways within the family at the expense of other family members.

TYPES OF MOTHERS

What are the mothers of these incestuously violated children like? Who are the wives of men who sexually abuse their own children? How do these women feel, react, and think, having had this act occur either with their knowledge, and sometimes consent, or without their awareness, when the women were out of the home working, performing family chores, or engaging in social activities? The questions are haunting ones.

There appear to be two major categories of mothers involved in the incestuous family: the woman who is a nonparticipant and the woman who engages in incest herself (Justice & Justice, 1979).

NONPARTICIPATING MOTHERS

Of the nonparticipating type, there are generally two subcategories. One is the woman who discovers or is told of the incest and acts immediately to bring it to a halt by any means at her disposal, including legal or violent acts. The other type is either one who knows what is going on and does not attempt to stop it, or one who has no conscious knowledge of the behavior but is relieved when the daughter takes over many of the roles typically performed by the mother of the family. Except for the first type, all of these women are directly or indirectly responsible for part of the problem. Each appears in some way to have abandoned her responsibility for establishing and maintaining a healthy, functioning family.

Just as there are pathological traits in the men who commit incest, so are there pathological traits in the women of these families.

Dependent

As shown above, some women seek to give up many of the roles typically held by the mother. This type of woman is herself starved for affection and has great dependency needs that are not being met. She turns to the oldest daughter, seeking from her the nurturing and caring that she never received as a child. She abandons the role of mother and attempts to become her daughter's child. This type of mother is similar to the symbiotic type of father described earlier. Each is a child in an adult body, eagerly seeking succor and nurturance wherever it can be found. Unfortunately, the policy of the military community, to place spouses in a dependent role and formally label them "dependents," does nothing to break down this pattern.

"Mom"

There is a strong corollary to the aforementioned type of woman who rejects her husband, and that is the woman who becomes just "Mom" to him. If the couple continues to have some sex while the woman is in this negative psychological state, it seems that a different incestuous type of relationship is forming. In either case, the "Mom" takes herself out of the sexual area, becoming the caretaker for the entire family. The husband tends to become even more dependent on her, which eventually may leave him with little responsibility for his behaviors, including those of turning to the daughter for his sexual outlet.

There are many women in this subgroup who are married to alcoholics and can be described as being coalcoholics. They tend to support their alcoholic–dependent counterpart husbands in their drinking and/or dependency needs by taking care of them and relieving them of their responsibilities—a very unfortunate combination for the adults as well as their children.

Submissive

A type similar to the symbiotic "dependent" woman is the mother who is weak, submissive, and ineffectual. The structure and functioning of the family rests entirely on the shoulders of the father, who encourages all other family members to be totally economically and emotionally dependent upon him. This category of woman complements the macho tyrant discussed previously. He rules with an iron fist, often physically abusing his wife and sometimes the children, except for the favored one. In order to prevent his wife from becoming economically and psychologically self-supporting, he does not "allow" her to have a job. His fear is that if she did have a job, she might leave and take the children with her.

This husband–wife combination is frequently found in military families, most prevalently in the young sailor who marries a young Asian woman. When he brings her to the States she has little cultural or English language education. He keeps her a virtual prisoner within the house by not allowing her to drive the car, go out by herself even to grocery shop, or entertain any non-Asian women friends. Even if he is willing to allow for the growing independence of the wife, these marriages spawn many problems which take many years to solve, if indeed they are resolved.

Cooperative

The final major type of mother who is a nonparticipant in incest herself, but who may have some knowledge of the activity, is the woman who is generally absent from the household, either physically or psychologically. She appears to have abandoned the children, especially the affected daughter, and engages in a life of her own outside the family as much as possible. She may be promiscuous, put in extra or unnecessary hours at work, or just generally be absent, thereby leaving the father to his own devices with the daughter. She may not be physically absent, but in being there may provide a poor role model of normal sexual restraints within the family. This behavior often leaves the family to do whatever it wants to do, like getting involved incestuously.

In all of these categories, it is clear that role reversal or role slippage, absenteeism from the household, a lack of clear sexual roles, and often, mental or physical exhaustion on the part of the mother, contribute to the deterioration of her expected sexual role within the family. Certainly, the woman is not responsible for the actions of her husband, but she is usually an accomplice, wittingly or not.

INCESTUOUS MOTHERS

There are cases of mothers participating in incest. The first kind of incest usually occurs with the oldest son and often is somewhat situational. In the military context, this type of activity is most apt to occur when the husband is away for extended periods of time. The son is literally given the directive to be "the man of the house while Daddy is gone." Frequently, this directive describes exactly what occurs, and the mother and son become sexually entangled, although originally attempting only to lend psychological support to each other. The difficulty may develop when the mother, who begins sleeping with the child in the father's absence, wants to relieve her own feelings of abandonment and loss through some physical contact with another human being.

This second type of typical mother–son incest results from a gradual, growing mutual support system. On the one hand the mother gives encouragement to the oldest boy, who may be hard pressed to meet the father's expectations of his being a "chip off the old block," a "hard charger," a "real man." Simultaneously, the son begins to fulfill the emotional needs of the mother who feels abandoned by a husband who is "married" to his career. This bond between the mother and son can become quite strong as they attempt to protect each other from the growing isolation of the military father/husband from his family as he pursues his career. In moments of stress, the relationship may be redefined and become a sexual bonding as well as a psychological one. A recent motion picture about a Marine flyer, *The Great Santini*, portrayed portions of this process, but without the obvious sexual overtones that have been described here. While it should be noted that some same-sex incest occurs, mother–daughter, father–son, and other familial (i.e., homosexual) combinations occur with less frequency (Kaslow, Haupt, Arce, & Werblowsky, 1981) or else are underreported.

DAUGHTERS

Finally, what happens to young girls who are the victims of incest? How is it that the innocence of childhood and the young girl's desire for affection and nurturance become corrupted into an incestuous relationship with her father? What part, if any, does the girl herself play in this family scenario?

First, it should be noted that while most daughters do not encourage or actively engage in the instigation or the continuance of the incest, only a fairly small number of children are violently forced into sexual activities. Usually, the behaviors begin rather innocently with touching, caressing, and snuggling being the original activities. As time passes, the child learns to "act cute" to please Daddy, thereby getting from her father the attention she wants. At that point, the scene often changes to more obvious sex play, with the father caressing her genitalia and breasts and telling/asking her to fondle him in the same areas. The pattern is often thus set and change becomes difficult.

Some young girls passively accept this new behavior; others find that they can gain special favors from their father in exchange for these activities, and do not attempt to resist; and still others learn to encourage the sexual behavior to secure a place of power within the family. The veiled threat that she might tell authorities about her father's behavior gives her a tremendously potent leverage in family affairs. Also, the daughter may be unwilling to give up the only source of affection and attention available to her in the family. She may have real caring for the parent in spite of the incest. Once the redefining of the activity occurs, it is difficult to reverse, and outside intervention is needed.

CHARACTERISTICS OF VICTIMS

There are several characteristics typical of the incestuous daughter. She usually has a poor relationship with her mother. Often there is fighting, rejection, suspicion, and competition between them for the father's attention. Viewed in psychoanalytical terms, the daughter may be seen as living out the Oedipal fantasy, that of supplanting the mother and actually having a sexual relationship with the father. If the father deploys for long periods of time, his return intensifies the competition for his attention between the mother and the daughter, causing a deepening of their schism.

The daughter is searching for love, affection, and nurturance. Any overt manifestation of attention or affection from the father can bond the child to him, increasing her ineptitude at making friends and reinforcing her social isolation at school. This alienation and isolation often are also a consequence of having to move with the family from one duty station to another.

The daughter generally has poor self-esteem. She pictures herself as unworthy of affection and finds the attentions of her father irresistible. She attempts to act mature beyond her years and gladly takes on the role her mother partially vacates to her in exchange for attention from her father.

Sometimes she may learn to be seductive in order to squelch any competition from her mother or siblings who might attempt to take her favored status away. She may even eventually make overtures to the father, knowing what pleases him and giving her great favor in his eyes.

RESPONSIBILITY

In my opinion, the responsibility for the incestuous behavior is still squarely placed on the older person, whether father, mother, uncle, or sibling, not on the child who is only mimicking behaviors taught by the incestuous adult. However, as one looks at the dynamics of the relationship, there are additional issues that evolve out of the original situation. Even though the child is initially unaware of the ramifications of the incestuous situation, there often comes a point at which an awareness does dawn on her that, although she did not instigate or seek the relationship, often she has gained new power in the family, or at least with the father. Some incest victims who have sufficiently worked through the trauma of the event report that in objective retrospect, they realize they sometimes began to perpetrate the relationship in order to gain power or to receive "love," even if the emotional cost to them was quite high. There are even some victims who state they knew they were experiencing this ambivalence of power versus pain, fear versus "love," but that this situation was better than no attention/affection at all (Crigler, 1982).

RESCUER

Finally there is the daughter who not only takes on the role reversal pattern with the mother, but who also becomes the rescuer for the entire family. Indeed, she may feel that only by keeping the father happy, and the rest of the family quiet, can the family remain intact. She literally becomes the keeper of the family, the family heroine. In many military families that are isolated, this need to maintain an intact family is critical. The other family members are all each person has to rely on as they are transferred about.

UNCOVERING INCEST

How can incest be detected? What clues can be spotted that allow for early detection and, in some cases, possible prevention?

FATHER'S BEHAVIOR

Jealousy of his daughter's activities and friends may become readily apparent. The father may be extremely protective of his daughter and even follow her around town when she is on a date. Sometimes he will not allow her to date. Hallmarks may include overt displays of affection and touching, both in public as well as in semiprivate locations, such as hand-holding in an automobile. Father and daughter may go places in a dating fashion and he may buy her presents as if courting her. He may appear to interact with her in an even younger fashion. The father can even take on childlike behaviors, such as temper tantrums, shouting, or pouting when he cannot get the sex he wants from her. Any behavior that brings about an alliance between the father and daughter may be attempted. Sometimes even confrontation or complaints from the mother are to no avail and only serve to bind the pair closer together in their conspiracy.

MOTHER'S BEHAVIOR

Role reversal between the mother and daughter is a clear red flag, indicating that a possible incestuous triangle exists or that one is in the making. The mother often verbally maligns her daughter, for example, calling her a troublemaker, a tramp, or no good. Mom feels something is wrong but can't quite figure it out, saying she doesn't "understand" her daughter.

Competition between the two for the father's attention and affection is often keen. The mother may even dress similarly to the daughter's taste or age group. In an attempt to turn back the biological clock, the mother may resort to stringent dieting, exercising, and cosmetic plastic surgery.

DAUGHTER'S BEHAVIOR

Perhaps the clearest indicator of incest on the child's part is her taking a parent's role in the family. This trait is often present, even in the young child who, if not physically taking care of the family as if she were the mother, will become the emotional support for Daddy (Bernstein, 1979). There can be a sexually charged aura around the child and she may act in a sexual manner. Another clue is a seductive manner that the daughter exhibits to most males, but most obviously toward her father. This behavior often takes place blatantly in front of the mother as if to goad her into competing with the daughter for the father's attentions. An emotional deterioration of the child can sometimes be noticed. This behavior can be exhibited either as a hyperexcitability or as a depressive mood with flattened affect and loss of the joie de vivre that children usually have. When questioned about earlier childhood activities, there may be gaps in her memory, a symptom of a blocking mechanism being used to cut off conscious awareness of negative experiences.

Often the openness the daughter once exhibited diminishes and she becomes closed off, secretive, or even slightly paranoiac. These traits develop as a method of hiding the secret of the incest. She withdraws from siblings, who may be already snubbing her due to her favored position with the father.

The child may begin somaticizing her problems, resulting in frequent doctor visits for vague complaints, such as abdominal pain or gynecological problems (Gross, Doerr, Caldirola, Guzinski, & Ripley, 1980). Interestingly, the child may look significantly younger or older than her years.

School difficulties often arise, in the form of a dramatic or a steady decline in the child's grades, attitude, and/or attendance. She may become a disciplinary problem or change her peer group to a less stable, less socially and/or academically desirable set of friends. A deterioration of performance or attitudinal level may be symptomatic of sexual abuse if no other obvious explanation is evident.

Another manifestation may be a change in the sleep pattern. Some individuals respond by having difficulty getting to sleep, while others have trouble sleeping through the night or may experience early waking. Children who are victims of incest often use nightmares to dispel some of their anxiety and anger over their abuse. Many times the child is hesitant to describe the dream even though she will report having nightmares. Asking subtle, gentle but probing questions can pry loose valuable information. Frequently the dreams are highly symbolic, but with younger children the nightmares tend to be quite realistic to the actual situation and provide many important data.

A reluctance on the youngster's part to spend time alone with Daddy may be of significance. If this feeling is a change in the child's attitude and is coupled with a new or much stronger desire to be physically close or "clingy" to Mom, or to another adult who might be seen as a possible advocate or rescuer, further questions should be asked.

In sum, the three overriding traits are as follows: (1) a blurring of intergenerational parent–child responsibility lines, illustrated most obviously by a role reversal of the child and the mother; (2) an emotional/behavioral personality change in the child; and (3) premature sexual preoccupation.

BREAKING THE SECRET

Given the prevalence of incest, its existence in all social classes including the miltary community, the recent knowledge amassed about the composition and dynamics of these families and their individual members, and the ensuing psychological damage incest causes, there is little question that intervention is required. How can we come to the aid of these families who are in need of outside help to stop their pathological behaviors?

Working from a family system perspective, the cardinal rule concerning cessation of incest is to break the secret, to bring the information out from behind the family's protective walls. Research and clinical experience clearly show that very few families can remedy this problem on their own. Due to the complex and entangled dynamics described above, it becomes necessary for some outside person or agency to step in, analyze the interlocking and reciprocal relationship, provide protection for the child, and get the family into treatment.

Many mental health professionals, religious authorities, and medical professionals have believed erroneously that to report these incidences of suspected sexual child abuse will so thoroughly break down their rapport with the family, that the consequences will terminate any further therapeutic effectiveness. This result is sometimes the case. However, *not* to intervene is, in effect, to condone the behavior; the outside person may be the only protector the child can acquire. As we have seen, the damages to incestuously involved children are extensive, deep-rooted, and long lasting. In my opinion, *not to intervene is not only illegal, but unethical, and chooses the side of the adult over that of the "defenseless" child.*

EFFECTS OF INCEST ON THE CHILD

There is a myth that must be demolished about incest: that the degree of involvement equals the degree of impact. This is incorrect. It is *not* the degree of sexual involvement that determines whether there will be psychological damage, but that there was involvement at all! Fondling can lead to as much emotional trauma and later dysfunctions as more extensive involvement such as fellatio, cunnilingus, or intercourse (Hirschman, 1979).

Another misconception is that incestuous activities between a stepparent and child are not devastating because there is no *blood* relationship to be broken. This fine point is lost on the child who has been told she has a "new Daddy," whom she can trust and who she believes will assume the role of protector and supporter. When she finds she is being used, sexually violated, instead of being cared for by this new authority figure, she feels betrayed. This event also increases her distrust of her mother for bringing this new, powerful, and harmful person into her home, the one place she should feel completely safe. She feels further betrayed by her mother for not protecting her from him. In reality, Mom may even use her too, as bait to keep the new husband interested in staying in the family.

Much evidence has been gathered that clearly indicates that even very young children know on some level that incest is not appropriate. Even when the sexual activities are physically and socially benign, the victim begins to sense that the relationship between Dad and herself is not quite right. Possibly this awareness arises when father tells daughter that secrecy is of paramount importance, that the rest of the family must not know what is going on.

This awareness plants the seeds of discomfort and uncertainty that later mature into guilt. It seems from both clinical work and extensive literature review that almost all incest victims are significantly guilt ridden. Each girl/woman in her own way feels responsible for the majority of the involvement, even though it was initiated, executed, and continued by the father, stepfather, or other male relative(s).

A FEELING OF BEING DIFFERENT AND POOR INTERPERSONAL RELATIONSHIPS

Another prominent feature of both female and male victims is a belief that they are "different." This awareness of difference appears to be a combination of feelings of guilt and of the psychological, and sometimes physical, isolation they experience from their siblings and/or peers. As a survival technique, they use this difference to distance or dissociate themselves from the act and/or emotions concerning the incest. They, in effect, dichotomize their behavior into "me"–"not me" categories to disengage from their feelings of shame, guilt, embarrassment, and/or confusion. By using this dichotomization technique they do, indeed, become "different"; they believe that somehow they brought this experience on themselves either by being different prior to the incest, or by becoming unique because of the incest. In either case, isolation occurs and brings still more emotional trauma to the victim.

Because these victims believe they are different, they often begin to punish and berate themselves for being party to an activity they somehow know is inappropriate. This phase of the condemnation leads to low self-esteem, a psychological hallmark of an incest victim. Unless some therapeutic intervention takes place, this debased self-image is almost always a lifelong legacy of the incest. Depression is often a concomitant of this poor self-esteem. Victims 50 and 60 years old may still experience feelings that are coupled with guilt and self-deprecation.

Such feelings provide the negative groundwork that cultivates a psychological mind-set which leads to poor interpersonal relationships. The young victim and her seducer have a level of trust, and she fears that, if the incest is disclosed, she will be judged as unacceptable, tainted, and at fault, and will be abandoned—again by someone she should be able to trust.

Many incest victims go on to have rocky marriages, often evidencing significant sexual dysfunction. The sexual side of marriage is marked by a lack of consistent orgasm, feelings of being used and sexual dissatisfaction, absence of lubrication, severe vaginismus, and/or loss of interest in sexual activities. There may be extramarital affairs used as a method of avoiding real intimacy with the spouse for fear of still further betrayal of trust. The intimate side of life for an incest victim and her spouse can be very difficult.

INCEST AND ALCOHOLISM

Another spinoff of the impact of incest on the victim is excessive alcohol use and drug abuse. Many youngsters use chemicals to dull their feelings so as to deal less consciously with this trauma. As she grows older, the woman will most often use alcohol and/or food compulsively and become alcoholic or grossly overweight. She may also turn to the addictive use of prescribed drugs, such as Valium or Librium, usually prescribed by a father figure.

In a recent study, I discovered that 80 to 85% of women treated for alcoholism in California reported being sexually abused. The vast majority, 90–95%, stated they were victims of incest at the hands of their fathers, stepfathers, and/or an older brother (Crigler, 1982). This awareness of molestation may occur prior to admission for alcoholism, during the treatment process, or following treatment. It is not unusual for recovering women alcoholics to uncover this part of their past 2 to 5 years posttreatment. Sometimes the awareness may dawn slowly. It comes quite often first as great discomfort about the subject of incest, perhaps followed by dreams and/or flashbacks of the incestuous scene. Finally, most women do reach a fairly complete realization of what happened. When this knowledge becomes conscious, it *must* be dealt with. If it is ignored or repressed, the woman's sobriety is in great jeopardy, as are her current and future intimate relationships.

Teenage victims of incest sometimes run away from home because they themselves cannot stop the abuse or get sufficient support from other family members who are unwilling to intervene. Often, these youngsters drop out of school, take to the streets, and end up as prostitutes, thieves, "druggies," and/or welfare recipients (James, 1980). Many young girls have no skills other than those acquired through sexual experience, so they use their sexuality to survive economically. These young victims have such low self-esteem, coupled with a strong sense of abandonment by their families, that it seems a short, natural leap to become prostitutes. Even one act of incest has many damaging and long-lasting effects.

Finally, it should be noted that while male adult–female child is the most prevalent form of incest, there is a growing awareness on the part of mental health professionals that same-sex incest occurs with greater regularity than was previously reported (Kaslow *et al.*, 1981). In a review of the literature, Kaslow *et al.* illustrate clearly that homosexual incest, which they define as at least one partner being over 13 years of age in order to preclude sibling exploratory behavior, does occur and appears to have long-term negative effects. Indeed, the results may be doubly impairing because the person has experienced the breaking of two taboos, incest and homosexual relations. These victims often experience significant sexual maladjustment, a profound sense of guilt, and/or confusion as to their sexual identity/preference. Simply stated, the more taboos broken, the more complicated the problems and the recovery.

EFFECTING CHANGE

Perhaps the single most important action that can be taken by anyone who becomes aware of an incestuous relationship is to bring the issue out into the light of day. As adults, we must take the role of protectors and supporters of the victim, the child or youngster who is experiencing something that will affect her potentially for the rest of life. Quick action is particularly critical among military families who are highly mobile. Sudden transfers often block detection or remedial work that is so severely needed by both the child and family.

Interviewers of incest perpetrators as well as rapists quote the men as stating that they themselves believe public exposure is the most powerful step that can be taken to stop them. Many men know that incest is wrong but, until publicly confronted, cannot or will not stop (Groth, 1980). They, as well as the victims, need help.

Exactly what must be done depends on individual state law. In general, three steps must be taken:

1. Report the suspected or acknowledged incest to a legal authority such as the police or child protective services. They will generally take over from this point.

2. If you are in a position to be of support to the family, insure that an advocate provides consistent information and assistance to the family concerning legal and social work–mental health services available. An advocate also can assist the family members in dealing with their own feelings. Military members and their families can be in double jeopardy as the perpetrator may be charged and tried in both military and civilian legal systems. The entire family needs a consistent contact person to keep them reasonably intact and performing certain required activities while they undergo this experience. The Command can be of great assistance by providing a military sponsor, such as a social worker, during this delicate time. (See Chapter 2 for a more thorough discussion of legal issues.)

3. Therapy for the entire family is most strongly recommended— indeed, it should be mandated (Neill & Kniskern, 1982). The passage of time and cessation of incest will not be sufficient alone to heal the wounds suffered by all members of the family. Betrayal, fear, confusion, and anger must be dealt with openly. Trust, acceptance, and understanding must occur before forgiveness and love can come to the family.

In conclusion, the therapist needs to view any occurrence of incest from two perspectives: (1) the effect the incest has had on the child and

(2) the pathology of the entire family. Each member of the family unit must be given assistance. To treat only the child and/or to punish only the offender will not solve the continuing problems manifested by the people involved. A family system is in trouble and each member of the unit has an integral part to play in the problem and in the solution.

REFERENCES

Bernstein, G. A. Physician management of incest situations. *Human Sexuality*, 1979, *13*(11), 67-87.

Brinbaum, H. S. Personal communication, Annual Conference on Violence in the Family, University of Arkansas, Little Rock, October 1980.

Crigler, P. W. *Prevalence of incest in alcoholic women*. Unpublished manuscript, 1982. (Available from P. W. Crigler, Box 126, Naval Hospital, San Diego, Calif. 92134)

Crigler, P. W., & Pattinson, J. A. *Alcohol abuse: A symbiotic partnership*. Unpublished manuscript, 1982. (Available from P. W. Crigler, Box 126, Naval Hospital, San Diego, Calif. 92134)

Finkelhor, D. *Sexually victimized children*. New York: The Free Press, 1979.

Gottlieb, B. Incest: Therapeutic intervention in a unique form of sexual abuse. In J. G. Warner (Ed.), *Rape and sexual assault*. Denver: Aspen Publication, 1980.

Gross, R. J., Doerr, H., Caldirola, D., Guzinski, G. M., & Ripley, H. S. Borderline syndrome and incest in chronic pelvic pain patients. *International Journal of Psychiatry in Medicine*, 1980, *10*(1), 79-96.

Groth, N. Personal communication, Annual Conference on Violence in the Family, University of Arkansas, Little Rock, October 1980.

Hirschman, L. N. Incest and seduction: A comparison of two client groups (Doctoral dissertation, University of Michigan, 1979). *Dissertation Abstracts International*, 1980, *40*(9), 4485-B. (University Microfilms No. 8005251, 1979, 203)

James, J. Self-destructive behavior and adaptive strategies in female prostitutes. In M. Farberow (Ed.), *The many faces of suicide*. New York: McGraw-Hill, 1980.

Justice, B., & Justice, R. *The broken taboo*. New York: Human Sciences Press, 1979.

Kaslow, F., Haupt, D., Arce, A., & Werblowsky, J. Homosexual incest. *Psychiatric Quarterly*, Fall 1981, *53*(3), 184-193.

National Center on Child Abuse and Neglect, Childrens' Bureau. *Familial incest and intrafamily sexual abuse of children*. Washington, D.C.: U.S. Department of Health and Human Services, 1980.

Neill, J. R., & Kniskern, D. P. (Eds.). *From psyche to system: The evolving therapy of Carl Whitaker*. New York: Guilford, 1982.

No home safe from the tragedy of incest. *Long Beach, California, Press-Telegram*, April 5, 1981.

6

Violence in the Military Family

MARIO R. SCHWABE

FLORENCE W. KASLOW

The family is an evolutionary development which insures the cooperation of the parents and the extended family network in the protection, nurturing, and education of the offspring. Love, patience, and the willingness to give of oneself generously to and for the others are closely associated with family bonding.

In a nomadic society, violence, a destructive form of aggression, is useful in providing the family with protection against enemies and in hunting for food. We wish that it were possible to believe in the myth that violence is not found within the civilized, contemporary family, except among rare maladaptive individuals. This myth has been supported for a long time in folklore, literature, custom, and law. The concepts that a man's home is his castle and that all parents act in the best interest of their children presume that all danger of violence is external. Even fairy tales have fostered the projection of danger onto an outside devil, witch, or ogre, and preserved the image of the loving, nurturing family.

Since the early 1970s mental health professionals and feminist groups have challenged this myth, and with the help of the media have exposed the often brutal reality that family violence is very common, and that it is a contributory source to other major social, emotional, familial, and ultimately even political problems.

The opinions or assertions contained herein are the private views of the authors and are not to be construed as official or as reflecting views of the Department of the Navy or the Department of Defense.

Mario R. Schwabe. Captain, U.S. Navy, and Chairman, Department of Psychiatry, National Naval Medical Center, Bethesda, Maryland.

Florence W. Kaslow. Private practice, West Palm Beach, Florida; Director, Florida Couples and Family Institute, West Palm Beach, Florida; and Adjunct Professor of Medical Psychology, Department of Psychiatry, Duke University, Durham, North Carolina.

Studies of the behavior of animals in the wild reveal that violence is a common element in the family life of mammals. It appears to be an integral part of sexual rituals and of the educational process whereby animal parents teach their offspring adaptation skills.

Young children tussle with one another, enjoying the physical contact, animated activity, release of energy, and jockeying for power and control. Play fighting among juveniles helps them establish a social and power hierarchy or pecking order that eventually provides the leadership skills they bring to bear in their respective families and the community. Maladaptive acting-out violence is not uncommon, with weaker teenagers providing targets for the release of tension for stronger peers who displace their annoyance or rage at family members onto those their own age and size whom they fear less.

Instead of having eliminated violence from the fabric of life, humans have developed and expanded the use of force with increasing sophistication and destructiveness in the family and the community, and on the international scene. The threat of a nuclear holocaust is ever present, hanging heavy like an ominous cloud representing the collective urge of many to hurt and even annihilate others. Much of this mass rage is a spillover from wrath accumulated and inadequately resolved in depriving, depressing, abusive, uncaring families.

Verbal abuse in particular has become a significant new weapon. Although the animal's bark never quite matches the destructive impact of its bite, with humans, verbal assaults sometimes can be more painful and lead to deeper emotional scars than physical assaults. Insults, taunts, and humiliating deprecation take their toll.

It is easy to find anecdotes about family violence. Stories of incredible brutality between family members appear frequently in newspapers and television. Noting them has served to bring widespread attention to the problem. This concern has led to passage of beneficial laws establishing funding for agencies and programs to help identify victims and then move beyond identification to constructive interventions. Just as the civilian sector began to set up shelters and special services for abused wives and children in the 1970s, the military established its Child Advocacy Program in 1978 to protect children from abuse and to help turbulent families learn to cope in less violent ways. About a year later the concept was expanded to also include those involved in spouse abuse and rape-sexual assault, and was renamed the Family Advocacy Program. The agencies designated to carry out the advocacy program are charged with the tasks of prevention, identification, treatment, and follow-up care. Headquarters are lodged within the Bureau of Medicine in Washington, D.C. By way of illustrating the possible magnitude of the problem, the Navy Family Advocacy Program in San Diego has indicated that during 1981 approximately 100 child abuse cases were seen, they were asked to provide assistance in 250 spouse abuse cases, and their counsel was sought in 20 cases of rape–sexual assault.

NATURE AND EXTENT OF FAMILY VIOLENCE

A truly scientific approach needs to be predicated upon knowing something about the problem. How many families are involved? Is the rate increasing? What factors make families vulnerable? What are the consequences?

Violence is hard to describe and measure. It is not a specific behavior qualitatively different from other forms of aggression. Some believe that whether or not an act is violent depends not only on what was done but also on the intent and the consequences. The proponents of this position hold that there are no agreed upon objective criteria that clearly identify a behavior as violent. Instead they indicate that what constitutes violence is a matter of subjective judgment which depends on the beliefs and attitudes of the reporter (Steinmetz, 1977).

Destructive acts of aggression happen in many families some of the time. Sometimes they are executed impulsively and are unintentional. Occasionally they are alleged to be trivial in consequence. Other actions are malicious in intent and lethal in results. Between these two extremes there is a large continuum. Where does each society draw the line between socially acceptable physical discipline of children and punishment that is abusive? How does this demarcation differ from where experts on child psychology and mental health professionals would place it? How does it differ from where lay people, in different subcultural populations who believe child beating is a necessary part of child rearing if one is not to raise "brats," would place it? How one defines what constitutes abuse is most salient not only in the family, but also in the classroom and school-yard, as it determines what measures teachers can legally and ethically use to discipline unruly students. The decision is again subjective and makes the gathering of useful data very difficult.

Even if we had a reliable objective definition and a consensus on how to measure violence, we still would face the problem of getting family members to report the incidents. No one likes to talk about unpleasant or embarrassing private events. There is also the fear that the identified abuser will retaliate with further assaults. Punishment for the abuser may well result also in aggravating the financial problems that may have precipitated the violence in the first place.

Despite these difficulties, numerous statistics are becoming available. Whatever their limitations, they serve to illustrate the scope of the problem. Representative of the best of these studies is the one by Straus, Gelles, and Steinmetz (1980).

They conducted over 2000 interviews and concluded that, with the exception of military combat and urban riots, "Americans run the greatest risk of assault, physical injury and even murder in their own homes by members of their own families" (Straus et al., 1980, p. 32). Sixteen percent of husbands and wives engaged in at least one act of violence during the year they surveyed. Twenty-eight percent engaged in at least one act of violence against a spouse sometime during their marriage. Eight percent of parents admitted to having kicked, bitten, or punched their child at some time. Four out of every five children carry out at least one violent act toward a sibling during a typical year.

Straus et al. (1980, pp. 181–190) also found a close relationship between the amount of stress being experienced and the potential for violence. People instinctively respond to stress by mobilizing physiological and psychological resources. Physiologically there is an increase in muscle tone, pulse, blood pressure, and respiratory rate preparing the person for a sudden outburst of physical activity. Psychologically there is a focusing of attention on the threat with disregard for peripheral concerns with pain, fear of injury, or consideration of likely consequences.

Unfortunately, in civilized societies one can rarely deal effectively with stress through immediate physical activity or by taking flight. Economic problems, bureaucratic delays, traffic jams, insufferable bosses, all take their toll. Public displays of anger are discouraged. The tension is frequently suppressed and may be released in the privacy of the home with weaker family members as recipients of the displaced anger.

Yet not all families are equally at risk. The potential for violence in a given situation depends on the severity of the threat, the quality of the individual's inhibitions against violence, his appropriate impulse control, and the opportunity to attack a vulnerable person. For example, one of the most destructive stressors is unemployment (Thorman, 1980). It threatens the financial security of the man and his family. It also lowers his constraints against aggressive acting out by injuring his self-esteem and lowering his confidence and his investment in the social system. Finally, it increases the opportunity for domestic violence by giving him long hours with little to do but lie around the house, at a time when his frustration tolerance may be minimal.

We found no statistics comparing the incidence of family violence in the military family with that of the civilian community. Nevertheless, the visibility of military families and the uniqueness of the stressors and opportunities that confront them have made them the subject of much attention and discussion, and as indicated earlier, contributed to the recognition of the need for the establishment of the Family Advocacy Program.

Some authors have noted that military families are at greater risk because military men are somehow more violent. Del Martin, for example, while admitting the lack of empirical studies or statistics, states: "The military is, after all, a school for violence. No matter how peaceful or sensitive a man may be before he enters the military, once in he is processed by a totally male machine to become an agent of war." She adds, "Violence becomes his daily bread; brutality is often his means of survival" (Martin, 1976, pp. 55–56). This concept of military life may have applied to the tribesmen of Attila the Hun. Most present-day military men are technicians and bureaucrats. For them violence is not "daily bread" but something they watch on weekends in television football games. It is true that there are some small government-organized fighting forces specializing in intense physical combat. The men in these units are highly disciplined and professional and there is no evidence to support the assumption that they are at a greater risk for family violence than anyone else.

There are statistics, however, that show military families to be demo-graphically at risk. Over 55% of active duty personnel are 30 years old or younger. This age group is twice as likely to engage in family violence than the 31–50 age group (West, Turner, & Dunwoody, 1981).

Many characteristics of military life affect the risk for violence. Perhaps the most significant is the removal of the military family, usually young and inexperienced, from the support systems of the extended family and family friends. They are distanced from parents, grandparents, uncles, aunts, siblings, cousins, friends, and neighbors who usually pro-vide support, instruction, companionship, and a sense of perspective to young couples. Frequently, military couples have to live in quarters assigned according to rank. Their neighbors, therefore, are also young people with little more experience in marriage and parenting than they have.

A recruiting artifact may indirectly contribute to family violence. Enlisting in the military beckons as providing solutions to many personal problems through rapid environmental change and a socially sanctioned escape route. The young man who cannot find a job, is tired of his parents' nagging him to clean up his room and get a haircut, or who has just broken up with his girl friend is a prime candidate for recruiting. No government agency can move faster than a recruiter in pursuit of its man. The recruiter provides friendly fatherly attention, a ticket to leave town, a job, money, and the promise of a new life.

Unfortunately, although the military attracts people who want fast solutions with environmental rather than personality change, it places these recruits in a highly structured, slowly responding system with little opportunity for privacy or independence. Impulsive young men and women find themselves trapped in a system best suited for those with considerable patience and a compliant nature. Getting out of the military is considerably more difficult than getting in, since enlistments are for given, required time periods.

On the other hand, the military provides structure and financial security often missing in civilian life. Most military men are kept busy at work and all can count on a paycheck twice a month. Health care is free and programs are available to assist families with their problems.

Initially, programs for the identification and treatment of child and spouse abuse developed spontaneously in different bases. By 1972 over half of all military bases had established programs concerned with child protection. In 1975 the Air Force established the first service-wide child abuse and neglect program. In 1976 the Army and the Navy also established service-wide programs. As with the civilian community, spouse abuse programs lagged behind. In 1979 the Navy instituted the Family Advocacy Program which included child abuse and neglect, spouse abuse and neglect, and sexual assault and rape (Department of the Navy, 1979).

In 1981 the Department of Defense (DoD) established a comprehensive Family Advocacy Program which applies to the Army, Navy, Air Force, Marine Corps, and Coast Guard (an agency under the Department of Transportation). This program coordinates military activities for the prevention, identification, evaluation, treatment, follow-up, and reporting of child abuse and neglect and spouse abuse (Department of Defense,

1981). Whereas all states require the reporting of child abuse cases, most do not require reporting of spouse abuse as does the military.

A considerable advantage in the military is the ability to order the husband into evaluation and treatment. The husband is the missing link in most studies of family violence. His absence from the assessment and therapy process has contributed to a marked bias against the male among agency staff and in the literature. Unfortunately, this bias contributes in turn to the reluctance many men have toward participating in the process. Without the availability of the husband, agencies can do little more than plan for the protection of the wife and children.

Coercion of the husband into treatment combined with his initial lack of motivation do not preclude successful therapy. In fact, excessive submission toward treatment may indicate an expectation that the therapist will solve all the problems. Reluctance to submit himself to the control of others may indicate a willingness to accept responsibility for his situation. Furthermore, people who use force frequently respect force, and after an initial resistance can become engaged in a successful therapeutic alliance. In our experience, initial resistance is often a good prognostic sign. This impression is consistent with military studies that show draftees do better than volunteers as members of the Armed Forces.

SYNDROMES OF FAMILY VIOLENCE

Although each family is unique, certain syndromes of family violence can be identified, and these are discussed in the following section. These syndromes are not distinct, and each family may evidence components of two or more of them. Recognition of these patterns is useful in suggesting what the treatment of choice may be.

FAULTY EDUCATION

Many people still believe that the family is the property of the husband. According to this life view, he has the authority to use his family to satisfy all his needs, including his sexual and aggressive drives. Further, the wife and children may be used as punching bags to relieve his tension or may be raped for his sexual gratification.

Reputedly, some people think that the husband has a duty to discipline and educate his wife as well as his children and believe he is entitled to use physical punishment toward them for any mistake or transgression they may make. Although our culture professes equality between marital partners, considerable vestiges of the primitive concept that a husband/ father may kill transgressors persists. Women's rights advocates have done a great service to our society by their insistence on challenging these archaic concepts.

Unfortunately, many wives still accept this situation and prefer to be mistreated as the personal property of their husbands rather than accept the dishonor of being repudiated or the prospect of loneliness and having to be self-sufficient. Leaving the husband is often unacceptable not just because they do not have sufficient financial and emotional resources but also because it represents a failure in their perceived roles as women. Sometimes their family of origin and/or church may totally disapprove of separation and divorce.

Providing shelter and protection for these women may be life saving, but frequently it is not enough. Unless their concepts about femininity, sexuality, marriage, and their ability to pursue various options change, they often return to their husband and the violent situation is perpetuated despite all efforts by professionals and/or friends who try to help. Often the acquisition of saleable work skills and the building of a better self-concept which enables a woman to comprehend that she does not have to remain in an odious one-down position must occur before she is strong enough to either change markedly or leave the relationship.

Little consensus exists concerning physical punishment of children. "Spare the rod and spoil the child" still has many adherents as well as detractors. Does violence have a constructive part to play in the education of children, or does it imprint them with the message that violence is an acceptable solution to problems? Educators, philosophers, behavioral scientists, lawyers, and other professionals still debate the subject. Without scientifically valid, properly controlled studies we are not likely to arrive at a consensus. However, humane, civilized people agree that injury has no place in the child-rearing and educational process, and that discipline has to be tempered with affection and consideration if it is to have constructive results. Certainly, children should not be used as punching bags to satisfy their parents' need for an outlet for their tension, hostility, and sense of futility. Most mental health professionals probably advocate nonviolent limit setting and rule enforcement and positive reinforcement of desired behavior as much more effective ways of socializing children than any form of corporal punishment or discipline.

PROXIMITY

Men who handle tension through periodic violent discharges will frequently beat their wives and children. Weaker family members are simply the most easily available targets for the aggression. They are physically near for long periods of time, and no witnesses are likely to be present. Frequently female family members are virtually defenseless and loath to prosecute. Although the man often claims that he cannot remember the event because he was intoxicated, or that he could not control himself, it appears more than coincidental that few of his violent outbursts ever occur against bigger, tougher men capable of retaliating in kind. Somehow he manages not to lose control and "haul off" at them.

Often these men are insecure and feel inadequate in the face of stress. In a desperate attempt to deny their helplessness they strike out aggressively against inanimate objects, family pets, weaker family members, or themselves. Women may unwittingly contribute to the problem by crying, cringing with fear, or taunting and disparaging. Their demonstrations of helplessness or derisiveness further threaten the men, thereby compounding the problem. Beating them becomes the men's way of expressing mastery over the women's helplessness or sarcasm.

Alcohol and other intoxicants disinhibit the expression of violence. They make it easier to overcome any constraints the aggressor may have, and they provide him with a convenient excuse afterward. Unfortunately, they also provide the victims with an excuse to rationalize and tolerate the behavior since "he was drunk and did not mean to do it" (Thorman, 1980).

Mandatory reporting and the availability of responsive and effective agencies have increased the likelihood that the cases will come to the appropriate authority and then be properly handled. Additionally, neighbors and other concerned parties are increasingly likely to step forward and help identify child abuse cases.

The next consideration concerns the possible removal of the child from the family. The decision usually rests with the courts, although the input of health professionals is often welcome. Although we believe families should be enabled to stay together whenever possible, in extreme cases when persons' safety and sanity—in fact, their very lives—may be at stake, protection becomes the overriding concern. The trauma of separation is less painful than the trauma of severe injury and residual physical and/or emotional impairment.

When the problem is primarily one of the child's proximity to a parent with inadequate control of violent impulses, and the child is being used as target for the acting out of the abusing parent's psychopathology, it is unlikely that the child can remain successfully with the family. It should be stressed that the entire family has to be evaluated, not just the child and the abusing parent. Contribution to the crises by the nonabusing adult or adults either by commission or omission may be critically important.

If the basic problem is found to be one of faulty education or defective parenting skills, there is hope that with adequate treatment the family may remain intact. Both group and family therapies have been used with reported effectiveness.

In addition to spouse abuse and child abuse there are other forms of family violence that require attention. Violence between siblings is so common that many erroneously consider it normal behavior unless it results in severe injury. This may be true with friendly wrestling matches and innocent verbal sparring, but more dangerous forms of sibling violence may result in serious developmental injuries and lifelong hatreds.

Of particular interest to the study of the military family is the problem of delayed stress response syndrome (DSRS), commonly associated with but not limited to Vietnam veterans (Figley, 1978). Most Vietnam veterans, even many with DSRS, do not beat their wives or children. Many are not violence prone. However, those who do deal with DSRS through violent discharges present a severe problem for their families. Characteristic of these men is their idea that no one can understand them and their difficulties unless they have experienced the same intense stress. This requirement excludes their families and contributes to their unwillingness to seek assistance from mental health professionals, unless they too had been to "Nam."

Although the literature and health care professionals and volunteers frequently focus on the husband as the aggressor, it is more accurate to describe any family member as vulnerable to the violent discharges of those stronger than he or she is. Certainly some mothers are also likely to beat their youngsters. Children are frequently beaten by their bigger siblings. Even elderly relatives may be victims of family violence.

INADEQUATE FAMILY SKILLS

Becoming a "successful" spouse and parent requires the acquisition and development of considerable interpersonal skill. Without these skills and a modicum of self-control, problems will arise and violence may be used to cope with the ensuing tensions. A couple that lacks the skills to communicate without hurting each other may resort to violence as an alternative means of relating. This frequently happens when the woman is more skilled at verbal battles than the man. She argues him into a corner where he must either submit or strike out. Men who are brought up in an environment where they must fight physically or submit abjectly when provoked seldom learn the speech skills useful in verbal confrontations. "She just kept on talking and talking and there was nothing else I could do" is a refrain frequently heard from men who lash out physically to silence their talkative mate.

Sometimes the woman has interrupted the argument with tears. Feeling unable to cry to express his pent-up emotion, the man may resort to physical aggression. It is more congruent with the servicemember's "macho" self-image.

Parenting is learned from observing and talking to experienced relatives and friends as well as from memories of how one was brought up personally. Unskilled parents will often raise hard-to-manage children, will be frequently frustrated by them, and resort to aggressive assaults to establish their power. If the cycle is not broken, it is passed on to the next generation (Kempe & Helfer, 1980).

A crucial skill in parenting is the development of realistic expectations. Many parents have little knowledge of developmental milestones and are thwarted by what they perceive as intentional failures or obstinacy in their children. Unrealistic expectations are also a frequent source of frustration between spouses, as are life's normal exigencies for those with poor coping skills and quick, explosive temperaments.

UNCONSCIOUS PSYCHOPATHOLOGY

The most difficult form of family violence to treat occurs when unconscious psychopathology is involved. The relationships tend to be intense, stormy, and repetitive. Even after they have divorced, if they do, each partner frequently attaches to someone similar to the former spouse to form yet another pathologic relationship (Hyatt, 1977). Remarrying the same spouse is not uncommon.

Frequent among these ill-fated matches is that between the histrionic woman and the "strong, silent type" man. She is articulate, seductive, uninhibited, and volatile. He is quiet, strong, serious, seemingly unflappable, often obsessive–compulsive. Actually, their superfeminine and supermasculine exteriors are misleading. They are a facade masking their inner weakness. Once married, they fail to give each other what they need; disappointment, disenchantment, and anger rapidly ensue (Kaslow, 1981). He wants, by possessing her, a confirmation of his masculinity. He seeks the support and comfort of a mother. Instead of supporting him, she constantly prods and challenges him, making his weakness all the more apparent and painful. She wants strength from him as well as attention and demonstrativeness. She soon finds that his silence merely represents his way of denying his emotional helplessness and aloofness and his tendency to discharge his tension violently.

Typically she provokes and irritates him to "get a rise out of him." She is looking for him to respond and confirm his strength. He responds with further withdrawal and often with impotence. His original silence was not a manifestation of confidence and security but of weakness and inability to express feelings. As her provocations increase and threaten his concept of adequacy and masculinity, he finally loses control and beats her. After experiencing considerable relief, he may finally be able to consummate sexual intercourse.

One of the most dramatic examples of this process to come to my attention (M.S.) was that of a Marine sergeant who was hospitalized in a psychiatric unit several times following explosive attacks on his wife. He gave the appearance of being a tough man but was virtually inarticulate. He was actually very scared of his aggressivity. Only his physical appearance and reputation kept those around him at work from taking advantage of him. He was usually unresponsive toward his wife and frequently impotent. She provoked him with increasing ferocity. Eventually she would pick up another man and have him escort her to the bar where her husband worked as a bouncer. Her husband would try to control himself by having a few drinks. Finally he would beat up the other man, drag his wife home, beat her, and then be able to have sexual intercourse with her. The day following such an episode, he would present himself to the hospital full of remorse, threatening to kill himself. Within a few weeks he and his wife were back together again and the drama would be replayed.

There is a healthy part of both husband and wife that sincerely regrets the violent relationship. Following the beating they are both consciously determined never to let it happen again. But since the process is largely unconscious they are bound to repeat it over and over with the same partner or substitutes, until and unless they undergo good therapy which brings about some profound personality and behavioral change.

Children may be used by one or both parents as scapegoats against whom they act out their unconscious psychopathology. The child selected may be particularly vulnerable because he or she is the product of a troublesome pregnancy, or is deformed, sickly, hyperactive, or learning disabled. The child also may remind the parent of some other person from their past with whom there is an unresolved conflict. The child's very existence may be taken by the insecure parent as a competitive threat challenging his or her exclusive possession of the other parent.

Whatever the mechanism(s) by which violence is introduced into the family, the physical abusiveness soon sets in motion its own pathologic process. Once the taboo against such assaultive behavior is broken, it becomes easier and easier to break it again. No matter the initial reason for the violence, once the perpetrator has discovered that he can "get away with it," he is likely to continue his batterings with increasing frequency and severity.

Additionally, the violence is apt to trigger a series of related pathologic processes that facilitate its recurrence. Peering into the cycle at the instant of violence, we find the husband releasing all his anger and tension at his wife. Following the attack he is relieved of anger, typically calm and contrite. The wife, however, has just been hurt and humiliated. She is furious and vengeful. As time goes on she gradually discharges her anger at him by verbal attacks, stirring up guilt feelings, and/or withholding favors. He is virtually helpless at this point since he is angry at himself and eagerly accepts punishment. Instead of opening lines of communication, she typically encourages him to suppress his anger. At any sign of his irritation she often responds, "There you go again, next thing you'll do is beat me." As time goes on he builds up more and more resentment as she in turn expresses her hostility. Eventually he explodes again, releasing his tension on his "helpless" wife and starting the cycle anew. These observations are in keeping with the concepts of circular causality posited in family therapy literature and clinical practice.

Although the cycle is ignited by the husband's violence, it is perpetuated by the wife's lingering resentment and provocativeness. After many such incidents, when his fury and tension again become clearly evident, the wife can frequently recognize the danger signals and predict the imminent beating. Often, in order to avoid the suspense she will consciously provoke the beating in order to "get it over with." An outside observer might wonder why she doesn't leave, at least until the storm blows over.

TREATMENT

The first issue in the treatment of spouse abuse is detection. For years a *conspiracy of silence* by family members, health professionals, and the military allowed cases to go unreported, undetected, and/or unresolved. The beaten spouse would get her injuries treated after giving either only a perfunctory explanation of the causes or no explanation at all. The police, medical personnel, and other helping professionals would tacitly support the victim's reluctance to reveal the source of the injuries; they were trained "not to make waves" and to protect patients' confidentiality.

With the increase in public attention, the passage of pertinent laws, and the creation of child and spouse protection agencies, it is now more likely that the problem will be identified. A question properly asked in a nonthreatening way may be sufficient to encourage and enable a woman to talk about the problem. The index of suspicion of abuse should be heightened among all professionals likely to come in contact with the victim. In addition to the obvious signs of injury, suspicion should be aroused by evidence of chronic tension such as unexplained insomnia, violent nightmares, anxiety, fearfulness, and psychosomatic complaints in the spouse or the children.

Once the problem has been identified the most important principle of treatment is to *get the violence to stop.* Whatever maybe the cause and whoever may seemingly be at fault (e.g., society, husband, wife, relatives, children), no treatment will succeed as long as the option to be violent is viable (Thorman, 1980). The availability of shelters for the wife and children and cooperation from the police and the courts in restraining destructive behavior and protecting potential victims have been identified as having crucial importance.

Law enforcement officers are usually reluctant to arrest the batterer. They would not hesitate to arrest him if his victims were not family members. They cite as reasons for their double standard the fact that the wife is very likely to drop charges (Martin, 1976). They also want to avoid "embarrassing" the husband, thereby potentially getting him so angry he will do it again.

In the military, a common means of stopping the violence is the hospitalization of the husband, particularly if he is the active duty member and comes to the attention of the medical staff. In the absence of inpatient hospital facilities, if charges are pressed, the brig will serve a similar containment function. Merely ordering the husband to move into the barracks is usually ineffective since both spouses may conspire to get together again, unless he willingly agrees to stay away.

However, if he comes to the attention of the social work staff, they are likely to suggest that the wife go to a shelter or that the husband move out so they have a cooling-off period during which to gain control over the noxious behavior and for treatment to take hold. Point of entry will be one determinant of intervention strategy, as will background discipline in which the health professional is trained and branch of service of which the person is a member.

Hospitalizing the wife is not a good idea unless her injuries or her mental condition clearly warrant it. It identifies her as the victim, and perhaps also as the patient, and may further aggravate the man's guilt and lower his self-esteem, while also relieving him of the pressure to recognize that he desperately needs to become the patient by seeking treatment. It also facilitates a temporary "honeymoon" period (Barnett, Pittman, Ragan, & Salus, 1980). It is not uncommon for the husband to visit his battered wife and for the hospital staff to find the couple together in the hospital bed, blotting out the violent episode and the causative event leading to her hospitalization.

Instead, removal of the husband is often necessary even though the likelihood of further violence at the time may be quite minimal. The removal is necessary to break the cycle and therefore provide time and neutral space to facilitate treatment. Following the beating, the husband is likely to be relieved of anger and tension. He may also be feeling contrite and desirous of making amends. Still in crisis, he is apt to be highly suggestible and, therefore, more accessible to treatment. In accordance with crisis theory, it is important to intervene at the height of the trauma and capitalize on the person's vulnerability to therapeutic input (Bellak, 1963; Caplan, 1959).

The immediate aftermath period may be a "honeymoon" time, but only from the wife's perspective, as it is a time free of fear of impending abuse for her. The husband is often miserable. It is of crucial importance that he should *not* be imprinted further with messages of hatred, belittlement, or hostility from his wife or the treating person or agency. It is difficult to resist feeling indignation and playing into the husband's need for punishment to assuage his guilt. Yet, he needs protection from his wife's vengefulness if there is to be any chance of preventing the cyclical recurrence of the violence. In the early stages of rehabilitation, contact between the spouses should be kept at a minimum, and then closely supervised. Pathologic imprinting can then be avoided and the extent of their dysfunctional, destructive dependency on each other can be assessed. The next step is to carefully evaluate the nature of the interactive, transactional processes that have led to the violence. The marriage should be examined for the presence of any elements from the four syndromes described above. How much of the violence is due to faulty education, proximity, inadequate skills, or intrapsychic–interpersonal pathologic processes? Such an assessment can be best accomplished by interviewing the couple conjointly.

If the problem is primarily one of *proximity*, that is, if the wife and/or children are simply convenient victims for the husband's uncontrollable violent outbursts, every effort should be made to make it emotionally and financially possible for the wife and children to physically remove themselves from him. Although improvement in his behavior is theoretically possible, in practice it is unlikely, particularly if the pattern is deeply entrenched, long standing, and compounded by substance abuse. Trying to keep the family together, even with treatment, is usually a losing cause. Visitation with the children should be possible, but only under nonprovocative supervised circumstances for their protection. When psychopathological interaction patterns are evidenced and it is apparent that the violence is related to the nature of the interaction of these factors, reasonable goals of treatment may be to facilitate divorce in the most humane manner possible (Kaslow, 1981a) and to enable the couple to attain enough insight and growth not to remarry the same or a similar partner. This is difficult to accomplish since even though they cannot live together, they also cannot live apart and will usually conspire to get together again. Ultimately, it is *their* lives, and they must decide how they choose to live. Therapists can help them explore their options, the probable consequences of each choice, what they want, and how best to seek to obtain it.

The prognosis for those couples whose violence stems primarily from educational defects and lack of necessary skills is fairly good. Group therapy may constitute the treatment of choice and both husband and wife should participate in the same group (Kaslow & Lieberman, 1981). If one member refuses treatment or drops out, it is useless to continue with the other. The group would become a distancing element between spouses and a further source of discord and miscommunication.

Group therapy for spouse abusers can be very effective. The most useful thing they discover is the cyclical nature of the problem. They cannot see it in themselves but can readily see it in the others and can often predict when violence is imminent (Kaslow, 1982). We believe the group is most effective when led by a heterosexual cotherapy pair. The therapists should be articulate, direct, and have a healthy relationship with each other built on mutual respect, trust, and fondness. Treatment by one therapist or by therapists of the same sex tends to bias the process. Additionally, modeling how two adults of opposite sexes can disagree and successfully resolve or accept their differences is of great value to the group (Kaslow & Lieberman, 1981).

Treatment consists of helping patients to achieve a healthier perspective on marriage, on their own identity, individuality, and self-worth, as well as to enhance coping skills, particularly communication. It is usually a mistake to focus a group consisting of a population of abusers on encouraging the expression of anger. It is more important to facilitate the expression of the underlying feelings that the anger tends to mask. Fear of rejection, abandonment, weakness, insecurity, loneliness, and risking caring are considerably more important to bring into awareness and out into the open to be discussed and attended to.

A main theme can be the verbal argument. Couples should learn to fight verbally, perhaps frequently, always fairly (Bach, 1974). Avoidance of arguments leads to a building up of tension and misunderstanding. The argument, however, should never be used as a means to relieve previously built-up tension, exert dominance, or obtain revenge. They should be taught to focus on the matter at hand, not many tangential issues that divert attention from the real concern. An argument is not successful when one adversary "convinces" the other. Success comes when each partner has expressed his or her position (both facts and feelings) clearly, has listened to and understood the other's position, and no one has gotten hurt in the process. A cooperative win is the goal. Agreement is not necessary, although there should be movement toward a resolution which may consist of agreeing to disagree. With some practice, group members can become quite effective first in judging the success or failure and the unfair tactics in other couple's arguments and then in judging their own.

Another task of the group is to identify instances or circumstances where violence is imprinted on the physically violent spouse. A common example concerns the crucial time when the husband arrives home from work. He has had a long day at his job, and has just faced the commuting traffic. He finally gets home ready to shift gears into a relaxed, peaceful environment. Because his defenses are lowered, he is highly suggestible for several minutes following his arrival home. Too often his wife greets him with a litany of things gone wrong, appliances that need fixing, and the latest trouble that the children have caused. He perceives this reception as an attack and withdraws angrily. For hours he remains belligerent, on guard, and either inaccessible or perched to attack.

The wife can be taught that although she too has had a rough day and can hardly wait to ventilate her frustrations, *if she can postpone it for half an hour, she will probably get very different and better results.* If she can welcome the husband and wait until he is comfortable and receptive before bringing up all the problems, his willingness to be sympathetic and helpful will increase. However, the husband should come to understand that *sometimes her needs must take precedence* and his need to unwind will have to wait. Otherwise, the wife is forced into the handmaiden role of always considering what he needs first; some more egalitarian mutuality and reciprocity regarding need fulfillment and comforting might be the goal for many couples. For all, disrupting the destructive, unworkable repetitive cycle is crucial.

One-couple therapy, with its focus on just *this* couple, might be a better route for some couples, particularly if they are so needy that they cannot tolerate sharing the therapists' attention with others. Other possibilities are individual therapy of the spouse willing to be in treatment, or group therapy with members of the same sex. However, it is doubtful that a family can be kept free of violence without the commitment of all the members to change and try to make their family system function better; active involvement in therapy is one way to bring this about.

The brief outline of the treatment process for spouse abuse described above should indicate the magnitude of the commitment necessary from the therapists. Successful treatment consists of totally eliminating violence from the home either by treating the family or by facilitating the divorce. Anything less is unfair to the children as well as the parents.

Children are born helpless and remain for years substantially dependent on their parents for survival. Being smaller and unable to fend for themselves they are vulnerable to their abuse. Unfortunately, just as in spouse abuse, child abuse and being caught in the "world of abnormal rearing" generates its own violent cycle regardless of the causes (Kempe & Helfer, 1980).

The formation of healthy and successful coping mechanisms depends on effective modeling by the parents and self-confidence inspired by the environment (Kaslow, 1980; Walsh, 1982). The beatings, therefore, insure that the coping mechanisms that the child will develop will be pathological, unsuccessful, and likely to perpetuate the bad situation.

Again the first step in treatment is identification. Fortunately, attention by the media and a large number of medical and psychological articles have alerted physicians, emergency room staff, and mental health professionals to the problem.

Children acquire much of their understanding of the world and the skills necessary to get along with others through play and from television viewing. They also learn a sense of identity and of their place in the community. This learning can be distorted if violence is a regular part of their lives. Supervision of the playing and television watching should be distant enough to allow for the development of healthy curiosity and aggressivity. It has to be close enough, however, to prevent the emergence of violence as a preferred and frequent means of coping or communicating.

Violence between children may be the result of unconscious psychopathology in the parents. In several classic papers Adelaide Johnson described how parents may vicariously act out their unconscious antisocial impulses through their children's violent behavior (Johnson, 1949; Johnson & Szurek, 1952).

Finally, attention should also be given to the problem of battered parents. It is probably the most difficult type of family violence to detect. Parents are unlikely to report the abuse due to embarrassment, fear of being labeled as failures, and not wanting to cause their children to be apprehended by the law. Harbin and Madden (1979) conducted a study that showed that 1 out of 10 children between the ages of 3 and 18 attacks his or her parents. Clearly the hierarchical structure of these families is defective, and the abusing children may be pushing the parents to assert their rightful control (Minuchin, 1974).

CONCLUSION

As we have seen, every form of violence is possible within the family. What makes family violence particularly disastrous is that it destroys the family's capacity to provide for the nurturing of their young in a wholesome milieu, the development of a positive self-image in all family members, an optimistic outlook, effective coping skills, and a safe environment in which they feel attached and secure and from which they can depart equipped to make a positive contribution to the external world. Family violence generates not only its own cycle within the family but also a violent spiral that is handed down from generation to generation as a legacy. It is widely accepted that battered children often become child beaters and the children of spouse abusers often become spouse abusers themselves (Kempe & Helfer, 1980).

The consequences of family violence are tremendous in terms of actual injury, faulty biopsychosocial development of family members, and the carrying of the violence into the community, the military, and the larger universe. Treatment is difficult, lengthy, and costly. Clearly the solution lies in primary prevention. Our familial and educational systems must give children the necessary knowledge of mental health principles and the necessary skills of communication and parenting to cope with stress and frustration constructively and decrease the potential for violence. The sociopolitical environment and mass media must also create a much less violent context in which families can function more harmoniously, accepting the feelings that underlie violent outbursts yet expressing righteous indignation against these being acted out in this horrendous fashion and seeing that negative sanctions are applied and "victims" are protected until more constructive outlets are found and utilized. This is recommended as a posture to be taken by the community at large. Until all of this occurs, secondary and tertiary treatment strategies like those outlined above will need to be employed and refined to eliminate the otherwise brutalizing impact of incipient violence in some families.

REFERENCES

Bach, G. Creative exits: Fight therapy for divorcees. In V. Franks & V. Burtle (Eds.), *Women in therapy: New psychotherapies for a changing society.* New York: Brunner/ Mazel, 1974.

Barnett, E. R., Pittman, C. B., Ragan, C. K., & Salus, M. K. (Eds.). *Family violence: Intervention strategies* (Department of Health and Human Services No. OHDS 80-30258). Washington, D.C.: U.S. Government Printing Office, 1980.

Bellak, L. *Handbook of community psychiatry.* New York: Grune & Stratton, 1963.

Caplan, G. *Concepts of mental health and consultation.* Washington, D.C.: U.S. Department of Health, Education and Welfare, 1959.

Department of Defense. *Directive, Family Advocacy Program* (6400.1). Washington, D.C.: DoD Institute, May 19, 1981.

Department of the Navy, Bureau of Medicine and Surgery. *Family Advocacy Program* (BuMED Instruction 6320.57), July 11, 1979.

Figley, C. R. *Stress disorders among Vietnam veterans.* New York: Brunner/Mazel, 1978.

Harbin, H. T., & Madden, D. J. Battered parents: A new syndrome. *American Journal of Psychiatry,* 1979, *136,* 1288-1291.

Hyatt, R. *Before you marry again.* New York: Random House, 1977.

Johnson, A. M. Sanctions for superego lacunae of adolescents. In K. R. Eissler (Ed.), *Searchlights on delinquency.* New York: International Universities Press, 1949.

Johnson, A. M., & Szurek, S. A. The genesis of antisocial acting out in children and adults. *The Psychoanalytic Quarterly,* 1952, *21,* 323-343.

Kaslow, F. W. Profile of healthy family. *Focus Pä Familien* (Norwegian Journal of Family Therapy), 1980, *1.*

Kaslow, F. W. Divorce and divorce therapy. In A. Gurman & D. Kniskern (Eds.), *Handbook of family therapy.* New York: Brunner/Mazel, 1981. (a)

Kaslow, F. W. Group therapy with couples in conflict: Is more better? *Psychotherapy: Theory, Research and Practice,* 1981, *18*(4), 516-524. (b)

Kaslow, F. W., & Lieberman, E. J. Couples group therapy: Rationale, dynamics and process. In G. P. Sholevar (Ed.), *The handbook of marriage and marital therapy.* New York: SP Medical & Scientific Books, 1981.

Kempe, C. H., & Helfer, R. E. *The battered child* (3rd ed.) Chicago: University of Chicago Press, 1980.

Kennedy, D. Personal communication, October 1982.

Martin, D. *Battered wives.* New York: Simon & Schuster, 1976.

Minuchin, S. *Families and family therapy.* Cambridge: Harvard University Press, 1974.

Steinmetz, S. *The cycle of violence.* New York: Praeger, 1977.

Straus, M. A., Gelles, R. J., & Steinmetz, S. K. *Behind closed doors: Violence in the American family.* Garden City, N.Y.: Anchor Press/Doubleday, 1980.

Thorman, G. *Family violence.* Springfield, Ill.: Thomas, 1980.

Walsh, F. (Ed.). *Normal family processes.* New York: Guilford, 1982.
West, L. A., Turner, W. M., & Dunwoody, E. *Wife abuse in the armed forces.* Washington, D.C.: Center for Women Policy Studies, 1981.

7

C'est la Guerre:
Military Families and Family Therapy

DAVID V. KEITH
CARL A. WHITAKER

> They're never at home and they're always alone, even with someone they
> love.—Bruce and Bruce (1975)

Among the difficulties in working with military families is that of doing
psychotherapy with men in the world of men. There are two problems:
The first loyalty of the husband and father is to his work, the military
service. And men are rarely available for psychotherapy. When a man is
available, it is because he has access to the feminine components of his
character structure. The other time is when a man is desperate.

We started this chapter with the idea that military experience is
necessary in order to work with military families. It then occurred to us
that many of the problems involved in work with military families apply
to an endless list of occupational and cultural groups that provide considerable self-respect for their members and develop a process similar to
that of the military. Some of these groups include musicians, professional
athletes, truck drivers, financial wizards, physicians, dentists, airline
pilots, West Virginia coal miners, and Wisconsin dairymen. A person who
uses a group identity in place of a personal identity is much less available
for psychotherapy; men are more apt than women to do this. While the
men who serve in the military and the men who drive trucks have much in
common, the families of the truck drivers do not belong to the institution

David V. Keith. Department of Psychiatry, Park Nicollet Medical Center, Minneapolis,
Minnesota.

Carl A. Whitaker. Professor Emeritus, Department of Psychiatry, University of Wisconsin
Medical School, Clinical Sciences Center, Madison, Wisconsin.

in the same way that military families belong to the military. In the latter group there is less freedom for the family to fight the system. Therefore, in regard to the need for military experience for therapists, let us say it this way: It is helpful to have an appreciation of the military system and military maneuvering. A therapist who is too cynical about the military will be of questionable value as a therapist. Conversely, a therapist who is a member of the military may be locked into patterns of administration molded by the military which could serve as obstacles to helping families stay alive. For the civilian therapist, it is probably useful to have a consultant or cotherapist who knows something of the military and its impact on living patterns.

Our background with the military is sparse. Keith was an Air Force flight surgeon (1968–1970), and Whitaker was never in the military. Both of us have done therapy with military families and have provided consultation to therapists who work with military families. Our effort in this chapter is to look at military families from our right brains. Of course, we are also looking from a distance. From the standpoint of therapy we will paint an impressionistic picture of the men, women, and children, individually and in families. We will also describe the role of the therapist.

THE MILITARY SYSTEM

The military services understand and operate in terms of systems, not individuals. They know instinctively that they cannot pressure one part of the system without affecting other parts. For example, it is common knowlege that marital disharmony can have fatal effects on a pilot's performance. The system may be painfully nonpersonal at times but impersonal treatment is accepted. The Air Force stays pragmatic and nontheoretical in its understanding of life and living. The philosophic background of military families is often simple patriotism: "It is for me to do or die, not to ask the reasons why."

There are three components to every military mission. Listed in order of importance, they are (1) to get the job done; (2) to have some fun; (3) to survive. Surviving includes health maintenance. The military is wellness oriented yet it does not try to be therapeutic. "Shape up or ship out" states the orientation. (This attitude has implications for psychotherapy which we will expand upon later.) If someone has a crazy episode or in some way double-crosses the group he may be extruded by loss of honor or respect. The group makes few exceptions and rarely allows anyone to return.

There is a cultural myth that is involved in work with a military family. While the modern world is sometimes cynical about the military, there is a "warrior romance" that inhabits the heart of Everyman. Somewhere in Everyman's fantasy there dwells a Ulysses prepared to leave on a heroic journey to win dominance over the dragons of destiny, chaos, and death, with bravery and skill. For women there is the pleasure–pain of Penelope, divine in her loyalty to her hero husband, exciting in her potential for unfaithfulness. She yearns for his return, and is frightened of the changes he may have undergone. Likewise, he hungers for her. The marriage may go beautifully when he is off to war, but when he isn't, the marriage may become the battleground. Can family life compete with the excitement of the heroic journey?

The military services are divided into a men's system and a women's system. Children are included in the women's system. The family combines the two subsystems, but compared to its place in the civilian world, it has a subsidiary role in the military system.

THE MEN'S SYSTEM

In the last two decades it has become very difficult to stay "macho." The military services provide some opportunity, but the macho style can look ridiculous from the outside. The macho life-style does not have an inherently psychological side and the therapist who operates psychodynamically may be quickly excluded or disregarded. We talked earlier about the problem of working with men. It is easy inadvertently to make a fool of a man by matching him with the "do your own thing" ambiguity of the outside world. In civilian life we find ourselves involved in conversations that disparage the military and its value system. (For example, a not uncommon exchange may be: "What is the difference between the Air Force and the Boy Scouts?" "I give up." "The Boy Scouts have adult leadership.") It is easy to assume that this attitude is shared by everyone, but this is not so. The soldier may make fun of military life as one might make fun of his own family, but to ridicule or challenge the family too much as an outsider will be an insult to his honor. This can happen accidentally by the therapist playing with his kids or being overly supportive to his wife. *The military family does not come to the clinic to learn how to become a civilian family, but rather it needs help to live inside the military system.* Psychotherapy has long been held in low esteem by military personnel. Our guess about the reason is that to serve one's country well in an armed service a strong denial of death and craziness is essential. Conversely, psychotherapy always exposes patients to their fantasies about death or the possibility of craziness. Therefore, psychotherapy can be viewed as running counter to the aims of the military structure and its member families. At a simpler level, "seeking help" implies a personal weakness, a moral weakness as measured against the macho code. If a man cannot keep women and children in order, if he cannot manage his family, how can he be expected to command a complement of men?

By contrast to individually oriented therapy, family-oriented therapy is able to align itself with the values of the military because it has as its first purpose to intensify the family organization, increase the esprit de corps, and clarify the rank structure. Therefore, family therapy can be useful without pushing into the psychological vulnerability of the individual family member. When family therapy does push into the fear of death or the fear of craziness it can do so within the background of a structure that an organized family brings.

While Tom Wolfe's imaginative book *The Right Stuff* (1979) is about fighter pilots and astronauts, it provides a lively picture of the macho side of military life juxtaposed against the civilian culture. The "right stuff," which is a smooth blend of unusual bravery and fine-tuned competence, inhabits the souls of all military personnel. We think that the therapist who belittles or disregards this side of the man will have problems helping the family. Obviously in some, the flame burns brighter. In a dormant or atrophied state the "right stuff" consists of a stiff paranoia, colored with simple patriotism, religious belief, and a demand for order.

It seems that with rigid families the amount of intimacy possible correlates with what the most paranoid member can tolerate. The military is the paranoid edge of the culture. Usually the most paranoid member is the father. In the military the paranoid component is difficult to disrupt because the paranoia is validated by his profession. One way to liberate him and his family from his paranoia is to validate it, encourage it, expand it, and halt any effort by the family to minimize it. One definition of paranoia is unusual monocular honesty. To illustrate:

In a family where the wife is deeply concerned about the problem and the father is minimizing it and refusing to come back for the therapy, we agree with the father saying to the family, "Dad isn't anxious about it so why don't you live by his rules, let him take it over so you don't have to feel like something dangerous is happening until he tells you."

On other occasions it has been useful with men who get on their high horse about patriotism or moral values to say, "Dad, it is so hard to listen to you when you get on your high horse like that. I think it is because it is so impersonal. Each time you say it I hear less and less of it." Don't forget that the paranoia is equal in the system. It may not become apparent until you have been around the family for a while.

In many ways the work of the military is a kind of cultural play (Huizinga, 1950). The skilled warrior has deep respect for skill in his comrades and in the enemy, but his skill may be contaminated by involvement in the confusing world of Home. There is a boyish camaraderie that prevails among these warriors. I (D.V.K.) recall riding in the backseat of a fighter plane in the midst of a practice war in Texas. The pilot was a 42-year-old lieutenant colonel. When he rolled in to make a fake strafing run on some tanks hidden in a stand of trees I heard the pilot make the same machine-gun sound over the radio that I used to make playing cops and robbers as a child. This camaraderie is expanded when men don uniforms, and in the kind of language that evolves. It's fun; the play sure beats listening to a complaining wife or arguing with the children.

The gulf that develops between the military man and his children is one of the most hopeless troubles in family therapy. Too many times there is little to do about it. The father may be little more than a figure. One discouraging thing we have learned in doing family therapy is the extent to which men reduce the family tension by leaving the family circle. Often such men have no inner life. They have never been intimate with anyone and unfortunately may never achieve closeness with anyone. The military supports that pattern, and in fact endorses it. It is a very old warrior tradition that says, "We dare not love too much for soon we may die."

It is easy for the father to become a scapegoat in the military family. He is too impersonal, prudish, or bossy. For example:

A young, new major was in hot water with his wife. She was trying to reform her husband so that they could have a family more like her civilian sister's family. In addition to her anger about the present situation, she said that he should never have joined the military and that she had warned him about it. As a therapist, the first author became instantly angry with her. "You cannot blame him for that now, when you do you are double-crossing him because by your actions you agreed to go along with the military career in the beginning."

It seems that by defining and shoring up the official reality and its implications for the family, it gets the wife and her sergeants off of father's back. That may make it possible for him to soften personally in relation to his family. That applies in both military and civilian families. Fathers don't just leave; sometimes they are also driven off.

One young officer presented a vivid visual image of what it is like to be in the military. It is as if a sharp sword has pierced the family. "If we don't struggle, we can live fairly comfortably and in fact develop scar tissue around the wound like a pierced ear. However, if we try to fight the system too much we can cut ourselves to death with our squirming."

THE WOMEN'S SYSTEM

The women's system is much more complex, covert, and has more interfaces. It is difficult to stereotype a military wife these days. They have a greater responsibility for living with the children and they have a richer involvement with the civilian culture than the men do. We may sound old-fashioned, but women have a personal identity out of conceiving, bearing, and rearing children. It is possible to augment it by further careers, but men have no such implicit identity. As Margaret Mead (1949) said, "Fathers are social accidents."

Although informal, the wives' group is always available and fairly cohesive. Whenever a new pilot joins the squadron, moving in from another base or different assignment, his wife is immediately picked up by the wives' club. The group helps her into the community and guides her. I (D.V.K.) married while I was in the Air Force. When my wife came to the base she was greeted and oriented by the wives' group like an automatic sorority sister. She was a "sister" until proven otherwise. In this regard, there was a dramatic difference between our experience in the Air Force and our experience in the civilian world. In civilian life there was scarcely any effort to bring us into a group. The civilian "we" and "they" boundaries remain more ambiguous. The difference is in the community-group morale present in the military families. The squadron wives' group members were available to help one another through an assortment of crises. In addition to orienting a new family to the base whenever an officer was transferred away to a new assignment, there was a farewell party when they left. While the wives' group was supportive, it was not therapeutic. They upheld the credo that it was not theirs to ask the reasons why. While some did not actively support what their husbands did, they did not speak out against it. The men were allowed freedom to move in their world because of the morale in the wives' group. A case in point follows:

A copilot was killed in an aircraft accident. The fighter plane in which he was flying caught fire during a training mission. The aircraft commander decided that they should eject. The pilot survived. Investigation of the accident revealed that the copilot neglected to fasten his parachute harness. While he ejected successfully, he was not wearing a parachute and fell to his death. He had planned to begin his vacation on the day of his death. The flight commander had ordered him to complete this important training mission. The copilot's wife, in her grief, began to blame the flight commander for her husband's death. She received no sympathy from the squadron or the wives' group.

There is the constant assumption by pilots that a man only gets killed if he allows a lapse in his competence. If he has the "right stuff" he won't be killed (Wolfe, 1979). There is a corollary: If you have the right stuff you will never be in need of professional mothering as offered by any psychotherapist.

It is our impression that children stay in the background in the military. They are often the family members who express the symptoms for the family. The children more clearly belong to the women's system, less so to the men's system! Children can of course lead parents into craziness and feelings of mortality (mental illness is inherited; we get it from our children). Children are too aware that the emperor's new clothes are a group fantasy. They disrupt fantasies of authority and established hierarchy. To the extent that the soldier needs to retain a shield of psychological invulnerability and macho self-esteem it is difficult for him to be freely interactive with his children. So it is that the mother takes over the children and the father remains outside, sometimes as a consultant, often as a figurehead, like the unfinished portrait of George Washington in the schoolrooms of our childhood. Family therapy can be helpful in giving the father a way to discriminate between the outside reality of the military and the inner reality of the home. He can learn to expose his clay feet at home without losing his dignity in the military service. Successful psychotherapy with men may have to do with the precipitation of a multiple personality disorder.

THE FAMILY SYSTEM

In civilian life few groups are able to compete effectively against the family for a person's loyalty during stressful times. We think that the family has power, especially when mustered as consultants to the patient and his family troubles. It is our constant effort to bring in all three generations when we work with families. In the military world the civilian components of the family may have less influence because military rules supersede the past history. In other words, the bond of the military may take precedence over bonds to the family, past and present.

Together the men's system and the women's system become a "bunch of jocks"—the gangsters and their gun molls, the Hell's Angels and their women. Is the family in some way subsidiary to this world of honor and glory?

In a metaphorical way, a military man marries his military service. The bond is solid and must always be taken into consideration when dealing with a family's emotional struggles. The real-life male–female marriage is thus an extramarital affair. In the best adapted marriages the husband and wife stay in the same generation. In dysfunctional marriages the spouses move into separate generations. Several patterns are likely:

1. An affair between a cheerleader and a football player. She enjoys and participates in his little-boy antics, wears the right kind of clothes, makes the right kind of small talk, and participates in the cheerleading team's activities with enthusiasm. She likes football almost as much as he does.

2. A brother–sister affair. Here the partnership is stable but less sexual and less flashy. The couple stays joined, but outside the group.

3. The wife becomes the man's mother and he becomes her little boy. This marriage pattern is common and also pathologic; here a generation gap develops in the marriage. In this case both can use resentment to amplify the excitement of their infidelities. The infidelity may not be sexual. She may be emotionally closer to the kids than she is to him, while he may be in love with uniforms, bullets, bombs, or airplanes. In this arrangement his mother-in-law then becomes his grandmother if he is married to his mother. The son can then become the wife's husband (his father's father or his own grandfather). With father in the second generation, there is rich soil for such modern pornographic horrors as wife beating, child abuse, and incest. The symbolic son (real-life father) is then beating up his mother or his siblings out of his impotence, and having sexual fun with his sister. Extramarital affairs are then ennobled as a way to avoid participation in an incestuous affair with a real-life wife/symbolic mother. To add to the confusion, the general may be the grandfather, the colonel the father, and the top sergeant the brother.

When this is paraded out in front of the family, it may be confusing in the same way that it is difficult to keep these relationships straight as we write it. Symbolism always is a little out of focus. The boundary between what is real and what is symbolic is hazy—dreamlike is the most available metaphor. Symbolism is confusing and awkward, but still useful. When not acknowledged, these symbolic patterns can be emotionally crippling. We think of ourselves as playing with the meaning of relationships. What is important in play is distortion. We think that it is valuable to share fragments of our primary-process thinking even if they are not complete thoughts. They may be confusing to the family, but confusion is not harmful. Instead, it is often a precursor of change. Confusion is frequently for us the new symptom with which the whole family is afflicted. In one case we saw, the following transpired:

A parentified 11-year-old girl was defined by the therapy team as her brother's mother, later as her father's girl friend, and at another time as the family dog. "What's going on here?" she demanded incredulously with the tone of a mother to her children. "First I'm a mother, then I'm dad's girl friend, then I'm the family dog. I don't know who I am." Several interviews later when she was demoted to her own generation by a shift in her parents' posture, she left the office and said, "First you told me I'm my mother, then you called me my dad's girl friend, then you made me the family dog, but now I'm just a Karen." She playfully sucked her thumb as she exited.

It is possible to take these symbolic identities and extrapolate endless relationship triangles. For example, if the soldier's wife is acting like his mother he may have affairs with women in other ports in an effort to avoid incest. The pathology of most concern, but also to which family therapists have best access, is the triangular relationship problems. In the military, the triangle almost uniformly involves the soldier and his absorbing relation to the military system.

Thus, a wife's psychosomatic problems may have to do with her husband's overinvolvement with his work and her inability to change his loyalty patterns. His excessive commitment to duty provides a way for her to feed her dependency needs by allowing her frequent contact with her parents in the role of their little girl, and also with that malevolent–benevolent mother of the military base, the medical clinic.

Another slant on the military family is that for the wife, it is like being married to a man whose father is generous but demanding. The military service makes specific and nonnegotiable demands about time, but, on the other hand, rewards and compensation are forthcoming. While military pay may not match that for comparable jobs in the outside world, there are seductive compensations in the way of lower food and clothing prices, travel opportunities, and the "easy life" of retirement after 20 years.

Ten years ago, and we assume it is still the same today in the early 1980s, divorce could be a detriment to advancement in the military service. Thus, rather than heat up a marriage dispute, the military couple may prefer to effect a distancing emotional divorce only. The physical pattern of an intact marriage exists but there is no overt loving or hating. The partners may stay together but be turned away from one another. This pattern of marriage induces emotional flatness which stunts personal growth. It is this kind of marriage which may ultimately precipitate children into acting out against the culture as a way to rekindle affect in the family and to protect the family members from emotional contact with each other. They direct their outrage onto the community instead. This kind of family pattern may also result in nonverbal symptoms such as muscle spasm, coronary artery disease, cancer, and accidents.

Another interesting component of the military family is that it lives in a community in which no one dies from old age, only violently. A person leaves the civilian world to join the military world. After the completion of service they leave the military world to go back into the civilian world. This may lead to an illusion of eternal youth and vigor for members of the military and aid in the effort to repress the fear of death or madness and to maintain the delusion that time does not pass.

In our view of the world, the family provides a buffer between its members and the culture. In the military families it seems that the buffer is less effective. Informally, the whole family belongs to the military. The father may have the capacity to outrank his wife because he has a closer affiliation with the base commander. This imbalance in the parental authority and the permeability of the boundary between the family and the culture can cause problems when the pressure is on. Often, military families may be organized like a miniature army, complete with barracks inspection, clothing, and personal hygiene standards. The children are often required to call father "Sir." The children may respect their father as a fearless leader but often it is a charade played out only when he is there. Behind the scenes, as the chess queen says to the chess king, in an old *New Yorker* cartoon, "Your problem is that you can only move one square at a time." The fathers ought to know that the use of military manners are an act at home. Following this same line, most families are most apt to use scapegoating in the same way that the military does (Lagrone, 1978). The scapegoat can be transferred to another unit. It is possible for the therapist to ask the children if they would rather be transferred to another family.

PSYCHOTHERAPY WITH MILITARY FAMILIES

Metaphorical language helps give a picture of the military family's dynamics. Likewise, metaphorical language can be useful in talking about therapy or what has gone wrong.

The first problem to deal with is the question of the group morale. The group's spirit may be lost in a family which has lost too many battles. More problems emerge as dissension in the ranks start to build. The misbehavior in the youngsters may be a way to rally the family. When a family is unable to get all of its members together, it may be because the family is defeated and now it is every man for himself.

Another step in working with families is to clarify the rank structure. The parents have equal rank. Both are five-star generals, and neither can boss the other one around. One of the parents can be the officer of the day, but only if the other agrees to take a subsidiary role temporarily. The children are like the sergeants. They may have a rank structure of their own within their generation, but none of them can boss the parents around.

If one of the five-star generals is absent, it is possible for the chief master sergeant (oldest sibling) to take up some of the missing officer's administrative responsibilities but he or she can only do it with the agreement of both generals and the "as if" clause is always in effect.

The way father is handled in the early interviews is often critical as to how available the family will be for change. If ignored, he will feel useless. If confronted or criticized, he will feel outmaneuvered and not return to the therapy. If he is successfully courted, he may be scared and run off. If he wins the skirmish or one-ups the therapist, it may also end. The problem of how to deal with father isn't unique to military families.

Sometimes it is necessary for the therapist to side with a concrete exoskeleton of military life in order to be helpful to the family's alienating the father. It is rich in its fantasy of conquering the other. Truth is simple. What makes a man available for change is his desperation, and when that is gone, so is he. For example:

Chief Master Sergeant Cook was a highly competent Air Force communications expert with 22 years of service. His wife, 10 years younger than he, had never been a good military wife. She found civilian jobs off the base and was active in the Catholic church. After 15 years of marriage she told CMS Cook that it was either family therapy or divorce. He had been an excellent soldier except for two bouts of depression. She had run the home, raised the two children virtually single handed, and had been involved with her jobs. She was a captivating, exciting, grown-up woman going through an identity shift toward greater personal integration. He was a large man. In the office setting he was shy and noncommunicative. He spent most of the interviews looking at his shoes. He made virtually no eye contact with the therapist. The children, a daughter age 14 and a son age 11, were good kids, lively, yet well behaved. In essence the therapist was being asked to do nothing other than to provide a time and a place for Mrs. Cook to coalesce. They came for five interviews and she became even more lively. Next, she wanted him to change, to become excited about himself like she was about herself. He did not know what she was talking about. His philosophy about living was organized around two platitudes: "Live and let live," and "I don't think about the past, I just gotta get through today."

The wife in this family was the kind of "growing" patient that therapists relish. By contrast, the father was the kind of person that most therapists would like to work over, teaching him to be more feeling and self-expressive. We think it is a mistake to try to do psychotherapy with someone who is not seeking a change experience. The father is who he is and cannot change. Do not get us wrong, he has to come to the interviews, even if he does not wish to be a patient. One way to help the husband to become interested in family therapy is to get the wife and children off his back. The nonsubjective view of life goes against the grain of psychotherapists. But that is men—some do not have access to an inner self, and they never will.

VIPs, people whose self-respect is derived from their extrafamily activities, constitute a difficult problem for psychotherapists. Many assume that they are "in charge" everywhere, but that is a delusion. The VIP issue is clearly an issue in working with officers and their families. It is important to make clear that the office is the place where the therapist is in charge, even if outranked. Usually it is not a problem, but at times the therapist may have to make a move to establish his or her territory and authority. By way of example:

The colonel's wife was distressed about their marital pattern. She wanted to come alone to the first therapy session. I (D.V.K.) told her it would be a mistake, that she should talk with her husband about it and explain that I didn't work that way. He would have to come with her. If he had any problems with it he could call me himself. She called back the next day to say that he would come but they wouldn't bring the children. I asked her to tell him that would only mean that we would have to do the first interview twice, but it was their time and money so I wouldn't be upset about it. They arrived for the first interview. A medical student was my cotherapist. I began in my usual way, asking the colonel to describe how he thought I could be helpful. "The first thing you can do is ask her to leave," he said coolly, referring to the woman medical student working with me. I explained that I wouldn't do that because I never see a family without a cotherapist. He said that that didn't change his mind; he still would like to have her leave. I pointed out that this was my office, that I made the rules, and I did not think that it was appropriate for him to come in and tell me how to practice medicine. Having her leave was not one of his options. "What are my options?" My heart rate was approximately 130 as I replied with a calm smile, "First, you could start answering my question 'How can I be helpful?,' or second, *you* could leave." "Very well!" he said and got up and left. Immediately his wife began to cry and started to say something about him. I interrupted, "Listen, I know you're upset about this, but I don't want to be put in the position of seeing you by yourself, I think that it could be dangerous and cause problems in the marriage." She got up and left. At that point my medical student colleague began to cry. We talked some about what had happened and how she was upset by his authoritarian pressure. After we had discussed the matter for about 5 minutes I said, "Look at it this way: You saved me from having to work with these characters." At that point the colonel walked back into the office with his wife behind him and said, "We've decided to go ahead."

The value of this struggle which occurred in my office was that it showed him my strength, and as I learned in subsequent weeks, it gave him an opportunity to be dependent upon me. During the course of their therapy their marriage went through considerable turmoil, in the end they got back together in a way changed to their mutual satisfaction.

In the preceding example the battle was about who was in charge of the therapy. The next example is similar, it shows a confrontation between the macho world of the military man and the ambiguity-filled world of the psychotherapist.

The authors saw a family about their daughter who was treading the border line between psychotic fragmentation and trying to get a social work degree. The father was a colonel, sociable and friendly, and interested in doing something about his daughter's problems as well as about the anxiety that it caused his wife. A critical piece of the family history that came out had to do with the fact that the couple's first child died 3 days after birth. The mother was pale and tense as the interview reawakened this painful time in her life. She was evasive about the emotional side of the experience, but appeared thoughtful. Referring to the husband, Whitaker asked, "Do you think he was broken hearted at the time like you were?" The affable colonel chuckled, "What's that got to do with anything? You shrinks think everybody lives in the past like you do." Probably the best way to deal with a remark of that sort is to join with his criticism and agree with it, thus neutralizing it. I often do that, but in this case it would have been a lie if we had. "Look soldier, don't laugh me off. I have been sitting here for 20 years so don't get sarcastic with me. If you think the baby's death was nothing you are lying to yourself, but don't expect me to pretend your wife wasn't devastated about it." The colonel backed off thoughtfully. He had been relieved of his fantasy command of our office.

These two examples may be harsh, but it is necessary to be harsh at times in order to become important to the family. The therapist's authority is based on his or her integrity. The therapist cannot go one down if he or she has not been one up. Once the therapist establishes himself or herself as a somebody, then he or she can afford to be stupid and enjoy it.

If father cannot change his living patterns or intensify his subjective living, what is to be done with him? First, his dignity ought to be reaffirmed. He is not the wife's little boy. Boss's (1977) study of MIA families showed that a family with a psychologically present, physically absent father functioned better than one in which the father was absent both psychologically and physically. The fact is that the man's work world is restrictive. The coalition between the father and the military has to be acknowledged and respected. The family has to understand the importance of this coalition and reduce their expectations for the father (Lagrone, 1978).

It pays to define and even expand the reality of father's involvement with work. One might say to the wife, "It sounds to us as though he has more fun at work than at home, and I don't know how you can expect to change that." "How can you expect to compete with airplanes?" Reducing the expectations for change is helpful in two ways. If there is no change, then the family knows the limits of the father's availability. They can get out of the posture of waiting for him to change. On the other hand, the father may be able to glimpse the absurdity of his choice of functional adequacy over the warmth of the family, and it may precipitate a change.

We always look for common language descriptions of family troubles. "Battle fatigue" is an inevitable syndrome for mothers of young children. In its more severe forms, it becomes "stir crazy." The kid who is pushing the family around can be likened to the PLO attempting to push Israel around. Any family that moves goes through a period of culture shock. We assume that it would be a frequent problem in military families, especially when stationed in foreign countries.

Metaphorical language is very useful in interviewing. If the children do not answer when asked to describe the family, we ask if they had thought about getting transferred to a different family. Or, in a family with a parentified child we might ask, "Did mother court martial father when he was gone and then promote your brother to general?" If the parents are established as five-star generals, one cotherapist may wonder aloud, "Do you have any idea how generals make love?" Did the father go AWOL from the family or did he just retreat in the face of discouraging odds? Is the commander holding him hostage from the family?

There is a problem in trying to include the families of origin in the family therapy of military families. Often the families are displaced from their home region and it is difficult to bring other family members the distance required for an interview. Several years ago I (C.A.W.) hit upon the idea of using a speaker telephone and conference calls to do family therapy with extended families. In this arrangement, the therapist has a speaker telephone in his office. The grandparents call in and are present via the phone for the interview. Usually the first 10 minutes are awkward, but things cook up quickly and the afterwaves are powerful.

THE MILITARY THERAPIST

The family therapist with military families is in a difficult position, like all other psychotherapists. The civilian therapist has to have some way to understand and respect the value of the military system so that he or she does not inadvertently triangulate the family against the military. The military therapist, on the other hand, may be locked into patterns of operation, molded by the military system, which could serve as obstacles to helping families.

The flight surgeon is a good model for how to be therapeutic in the military. The flight surgeon is a member of the system, but he is covertly socialized to bend the system's rules.

Pilots do not like to go to doctors who do not have an appreciation of their right stuff (Wolfe, 1979). Outside of the system it may seem to be little more than the malignant macho of the sort seen among 13-year-old boys. As mentioned earlier, I (D.V.K.) was a flight surgeon in an Air Force fighter squadron. This is a fact which is inconsistent with my view of myself, past and present. When I was in medical school I was on the verge of becoming a conscientious objector as a way of avoiding military service. Because of Vietnam it was inevitable that I would be drafted after my internship. Instead, I signed up for Aerospace Medicine Training in the Air Force and became one of the pilots' physicians, a job which led to adventure in the inner sanctum of the Air Force. I learned more about systems from my experience in the Air Force than any other single source. After being in the Air Force for a year, my peacenik countenance had disappeared. The macho living-style had a seductive quality. I experienced strange impulses to stay in the military, to go to flight school, and discover my own right stuff. My socialization was complete. I was very much accepted as a member of the fighter pilot group. The pattern of my acceptance could be described thus: They thought I was a good guy who did not have quite enough of the "right" qualities to become a fighter pilot. But I enjoyed the pilots, and they were willing to orient me and to take me along in their world like a little brother. On the other hand, I was a revered, albeit feeble, grandfather because of my wisdom about health in relation to on-the-job functioning, an area of which they knew little but which was a great threat to them in that a physician's report could easily end a pilot's career. An illustrative vignette follows:

We were fighting a practice war in Germany, and eight of us went out one evening. One man said, "Hey, Doc. Tex slammed his finger in the car door. What should we do?" "Open the door" was my answer.

Thus, one key to psychotherapy effectiveness may be to join the men in their homosocial fun. We learn from miners about mining, truckers about trucking, but we stay clear about our function and expertise.

The Air Force flight surgeon allows himself to be placed in a double bind by the miltary. I think that the double bind is a component of successful therapy. If you cannot be double bound, you will probably be less effective as a therapist. For the flight surgeon, it works something like this: When I entered the military service straight out of medical internship I practiced by the letter of the law (University of Minnesota style). One of the laws was that you did not allow friends to become patients. The Air Force informed me that my first job was to get to know the pilots by socializing with them, which I did, and the pilots and their families became my good friends, but then they were also patients. It was at that time that I became a prostitute of Hippocrates, trying to maintain my medical practice standards and the Air Force's health standards for flying personnel, all the while enjoying the friendship of my pilot friends.

An excerpt from the casebook of a Hippocratic prostitute reads:

Andy was a 33-year-old major and regarded by his fellow pilots as a man of unusual talent in the art of fighter pilotry. He could do those wondrous things with a jet fighter plane that few outside of the profession were able to understand or appreciate. He was scheduled to go to Vietnam and then to a high-prestige appointment as an instructor at an advanced training school. While on a 2-month temporary deployment to Germany, Andy asked me if I wanted to go by F4 to Madrid for the weekend as part of a Navigational Proficiency Exericse and Boondoggle. A month after we returned, in the bar of the officers' club one night, Andy said, "Doc, how does a man know when he has an ulcer? Do you think he would be smart to have one of those upper GIs even if he didn't think he had an ulcer? Do you think there would be some way to keep the X-rays out of his medical chart?" Naturally, the indefinite man he described was himself. An upper GI evaluation was performed and showed no ulcer present. I treated Andy's symptoms and now, 12 years later, he is still in the flying business.

Officially he should have been grounded for the evaluation, but the Air Force sets it up so that the flight surgeon will protect the pilot as well as the Air Force. If the flight surgeon follows the letter of the law, pilots will avoid him. The Air Force wants to maintain high standards, but it does not want highly qualified pilots disqualified for small illnesses. Unofficially, they depend upon flight surgeons to bend the rules, within limits.

My primary point is that in working with military families it is probably important that the family therapist be double bound by the situation, but that he or she retain the capacity to acknowledge it when it happens. The physician who follows the letter of the law will be laughed off, regarded as an uptight square, and avoided. Conversely, a physician who fails to maintain his personal integrity will lose the respect of the men.

A cotherapist is invaluable in these situations, as the following example demonstrates.

A retired lieutenant colonel was on the Veterans Administration inpatient ward with his family. Following a myocardial infarction 5 years previously, he had had bypass surgery and was abruptly retired from the military. He told a long story of his illustrious career, and his many exploits as a fighter pilot. The family listened and never took issue with anything. It was a long story, I was hooked by it. I sensed that some of the others there were less interested and even bored. At the end of the man's story the psychologist cotherapist said, "I think you're a spoiled brat. You sound like you can't stand it if you don't get your way. I was just having the nicest fantasy of taking you over my knee and paddling your 55-year-old ass with that cane you carry."

I was surprised that I was not able to dissociate myself enough from my fascination with his story. In retrospect I think that we provided a balanced effort. I was seduced by the man. I sensed his vulnerability and could feel no confrontation from the family and I did not get anywhere. Then my cotherapist moved in and let him have it. This was a nice blend. It says that it might be smart for military therapists to be matched with a civilian cotherapist. As a twosome we respected his history but we were able to work on his personal structure as well. Alone, neither one of us would have been effective. I was too captivated by his exploits; the cotherapist would have been too confrontative.

Often, those who have the most access to family members may not be in a position to work with the whole family. In the civilian world, for example, the family doctor may know the family members and may have considerable information about the family accumulated over time, but because of closeness to individual members he or she cannot work well with the whole. The doctor has the old problem of the inability to see the forest for the trees.

It is possible to do family therapy with only one family member and it need not occur in an office setting. It can occur in an airplane, the officers' club, or at a routine medical checkup. This kind of family therapy is less potent but not impossible. If the practitioner is able to think and talk family dynamics he or she might be helpful by casual conversation in the medical setting or may be able to develop a preliminary staging effort to later therapy. In civilian life when we get referrals from someone who knows us and refers the whole family, it makes our work much easier. In this sense the person who does the family therapy would be wise to develop a professional and personal relationship with people who provide primary care services in the military so they become less suspicious of our brand of "witchcraft."

Family therapy can be done informally. One model would be the psychiatrist in T. S. Eliot's short play *The Cocktail Party* (Eliot, 1950/ 1962). That psychiatrist arranges events so that the persons have a therapeutic experience in the real world. A pediatrician friend of ours refers people from the golf course, as in the following:

Over a postgolf beer, Bill confided his concern about his son's suicidal thoughts to the pediatrician (Dr. P). An older son had been killed in an automobile accident 2 years earlier. Dr. P suggested that Bill bring his family into the office so that they could talk more. He suggested further that if they did not want Dr. P to work on it he could refer them to a good friend who is a family therapist. The man said that he did not think that the situation was that bad and he was afraid to upset his wife. Dr. P thought that the family sounded like the one depicted in the novel *Ordinary People*. He recommended the book to Bill. Five days later Bill called back. He and his wife wanted to bring the son in for a family interview. One of us (D.V.K.) was invited in as a consultant to the second and eighth interviews.

Haley's well-known book about Milton Erickson, *Uncommon Therapy* (Haley, 1973), is a useful one for thinking about therapy with military families. Erickson is delightfully creative in his use of reality to effect therapeutic change.

CONCLUSION

Family therapy with military families offers a blend of challenge and frustration. That is not what makes treating them different from civilian families. Rather, first, family therapy is more feeble than usual because of the power the military system has over its members. Second, the military family is separated from its family of origin. Nevertheless, we think that family therapy is a useful way to deal with personal problems in military personnel, be they on a biological, psychological, or social level.

The goals of therapy with military families can be very pragmatic. They include an effort to intensify the family's organization, increase the esprit de corps, and clarify the rank structure. An additional aim is to develop a boundary between the cold, rigid outside world and the interior of the family, where joy and human warmth can be part of living in any world.

REFERENCES

Boss, P. A clarification of the concept of psychological father presence in families experiencing ambiguity of boundary. *Journal of Marriage and the Family*, 1977, *39*, 141–151.
Bruce, E., & Bruce, P. *Mamas, don't let your babies grow up to be cowboys*. Nashville, Tenn.: Tree Publishing and Sugar Plum Music Co., 1975.
Eliot, T. S. The cocktail party. In *The complete poems and plays, 1909–1950*. New York: Harcourt, Brace & World, 1962. (Originally published, 1950.)
Haley, J. *Uncommon therapy*. New York: Norton, 1973.
Huizinga, J. *Homoludens, a study of the play element in culture*. Boston: Beacon Press, 1950.
Lagrone, D. M. The military family syndrome. *American Journal of Psychiatry*, 1978, *135*, 1040–1043.
Mead, M. *Male and female*. New York: Morrow, 1949.
Wolfe, T. *The right stuff*. New York: Farrar, Straus & Giroux, 1979.

8

Treating the Military Captive's Family

EDNA J. HUNTER

> . . . women and children—rebuilding their lives and perhaps building houses of cards with the hands they've been dealt.—Smith (1976)

Wartime loss is a significant source of stress for military family members. Such loss may be prolonged but temporary, as during armed conflicts, peacekeeping missions, or prisoner of war (POW) experiences. It may be ambiguous and indefinite as in the missing in action (MIA) or hostage experience, or it may be permanent, as when the servicemember is killed in action or has been presumed to have died in captivity. All these situations call for family adjustments to a severe crisis. Most family members adjust eventually; some do not do it very well and require help from the professional psychotherapist. All appear to benefit from group support from those in a similar situation.

This chapter deals specifically with families who were called upon to cope with the loss of a loved one during the Vietnam years from 1964 through 1973, and even longer for those whose husbands, fathers, or sons were listed as MIA or presumed to have died in captivity. Based on a 7-year longitudinal study carried out at the Center for Prisoner of War Studies in San Diego (Hunter, 1977; Plag, 1976) from 1971 through 1978, much was learned about how families cope with a prolonged, indefinite, ambiguous separation due to national conflict, and the process whereby families renegotiate marital and family roles upon the men's return. This chapter will also focus on programs, actions, and treatments for families undergoing crises such as a POW, hostage, or terroristic kidnapping, not only at the advent of capture or casualty, but during the indefinite period of separation and the time of reunion and reintegration.

Edna J. Hunter. Director, Family Research Center, United States International University, San Diego, California.

Because the situation was very different for wives, children, and parents where the men were eventually returned to freedom, in contrast to the situation where the men were presumed to have died or had been killed in captivity, or where their fate was or is still unknown, this chapter primarily addresses POW families. Although the studies at the Center included all Navy, Army, and Marine Corps POW/MIA families, I shall deal primarily, although not entirely, with research findings for the Navy POWs and their families since those men were the only ones for whom a carefully matched control sample of Vietnam veterans was available during the postreturn follow-up.

THE CENTER FOR POW STUDIES

There were over 130,000 American service personnel captured during World War II; over 7,000 were taken as POWs during the Korean War; and nearly 600 returned from Vietnam to United States control during Operation Homecoming in the spring of 1973. Add to those figures the wives, children, and parents, and it becomes obvious that thousands of individuals have been called upon to cope with this crisis. Moreover these figures do not include those whose loved ones remain in the MIA category. For some of the MIA families, the Vietnam war goes on today even though the fighting ended over a decade ago (Hunter, 1980a).

A Unique Research Opportunity

The Vietnam POW experience offered a unique opportunity to scientists to study the effects of prolonged extreme stress in real life rather than in the laboratory. It also afforded a chance to better understand the etiology of the excessively high morbidity and mortality rates in POW populations from other wars which had been reported in the literature (Beebe, 1975). For example, ex-POWs of the Japanese after World War II and of the Korean conflict showed a significantly higher mortality rate during the first 10 years postreturn, compared with those veterans who were not captured (Plag, 1974).

The men held in Southeast Asia were held longer (up to almost 9 years for some) than the POWs of World War II (4 years), Korea (3 years), or those held during the *Pueblo* incident or more recently by

Iran (approximately 1 year). Thus, when the men held in Vietnam were finally released, the worst was expected. Those who returned were *survivors*, since the men who could not cope with the long years of deprivation, torture, and degradation, or who were not given the opportunity to cope because of captor treatment, had already been plucked from the group. Moreover, all returnees had experienced extended weeks, months, or even years in solitary confinement during their captivity. Thus, at Homecoming in early spring of 1973 a group of exceptionally strong-willed individuals returned to their families. Antithetically, those very psychological characteristics or adaptive behaviors which made survival possible in captivity, tended to make the family reintegration process more difficult. These were qualities such as obsessive–compulsiveness, blunted affect, or tightly controlled emotions, rigidity and intolerance, extreme patriotism, "gearing down" and time-filling activities, mental gymnastics, the ability or preference for solitude, and a need for organization or "sameness" in the immediate environment.

During captivity these men went from high independence to total dependence; this was not so for the wives. One wife commented, "We needed very different kinds of rehabilitation when he came back but we didn't get it." Immature, dependent women had become capable, independent family managers. They had been forced to venture into the world outside, and after years of practice they found they enjoyed their independence and the newly acquired feeling of competence and increased self-esteem. True, they missed their husbands' companionship terribly. That feeling of loss did not diminish with the passage of time. Yet, on the husbands' return the wives were usually unwilling to relinquish their autonomy.

Many women had furthered their own educations and job skill training. Few worked during the men's absence because their children were their foremost concern and they had to be both mother and father. They became the family disciplinarian, a role few had filled previously, and they were hesitant to give it up when the men returned.

As for the men, when they finally came home, many had doubts. Would they be courtmartialed for actions during captivity, actions forced through hours or months of deprivations and calculated torture sessions? When they observed how the wives had grown and matured while they vegetated in a Rip Van Winkle time capsule, they sometimes wondered if they were really still needed. Children, through years of practice, continued to seek out mothers for permissions and allowances. When fathers tried to discipline, they found that even the slightest critical remark about the children's behavior evoked their wives' defensiveness because these innocuous remarks were interpreted as direct criticism of the manner in which the children had been reared during their absence.

In some families, rituals existed which the men had played no part in formulating. Teenagers were sometimes emotionally distanced; babies were complete strangers. However, other children welcomed their fathers back with open arms, waiting expectantly for them to be the "heroes" they had become in the children's minds. But the men did not feel like heroes; some even brought back guilt feelings about their actions while in captivity.

It was to be expected that all family members had many adjustments to make before the family system again achieved any sort of satisfying homeostatic balance. The younger the couple at the time of casualty, the shorter the marriage, and the longer the period of separation, the greater the adjustments necessary after reunion. Adjustment is a process which occurs over time. In this chapter four discrete periods will be addressed, since the needs of these families, the research findings, and the treatment implications differed during each of those time frames, which were (1) the precapture period; (2) the crisis of capture; (3) the advent of Homecoming; and (4) the family reintegration period. First, however, a brief description of the Vietnam POW population is in order before continuing.

THE VIETNAM POW STUDY SAMPLE

In early 1973, the United States ended its active combat role in Vietnam, and a total of 566 U.S. servicemen were released, some of whom had been held as long as 9 years. The military group included 325 Air Force, 77 Army, 26 Marine Corps, and 138 Navy prisoners. All returned Navy POWs were aviation officers (102 pilots, 36 bombardier/navigators); their average age at time of capture was 30.8 years, and the duration of captivity averaged 61.7 months (Berg & Richlin, 1977). All but two of the Navy men were shot down over North Vietnam. Thus the Navy POW experience described herein is basically that of a captive held in North Vietnam rather than South Vietnam. These two captivity experiences differed significantly. As a prisoner in the North, the Navy POW's potential for physical survival was perhaps greater, but torture, brutality, and psychological stressors were also much greater. Consequently, if one survived at all, the residuals of captivity were likely to be more psychological in nature rather than physical, as would be expected for POWs held in South Vietnam.

Over 70% of the 138 Navy POWs were married at the time of capture and most had children. Prior to February 1973 when the American POWs were released, a total of 215 Army, Navy, and Marine Corps POW/MIA families had been personally interviewed by the Center for POW Studies professional staff. Of those interviewed, 100 were families of POWs, and the remaining 115 were families of servicemembers classified as MIA. Interviews began in the spring of 1972 and were discontinued when word finally came through in January 1973 that the POWs would be released in the near future.

In this chapter, the discussion of the Center's findings concerning the families' adjustment and their utilization of professional assistance during the separation period is based primarily on this sample of 215 POW/MIA wives. Later, with the return of the POWs and the longitudinal 5-year medical and family follow-up, the subsequent discussions are based primarily on data gathered from a subsample of the total sample, the 60 Navy POWs who had been married prior to capture and whose families had been personally interviewed by the Center's staff prior to the men's release. Data were also obtained from the remaining 78 of the 138 Navy POWs who were not interviewed personally, through mailed questionnaires or questionnaires completed at the time of their annual medical examinations. A carefully matched control group became available in 1975 for the 60-family Navy POW subsample. Thus it was possible beginning with the third postrelease follow-up (1976–1977) to be more definitive concerning findings. With such a comparison group it was finally possible to answer the following question: *Are the problems or characteristics found in POWs and their family members any different from those found in any comparable military family with similar marital status, family structure, and military history?*

THE PRECAPTURE PERIOD

FAMILY PREPARATION PRIOR TO DEPLOYMENT

No one knows who will become a POW. All military personnel are candidates; thus all military families must be prepared for such a crisis. Any treatment plans or programs needed for families during the precapture period should entail taking what is known about routine military separation and reunion, incorporating the knowledge gleaned from POW studies of prolonged indefinite separation, and then implementing support services for all military families who are about to face deployment.

The Center's studies showed that the more active, socially oriented, working wives, and wives with children coped better with separation. Ironically, young military men often discourage wives from learning to drive or from taking an active part in wives' groups. The studies also showed that wives who were in a similar situation were the most helpful to each other during family disruptions. Thus self-help groups should be encouraged for wives coping with husband absence.

The immature, extremely dependent wife, foreign-born wives, and wives who are isolated within a civilian community are the ones most likely to experience severe problems during deployments. They are least informed about the services available to them. The husband may have intentionally neglected to bring home information on social activities planned for wives during deployment because he prefers that she stay at home, waiting for him. These young wives are also more likely than the older, more outgoing, experienced wives to believe that there is a stigma attached to reaching out for help. Further, they often neither drive nor have the money for transportation or child care which would allow them to go where support services are located.

Adequate preparation of the family for separation during the pre-deployment period has been found to be significantly related to satisfactory family adjustment during the husband's absence. Many questions should be addressed by marital couples prior to the husbands' departure. Based on findings from POW studies, most couples never discuss the possibility of the husband not returning, or of returning after a prolonged absence due to captivity. If necessary, the wives should take the initiative and ask pertinent questions. Is there a power of attorney? Do both spouses have a will? Wives may believe it is unnecessary for them to have wills drawn up also, and yet there were instances where children of POWs were suddenly without either a father or mother when illness or death of the mother occurred after the father was already missing or captured.

Being prepared takes away many of the anxieties and stresses for separated couples since they have already made joint decisions on important family matters. The Center's studies showed that POW couples who had open communication prior to the casualty and had been able to discuss such matters coped better with the separation period, had fewer problems, and were less likely to experience divorce upon the men's return.

In a recent workshop on the Quality of Military Family Life (Hunter, 1980b; Orthner, 1980), the issues of *money, education,* and *coordination of services* were repeatedly mentioned. Wives of deploying men should be well informed. They should know what bills must be paid, what assets are available to them. Routinely, prior to deployment, financial records should be brought up-to-date. Husbands should make certain that wives (or a bank trustee) have powers of attorney so that stocks, bonds, houses, and cars can be bought and sold, should the men be gone considerably longer than anticipated. Beneficiaries on insurance policies and pay records should be updated. When family assets are in the husbands' name only, if they are taken captive, wives find it impossible to make intelligent decisions or take appropriate actions on matters which affect the family. For example, during the Vietnam POW situation there were insurance policies, pay records, and bank accounts where a newly-wed POW/MIA had not changed the beneficiary or cosigner from the parent's or girl friend's name to that of his bride prior to departure. Such oversights increased family stresses and resulted in conflictual situations for those left behind. Research shows that egalitarian families with open communication cope better with stressful family disruptions. If couples are unable to communicate effectively, they should be advised to seek marital counseling or communication skills training prior to separation.

The "unknowns" surrounding any deployment or captivity are difficult factors with which families must cope. Thus, as far as possible, wives should be briefed prior to deployment concerning their husbands' military assignment. Not only should they learn about the predictable stresses they will feel, they should also be knowledgeable about the stresses, feelings of boredom, and loneliness their husbands will experience. Wives who feel they are part of the "team" are more willing to make the sacrifices necessary during family disruptions. Family commitment to organizational goals can be more important in a peacetime military than it is during time of national conflict.

COPING WITH LOSS

Wives whose husbands deploy typically go through various stages analogous to the process of grieving. Simply knowing in advance about some of the feelings they may experience after the husband leaves attenuates much of the stress that would otherwise be experienced. For example, military couples often argue immediately prior to deployment, perhaps to make parting easier or perhaps merely in anticipation of the separation to come. Unfortunately, if the husband later is captured or declared missing, perhaps even killed in action, the "Oh, why didn't I?" syndrome occurs, accompanied by ruminations, guilt, depression, and anger. If the wives understand their feelings are normal, they are less likely to worry unnecessarily, sometimes to the point of wondering if they may be losing control emotionally. Insight into these feelings may prevent the wives from turning feelings inward, or venting their anger upon children who will be puzzled by this phenomenon.

Wives should be informed about effective coping behaviors during the separation which facilitate reunion, such as closing out the husbands' roles partially *but not completely*; being willing to assume the disciplinary role so that children will not be lacking both parents; and maintaining family rituals and celebrations, such as birthdays, holidays, and vacations. Routine assists all family members, and especially the children, in coping during separations, as well as readjusting after the man's return.

Wives find it helpful to approach the separation as an opportunity for personal growth, a chance to further social contacts with other wives in similar situations, and a time to pursue outside employment or to further educational goals or technical skills. The POW studies showed that those wives who were more active in such activities coped better with the void.

SUMMARY OF PREDEPLOYMENT INTERVENTIONS

Suggestions for predeployment programs or treatment services are primarily of a proactive or preventive nature. One such recommendation is that a predeployment family check-up be instituted as a routine procedure. This check-up would *educate*, *inform*, and *update*, and would include both a financial and legal check-up. This orientation package would be under the guidance of trained professionals and paraprofessionals who are familiar with the network of civilian and military services, and are knowledgeable about the typical process of coping with military separations. Orientation sessions should be repeated immediately prior to reunion, both for families at home and for the men overseas. Although the need for the availability of family counseling during separation has long been recognized, research shows it is also necessary prior to deployment and even more so after the return of the husband.

Still another suggestion is that a "military family advisor" or "sponsor" be appointed for each deployed member *prior* to detachment, and that a "dial-a-regulation" hot line be available to wives for the immediate obtaining of information needed throughout the separation. These, plus other preventive services such as marital enrichment programs, communication skills training, and parenting skills classes, could effectively close the gap between the availability of family support services, families' awareness of them, and their utilization. Affordable child-care services must be made available to allow wives to utilize these programs.

Another suggestion is that wives' clubs be officially recognized as an arm of the military organization and that they be encouraged to provide group support for wives of deployed men. Moreover, the approach used by the clubs should be one of active outreach to facilitate contact with isolated or alienated wives who are more likely to need assistance, but who are without the personal resources to reach out to obtain it (McEvoy, 1982).

Finally, an evaluative research component should be built into all family programs to measure their efficacy over time to make certain they are meeting families' needs. The final outcome would lead to reduction in duplication and the elimination of weak programs, resulting in lower health-care costs for the military without decreasing the quality of service.

THE CRISIS

Man [*sic*, or woman] is an adaptive animal . . . and though he is a product of his environment, and may be subjugated and destroyed by a strange one, he must constantly attempt to work within it, to mold it, and to rise above it. It is the key to survival.
—Kushner (1974)

In combat the hazards are obvious, but however well prepared military men are to meet with danger, when they become captives, a common first reaction is, "This just can't be happening to me." During the initial hours after being captured they experience feelings of unreality, "It can't be true . . . I'll wake up and be back on the ship" (Stratton, 1978). Wives of captives or hostages also initially register disbelief and numbness when they learn their husbands are missing or prisoners. Both spouses use denial to cope with the unexpected crisis.

THE PROCESS OF GRIEVING

Among the families of the Vietnam POWs, the event of casualty meant sudden drastic changes for all concerned. At the moment of capture POWs were plummeted from independence to complete dependence; simultaneously, the wives went from almost complete dependence to unaccustomed independence. Both suffered great loss; both experienced extreme aloneness. One of the Vietnam MIA wives, commenting on the Iranian hostage families, expressed vividly what families go through in the weeks following capture:

> The families . . . are probably experiencing all of Kübler-Ross's steps of the grief cycle, on a "temporary" basis. They are bouncing back and forth within that cycle . . . experiencing a sense of helplessness. . . . They cannot take charge of the issue that has disrupted their lives; it is far too big. . . . Wives will experience intense fear for their husbands' safety. They will also be angry, because they have been left alone, and then they will feel guilty because they are angry . . . the final outcome is uncertain; the "limbo" could end tomorrow or next year. . . . Some wives may be able to reach decisions, based only on their husbands' pre-stated wishes. . . . Others may be able to demonstrate more independence or autonomy. Some may be paralyzed. (Foley, 1980, p. 2)

Ambiguity and indefiniteness characterize any captivity experience; thus relatives are also victims or "captives," and they find it difficult in the beginning to take positive actions to resolve their situations. Studies have shown that both men and women experience similar, parallel stages of adjustment in coping with their losses. Both pass through the classic stages of denial, anger, bargaining, depression, but with no final acceptance of their losses until release comes. In that respect, the process of grieving over the captivity of one's spouse may be even more difficult than dealing with death, because the POW situation is ambiguous and indefinite. The loved one may be alive or dead. He may come home in 1 month, 1 year, or never.

For these wives there will be loneliness, guilt, anger, alienation, isolation, and hostility, all mixed up together. These feelings may be directed toward the self, the husband, the military, and/or the therapist. But someone who is knowledgeable, who understands, is empathic, and who listens, is crucial. The family *must* be allowed to grieve. No "stiff upper lip"; no "everything is going to be all right"; or, "That's not the way a 'good' military wife acts." As mentioned earlier, other wives who have suffered a similar loss are the individuals most helpful in this early stage.

In the Vietnam captivity experience, most wives grieved and remained in their "limbo state" for 1 or 2 years before an apparently conscious decision was made that in order to survive they had to stop "marking time in place" and get on with living. They partially or completely closed out the husbands' roles within the families. They went about the daily routines, making major family decisions as if the husbands were no longer part of the family unit. Closing out their roles made for better functioning, although doing so may have made the reunion process more problematic. Wives who were unable or unwilling to close out the husbands' roles appeared generally to have coped less well with the years of separation. Each wife had to find her own unique way of coping, and only time and a personal history of successful coping led to resolution. Wives coped differently with their losses than did the parents of captives, and children tended to cope about as well as their mothers did.

TREATMENT IMPLICATIONS

The major treatment implication for the time of crisis is the importance of good organization/family communication lines. The "military family advisor" or "sponsor" designated for routine deployments, which was recommended earlier, could also serve a critical function at the time of a major crisis. He would be the families' liaison with the military organization, and would be there for troublesome administrative matters and to run interference with the media when requested to do so by the family. (Surprisingly, for some families, media contact was viewed as very helpful rather than as intrusive.)

During the Vietnam conflict, POW/MIA families were assigned advisors—CACOs (Casualty Assistance Officers in the Navy) or FASOs (Family Assistance Services Officers in the Army). Unfortunately at times these administrative sponsors tried to serve the role of professional therapist as well, a role which often they were not trained to fill.

Crisis intervention should be available when needed, and there should be close liaison with the family members, especially during the first few months subsequent to the crisis, a time when the families' needs and confusion are greatest. There should be a telephone hot line direct to a Washington contact which families can use at any time.

Even where there is absolutely nothing new to report, military officials should be urged to keep in regular close contact with the families.

The sponsor should emphasize that no news does not necessarily mean that nothing is being done. Phone contact, initiated by the military whenever world events warrant reassurance, explanation, or elaboration, supplies an "emotional stabilizer" which reminds the families that they have not been forgotten, and that someone cares (Foley, 1980).

Immediately after a crisis, families undergo extreme stress. Families should be made aware of the availability of professional and paraprofessional help. Family members must be urged to express their feelings, be it to each other, to understanding friends, to professional counselors, or to members of the clergy. Sharing emotions, whether they are viewed as "good" or "bad," is essential (Foley, 1980). Details concerning the casualty should be shared with the family members; they should not be "protected." Facing the possibility that the loved one may not return can assist in eventual resolution, especially if he does not. The captive is not the only casualty; the family is also a victim.

COPING WITH THE LONG SEPARATION

Waiting calls for patience, maturity, I don't do it very well. But you don't have to do it very well. You just have to do it.—Ebbert (1973)

The longitudinal study at the Center was designed to investigate the family as one source of stress for the returning POW which could affect his immediate and long-term adjustment after release (Plag, 1976). Those wives who perceived their marriages as highly satisfactory prior to their husbands' capture and who coped well during the separation period, it was hypothesized, were also likely to be the ones who would offer the greatest support to the men upon their release. If families were supported during the disruption, they could perhaps better cope with reunion.

During the year prior to the POWs' release, data were collected from a total of 215 wives, using a structured interview format. Single in-depth interviews, ranging in length from 2 to 8 hours, were conducted with these wives living throughout the continental United States, Hawaii, Puerto Rico, and Europe. At the time of these first interviews, wives' ages ranged from 20 to 49, with an average of 33.2 years. The educational level of the majority was in excess of 12 years; one third had received college degrees. Although the families averaged two children each, 20% had no children. The 405 children in these families ranged in age from less than 1 year to

25 years of age, with the majority between the ages of 8 and 15. Over 50% of the couples had been married over 10 years at the time of the first interviews.

FAMILY PROBLEMS DURING SEPARATION

Analysis of the initial interview data showed that the most difficult area of adjustment during the separation was the loss of the husband's companionship, followed by feelings of extreme loneliness, making decisions alone, lack of social outlets, and child discipline. Although physical health problems were not reported by the wives as one of the more difficult areas, a variety of illnesses were mentioned which had required medical attention during the husbands' absence, such as influenza and allergies (mentioned by almost half the group), respiratory ailments, and gastrointestinal disturbances.

Emotional and psychological adjustments seemed more prevalent than physical disturbances. Nearly three fourths of the sample reported having experienced five or more of the symptoms covered in the interview. The most frequently reported symptom was that of feeling depressed or "down in the dumps." Disturbed sleep patterns were also cited, as were feelings of jumpiness or being "uptight." Over half the wives either were taking or had taken tranquilizers. Over 40% reported frequent "feelings that life was meaningless" and that they had entertained suicidal thoughts. The impact of the husband's captivity on his wife was considerable. Over 30% of the wives were either receiving psychotherapy at the time of the interview or had been in treatment at some time during the husbands' absence.

Understandably, children's problems added to the mothers' stress. The most frequently reported physical health problems among the 405 children were common childhood diseases (41%), accidental injuries (18%), and surgeries (12%). Children's emotional adjustment presented more problems for these families than physical ailments. For families with children, the average number of emotional or behavioral problems was 4.3 per family. The most frequently reported symptoms were excessive crying, nightmares, rebelliousness, extreme shyness, nail biting, and fear of the dark. Among the social and interpersonal adjustments of the children, school behavior problems were most frequent, followed by poor relationships, and behavior problems at home. Of the 69 children judged by their mothers to have significant emotional problems, only 37 had obtained professional counseling for the child. Wherever possible, children were interviewed personally by the Center's professional staff. Of the 102 children personally seen, over 25% were evaluated as needing psychological or psychiatric counseling (McCubbin, Hunter, & Metres, 1974).

During the prereturn interviews, the wives mentioned many apprehensions concerning the reunion period, the major one being their husbands' reactions to the wives' increased independence. The wives' lack of frugality, having dated during the husbands' absence, and the manner in which they had raised the children were also major concerns. The majority of the wives were also apprehensive about their husbands' abilities to adjust to the rapid social changes which had occurred during the long absence, about their health, and about the renegotiation of family roles that was anticipated after the husbands' return.

There were many legal issues which arose because of the questionable status of the husbands, some of which were without legal precedent. Over 30% of the wives had no power of attorney from their husbands. Consequently, many problems were encountered in the purchase or sale of personal and real property during the years of the husband's absence. Other problems centered around obtaining credit, the husband having no will, and the decision to terminate the marriage when there was no method for "serving papers" on the husband, even where the wife was certain he had not survived, or when the marriage had been unsatisfactory even prior to the casualty. The legal difficulties experienced bring into focus the need for established guidelines for servicemembers which anticipate the wide range of potential problems inherent in a combat tour and the value of adequate preparation of military families *prior* to deployment.

Despite the wives' efforts to perform their roles well, during the indeterminate absence they received little satisfactory feedback and had to deal with the realization that there were few if any socially acceptable outlets for women in their situations (Boss, 1980). There was much guilt; even the most stable and mature wives experienced emotional problems at times. After the husbands' return, marriages were seen by some wives as "renegotiable," with demands that their husbands give consideration and recognition to their newly acquired abilities and skills.

Prior to the captives' release, it was predicted by the Center's staff that approximately 30% of the marriages would be terminated almost immediately after the return of the men (Hunter, 1972). The wives' apprehensions about the future of their marriages focused upon the specific period of reunion. The Center's data suggest that after release from captivity, families' adjustment during separation can indeed influence the families' adjustment and the men's personal adjustment. Thus the families' adjustment during separation and their apprehensions about repatriation must be considered important factors in the formula for the successful reunion and readjustment of returned captives.

During the Vietnam conflict the unprecedented length of the men's absences made for complex issues. When reunion looked imminent, those families who had had no word from their loved ones during the separation wondered whether to plan for the men's return or for a confirmation of death; in most cases, they planned for both. Anxieties ran high when word finally came through in January 1973 that the POWs were soon to be released.

IMPLICATIONS FOR TREATMENT DURING PROLONGED SEPARATION

The importance of having an effective support system for families in place prior to the separation has already been discussed. The data collected immediately prior to the POWs' release pointed up the discrepancy between the families' needs for services and their limited contacts with such services. The casualty assistance programs mentioned earlier appeared to have been fairly effective at the time of Homecoming for administrative matters. They could not meet the many emotional needs of these families, however. During the Center's interviewing, when wives were asked to list the characteristics they most desired in an assistance officer, they listed maturity, referral ability, empathy, and the ability to establish a professional relationship, as the four most important requirements. It appears that other services are needed in a captivity situation in addition to an effective casualty assistance officer who handles administrative matters. For example, legal assistance is needed prior to separation, during the separation period, and at the time of reunion. The military's traditional attitude that "if the family needs legal help, it will ask for it" was found to be a myth. Many families did not know they needed legal help until it was too late. A legal check-up is especially recommended for families experiencing deployments.

The need for a more effective approach to extending services to these families under stress was suggested by the Center's initial interviews, and an outreach family services plan was put into effect shortly after the men's release from captivity (Hunter & Plag, 1973). The Homecoming period is a particularly critical time for families. Adequate and accurate briefings of both the family members and the returning men prior to actual Homecoming should be made.

Prior to the release of the POWs from Southeast Asia, a recommendation was made by the Center's staff (Segal, 1974) that a short "decompression" period be instituted for these men prior to family reunion to allow them time for a complete medical examination and to adjust briefly to freedom after their long, stressful captivity. Operations planners, however, decided that logistically such a delay was impractical and the men were returned immediately with only a 24- to 36-hour stopover at Clark Air Force Base en route. When the men arrived stateside to greet their families, some had not slept for almost 7 days! Almost immediately they were caught up in a whirlwind of wives who had changed, children who had grown, relatives who awaited eagerly to hear their stories, members of the media, and thousands of well-wishers. True, the men were deliriously happy to be free, but they were overwhelmed, and they felt an obligation to speak at every function to which they were invited, to show gratitude for their freedom. Many were off on a "chicken salad circuit," as the POWs called it, for the next year, and family adjustments were often further postponed or made more difficult.

Future homecomings should include a planned "delay" before reunion with the family. Former POWs, when later questioned on this matter, said that although they might have raised some objection at the time about a delay overseas prior to family reunions, they now agreed with the Center's recommendation. Hindsight told them that a brief hiatus to catch their breath would have been better both for the adjustment of the returning POWs, and for their families.

Two other suggestions for future captivity experiences can be made based on the findings from the POW studies. First, *opportunities for small group support with other families in a similar status should be arranged almost immediately after the servicemember's capture.* The Vietnam conflict had already dragged on from 1964 until 1969—5 years—before the families, on their own initiative, finally got together for group support. Initially, the government had kept information from the wives and parents about others who were experiencing a similar loss.

Second, *wives whose husbands are missing in action should not be kept in an ambiguous status indefinitely.* After a reasonable time, perhaps

1 year, if no information is forthcoming to indicate the husband is definitely alive, the missing person's status should be changed to "presumed died in action" to allow families to resume "normal" living. Certainly, some wives may believe that their husbands are alive and choose to wait for them indefinitely, but that would be their option. Early in the Vietnam conflict, a decision was made by the military not to change any of the MIAs' status until the end of the conflict, undoubtedly a policy based upon the belief that the war would surely end within 6 months to a year. As the years passed, however, no one in the top echelon was willing, or had the courage, to change that policy. Many wives were firmly convinced that their husbands were dead. In some instances they were even told that the government also believed that the husbands were dead, and yet these wives were unable to have their husbands' status changed and proceed toward final resolution of their grief.

Psychologically, such a policy was damaging. It exacerbated the adjustments necessary when the status of the men was finally changed many years later. Yet, monetarily it was rewarding since the military continued to pay the husbands' full salaries, including flight pay if applicable, to the wives throughout the period while they were classified as MIA. Considered from a broader perspective, however, the policy was not equitable. There were many Vietnam widows, some of whose husbands' bodies were never recovered, who drew only one lump insurance payment of perhaps $25,000. The MIA wives, after 5 to 9 years, received that same amount plus another $200–300,000 in wages. These monies certainly alleviated financial problems for MIA families, but most MIA wives agreed that the added monies did not adequately compensate for the years of ambiguity the policy created.

HOMECOMING

Few men have the opportunity to be born again . . . to be able to stand in freedom again . . . to see the sun shining on the flowers, the trees, and the grass . . . to see clouds rolling past the hills in the distance . . . to hear birds sing . . . and more than that, to be able to share love with our families and friends again.—A returned POW (1973)

Five hundred and sixty-six men long referred to as "war criminals" by their captors, who had been underfed, tortured, and denied medical treatment for their injuries, returned home in early spring 1973, as *heroes.* Operation Homecoming had been in the planning stages for many years in anticipation of these men's release. There were few logistical problems encountered in carrying it out.

Although initial planning called for medical processing of the men at Clark Air Force Base in the Philippine Islands for 14 days prior to their return to the States, most of the POWs were winging their way home within 2 to 3 days after release from Hanoi. The excitement of release maintained most of the POWs at an emotional peak for several days. Nonetheless, the hectic pace had telling effects. Some families felt they desperately needed additional time to prepare emotionally for the POWs' return, and hospitals found many of the prisoners extremely fatigued upon their arrival. However, considering the men's surprisingly good physical appearance and their own and others' eager anticipation of their return to the States, the pressure to curtail the stay at Clark was irresistible. A directive to allow the prisoners to depart "as soon as medically feasible" served as a ready justification for the abbreviated stay. Although the consensus of the medical personnel in charge opposed a 14-day layover at Clark, most indicated that a delay of from 5 to 7 days would have been preferable to only 36 hours.

Prior to the release, a valiant attempt had been made to update the men's personal files which were to be used at Clark to brief each returnee individually on any changes which had taken place within his family during his absence about which he was unaware. Although "bad news" items had been periodically included in the files, many of the packets were inaccurate or incomplete. Chaplains and medical staff counseled and comforted those men who were immediately confronted with unexpected adverse information. Some experts felt that the bad news items were released before the men were ready psychologically. Certain POWs appeared incapable of assimilating the information. All men were allowed to call home from Clark shortly after arrival; some refused to call home, fearing the worst after hearing of fellow POWs' emotionally disastrous calls. For some POWs, the bad news was delayed and delivered personally by the wives or parents immediately upon arrival stateside as they were driven to the Regional Medical Hospital.

However, most families were ecstatic at reunion. Daddy was finally home; mother could get on with a normal existence. The question was, what is "normal" after families have been through an experience like this one?

Indeed, the deprivation and denigration the men had been subjected to, as well as their almost superhuman ability to cope with severe stresses, could have been expected to affect families which had coped admirably without the men. Although the focus of this chapter is on family adjustment to the captivity experience, since the men's physical and emotional condition at time of Homecoming could be expected to influence family adjustment, captivity effects on the POW must first be addressed before examining family reintegration postreunion.

The emphasis during Operation Homecoming was on the medical evaluation and treatment of the POWs, and a minimum 90-day period on the hospital sicklist was mandated for every man after his arrival back in the continental United States. The tally at the end of Operation Homecoming was a total of 1528 formal diagnoses for men from all military services, representing medical problems requiring treatment, or at least evaluation. Most of these diagnoses were still active problems at the time of Homecoming, but some, such as old well-healed fractures, were merely a notation in the medical record (Berg, 1974).

The average number of diagnoses per POW was 5.0 for the Navy POWs, 5.6 for the Marines, and 8.9 for the Army (the Air Force medical follow-up was not under the aegis of the Center for POW Studies). According to follow-up medical records (Richlin, 1981), there were significant medical problems: 90% had intestinal worms; 45% had orthopedic injuries which had not been treated by their captors; 34% had peripheral neuropathies; almost all had severe dental problems; and 30% of the Army POWs were positive for malaria screens.

There were four major categories of diagnoses: injuries, infectious and parasitic diseases, malnutrition, and psychiatric and adjustment problems. Since the latter are those which are most likely to affect family functioning in the postreturn period, the discussion here will be limited to psychiatric and adjustment residuals of captivity.

Psychiatric examinations were an integral part of the medical evaluation given the POWs. Most of the diagnoses were neurotic disorders; therefore, the prognoses were good. Five POWs, not Navy men, were diagnosed as schizophrenic. In each of these cases there was evidence of some precapture morbidity (Berg, 1974). (See Table 8-1.)

All POWs went through some degree of adjustment during repatriation. Medical staff noted the following typical pattern of adjusting to freedom. During the first few days after release the men were hyperactive; they were excited, euphoric, and voluble. They slept little, and bounced rapidly from topic to topic and activity to activity. That response was superseded by a few days of relatively subdued activity, followed by another period where they were eager to return quickly to active duty. They wanted to hurry and finish the medical evaluation, catch up with

TABLE 8-1. Psychiatric Diagnoses and Adjustment Problems in POWs at Time of Homecoming

	Number of returned POWs[a]			
Problem	All three services	Navy	Army	Marines
Situational anxiety	10	3	6	1
Depression	6	1	4	1
Schizophrenia	5	0	3	2
Other psychiatric problems	7	3[b]	4[c]	0
Career adjustment	23	16	4	3
Depression	22	11	5	6
Anxiety	18	13	4	1
Adjustment to injury	10	7	2	1
Hyperactivity	6	5	1	0

[a] Number in each service: Navy = 138, Army = 77, Marines = 26; total = 241.
[b] Alcoholism.
[c] Psychosis, 1; sociopathic personality, 1; dissociative reaction,; alcoholism, 1.

family matters, and finish all other tasks immediately so they could get back to duty. Eventually, after realizing they did not really have to "prove themselves" and make up for lost time, they tended to settle down to the mandatory 90-day convalescence requirement (Berg, 1974).

Looking back, not all of the men were ready to leave Clark in 36 hours; not all families were ready to reunite immediately; and not all returned POWs were ready to go back to duty at the end of 90 days. Others readjusted fairly rapidly. Perhaps the one major recommendation for future Operation Homecoming plans would be for more flexibility, and more tailoring to meet the needs of both the men and their families.

FAMILY REINTEGRATION FOLLOWING CAPTIVITY

Crisis? Hell, anybody can handle a crisis. It's this day-to-day living that gets you.—Clifford Odets, *The Country Girl*

The postreunion period was an extremely difficult one. Neither a captive nor his family could go through a situation like the Vietnam POW experience *without* being affected. The adjustment of Vietnam POW families was assessed by the professional staff of the Center each year for

5 years following the release of the men. All ex-POWs were given a complete medical examination annually, and all members of the Navy families in the follow-up sample (60 families) were personally interviewed in their homes. All other families of the POWs returned in 1973 were followed through mailed questionnaires. One hundred percent of the Navy POWs participated in the longitudinal medical follow-up (carried out at the Pensacola Navy Aerospace Medical Institute), and all but a handful of the Navy couples agreed to take part in the 5-year family follow-up. Due to space limits, only major conclusions concerning family adjustment at each follow-up period will be presented, together with implications for treatment derived from the study.

POW FAMILIES ONE YEAR AFTER REUNION

Each year data were collected to assess each spouse's personal emotional adjustment, the ex-POW's occupational adjustment, marital adjustment, and parent–child relationships. A brief overview of the major findings follows.

Personal Emotional Adjustment

One year following reunion, the variable which correlated highest with the POWs' personal adjustment was spousal agreement on the handling of family finances, followed by the level of the men's self-esteem, spousal agreement on the wives' career plans, parenting roles of husbands and wives, and marital adjustment. These relationships appeared to reflect the evolving renegotiation of family roles which was taking place during that first year back. Wives emphasized the importance they placed on the husbands' recognition of the wives' roles and responsibilities. Where the husbands were able to adjust to a more egalitarian family structure, their personal adjustment was better.

Career Adjustment

One might expect that men who received the worst treatment during captivity would have more difficulty getting back into their jobs. Surprisingly, first-year follow-up data showed that resistance toward the captor and the amount of harsh treatment meted out were not significantly related to the ex-POWs' subsequent career adjustment. Career adjustment had the highest correlation with high spousal agreement on family tasks or roles. Where the men were performing well on the job, they appeared to be experiencing good marital adjustment and excellent relationships with their children. Thus, men who were adjusting well in one area were likely to be adjusting well in all other major areas.

Marital Adjustment

The husbands' and wives' perceptions of the family and its functioning differed in many instances. Based upon wives' reports, the most crucial factor in good marital adjustment was spousal agreement on the husbands' future career plans. Another important factor for the wives was spousal agreement on family roles and values. The wives' levels of self-esteem played a part in how they judged their marriages. Higher self-esteem was associated with better marital adjustment. Other related factors for wives were spousal agreement on the amount of affection shown within their relationships and on sexual matters. For the husbands, good communication was the factor which correlated highest with their perceptions of good marital adjustment. As with the wives, the POWs' self-esteem was highly related to perception of high marital adjustment. For both, agreement as to who did what within the family was more important in explaining perceived marital adjustment than who actually performed which roles. It was not whether the family structure was traditional, egalitarian, or role reversed, but whether the partners *agreed* on those role relationships that was the important factor in perceived marital happiness.

Father–Child Relations

During the fathers' absence, generally, how well children coped was a direct reflection of how well the mothers were coping with the separation. Findings indicated that where mothers perceived either that they were the ones who made the final decisions or that decisions were made jointly by the parents, father–child relationships were perceived as better. Self-reports of both parents showed there was high agreement between them on how satisfactory father–child relationships were 1 year after release.

Results showed that the greater the discrepancy in parental perceptions on family roles and tasks, the worse the father–child relationship. Data also indicated that POWs who had received the harshest treatment during captivity were those who were most likely to hold divergent views, compared with those of their wives, with regard to how the children should be disciplined. More open communication was associated with minimal differences between parents regarding child discipline. Where the father viewed disciplining solely as his role, there was higher spousal disagreement. Here again, where the wife had been performing the role of disciplinarian for many years, she appeared reluctant to relinquish the role.

The ex-POWs' resistance posture during captivity was shown to have relevance for father–child relationships. *The firmer the resister during captivity, the more authoritarian a father he was likely to be after return.* Results showed that firm resistance during captivity was associated with more traditional sex roles for family members. If discrepancies between the husbands' and wives' perceptions of family roles and responsibilities reflect failure to renegotiate the marriage, then one may conclude that families of the firmer resisters were not reintegrating as quickly in this early postreturn period, compared with those POWs who had held less firm resistance during captivity.

However, another finding suggests an alternative conclusion. Resistance posture during captivity was not significantly related to the husbands' or wives' personal adjustment, marital adjustment, or career adjustment. Each family is a unique system, and perhaps those who were able to communicate openly concerning the changes which had occurred, or where the wives were willing to relinquish duties previously performed or, conversely, the husbands were willing for wives to continue performing certain roles, both marital adjustment and father–child relations were better. Families changed their roles and rules according to their own demands. Some families became more egalitarian; others quickly reverted to the traditional stereotypic sex roles found in typical military families. Husbands and wives alike were called upon to recognize that changes had taken place in their relationships over the years, and both partners had to change after Homecoming if family adjustment was to be achieved.

POW FAMILIES TWO YEARS AFTER REUNION

For the men, the "recuperation" period had ended by the 2-year mark, and a number of personal and career adjustment problems became more prominent. Over 20% of the POWs were showing symptoms of depression, and almost 30% reported they had experienced some degree of dissatisfaction with their military or civilian assignments during the preceding year. Several (12%) appeared to lack self-confidence in performing their jobs and had experienced difficulty in concentrating or in getting along with coworkers. A common observation of their wives was that the husbands held "unrealistic expectations" for themselves in relation to their military careers. Over 15% of the husbands were reported to have experienced adjustment difficulties which had either occurred for the first time, or had become major problems during the past year.

As for wives, although almost a third reported no problems with their personal emotional adjustment, interview results showed that almost one fourth of the wives indicated that jealousy was a problem for them. The wives believed their ability to communicate with the children was better than that of the husbands and many (one third) still indicated there were father–child relationship problems.

Nonetheless, the wives saw definite strengths in their marriages, specifically noting the financial security they enjoyed (mentioned by over 60%), their husbands' maturity, the emotional closeness between the marital dyad, and good family health. One fourth reported plans to have more children. These marriages appeared to have become more stable, and although divorces continued to occur, the numbers diminished each year.

By this time, there were fewer problems for these families in a number of areas. Significantly fewer wives had required medical attention or professional counseling than during the previous year. Not as many of the families reported they had sought financial counseling. Wives perceived their marriages were stronger, mentioning their mutual respect for each other as a contributing factor. Even the father–child relationships, regardless of birth order of child, were reported to have improved.

However, there were three areas which families mentioned as presenting greater problems for them than they had during the previous year. Making family decisions and planning for the future were seen as more problematic. Perhaps by then the men had decided it was time to step out of the POW role and had become more career-oriented. Perhaps decisions had been made for the men by the military organization with respect to future flying status or career assignments. Or perhaps they were viewing promotional prospects within the military with a more critical gaze. Significantly fewer men were on active duty at this time.

The major problems reported by these families 2 years postrelease, in order of decreasing frequency, were parent–child relationships (24%), the marital relationship (19%), personal adjustment of the family members (19%), and occupational adjustment (12%). According to the families, solutions had been found for over 60% of the major problems mentioned during the interviews, and although over a third of the problems remained unresolved, the families expressed optimism that things would definitely improve for them over the coming year (Hunter, 1977).

POW FAMILIES AT THE TIME OF THE THIRD FOLLOW-UP

Due to logistical and funding problems, the third follow-up spanned a 2-year time frame (1976–1977). Over the preceding 2-year period, whenever the problems of POW families were discussed, a question which was repeatedly asked was this: How do these POW families differ from the typical military family where the man had not been a captive?

At the third follow-up, for the first time a carefully matched control group was available for comparison purposes. In early 1975 procedures were initiated to select a comparison group for the 138 Navy ex-POWs. They were carefully matched on a number of variables, such as having flown missions in Vietnam within 1 year of the POWs' capture, age, year of commissioning, job designation, education, marital status, rank, total number of flight hours, and type of aircraft flown in Vietnam (Spaulding, Murphy, & Phelan, 1978). Within the group of 138 POWs, 101 POWs were married at the time of capture; 100 of the comparisons were married at the time they served in Vietnam. Sixty comparison subjects were selected from the total group of 100 to match the select sample of 60 Navy POWs who took part in the initial in-depth family follow-up.

Results of the third follow-up showed the divorce rate for POW families was at 32%, up from the 28% at the end of the first year. This rate was almost three times the 11–12% rate found in the comparison group. Other differences were noted. The POW families remained more matrifocal than the control families.

There was a decrease in the number of problems noted during the second year for POW families in the four major problem areas. The largest decrease was in the number of marital adjustment problems; the smallest decrease was with regard to personal or emotional adjustment of family members. The rank order of frequency of major problem remained the same as it was the previous year: parent–child, followed by personal, marital, and occupational adjustment. Between-group comparisons showed that the four major types of problems and their rank orders were the same for control and experimental group families.

The POW family members rated themselves as less independent and less cohesive than control families rated themselves, and wives of the POWs perceived their husbands' career adjustment significantly lower than did the control group wives. The health of the POW wives was comparable to that of control wives.

Other differences were that the comparison wives were more highly trained and more likely to be employed outside the home; POW wives were more likely to be full-time homemakers and planning for more children. Although POW wives reported more in-law problems, they also reported better sexual adjustment than control wives did. Moreover, managing the family budget was viewed as an easier task by POW wives, and POW families reported fewer financial worries.

Although parental modeling of appropriate behaviors for children now appeared less a problem, child discipline was reported as significantly more difficult than it had been previously—perhaps because the children were a year older and approaching their teens. When a problem did arise, however, POW families reported they felt more adequate to resolve it than they had the previous year.

POW FAMILIES AFTER THE FIFTH YEAR POSTRETURN

By the end of the fifth year families that had stayed together had fairly well renegotiated and stabilized the family roles and were well integrated. By the end of the Center's 7-year longitudinal study, family roles were again stable, families were future-oriented, and their concerns about what lay ahead were more an issue for them than any current problem. They felt adequate to cope with the latter. Nonetheless, because of their stressful prolonged separation and the treatment the husbands suffered during captivity, POW families may remain more at risk than other families to ordinary developmental family life crises in future years, such as the transition of retirement or of the "empty nest." Since the POWs have younger families or bimodal families due to the husband's long absence during the wife's child-bearing years, compared with controls, retirement may also prove more of a financial burden since children will reach college age much later. Also, wives of ex-POWs will be less likely to have the training or experience necessary to work outside the home.

Healthwise, after 5 years the Navy POWs were doing well, and a number of factors probably account for their excellent status. First, these men were a very select group—all officers, older than the Army and Marine Corps POWs, and strongly committed to their military careers. Secondly, under the guise of preventive medicine, they had been given excellent medical examinations and follow-up treatment postreturn, as well as having received social support services for their families. They had received survival training prior to captivity (Richlin, Rahe, Shale, & Mitchell, 1980). Delayed onset of physical or psychological problems in these former POWs could conceivably exacerbate personal or family transitions in the future. The outcome for the other Vietnam POWs who were held in South Vietnam is perhaps not as optimistic. This latter group, for the most part, were enlisted men who were younger, less committed to their jobs, and less highly trained than the Navy POWs we have been discussing.

What has been learned from this 7-year study is the importance of well-planned and carefully implemented medical and social support services for both active duty personnel and their families to assist them in coping with the crises of wartime stress such as POW or hostage-taking experiences, not only during family separation but also for at least 3 years after return (Nice, McDonald, & McMillian, 1981).

CONCLUSIONS

This chapter has examined implications for treatment of the families of captives or hostages based upon the findings from a 7-year longitudinal study of the adjustment of families of POWs during the Vietnam conflict. Specifically, the needs for treatment during four time frames were addressed: (1) the precapture period; (2) the crisis of capture; (3) the advent of Homecoming; and (4) the family reintegration period subsequent to the men's release from captivity.

Recommendations for the precapture period include a "pre-deployment family check-up" for each family; the assignment of a family sponsor to serve as a point of contact during the period of family disruption; and adequate briefings for all family members regarding available support services, and about the process of coping with the stresses of separation.

It is important that an adequate support system be *in place prior to the crisis*. It should be an outreach program which will be particularly responsive to the families' needs during the first weeks and months subsequent to the casualty. Not only should families be allowed frequent contact with knowledgeable military personnel, but also an opportunity should be available for group support from others who are or have been in a similar situation. Families should be given assurance that their emotional responses to the highly traumatic event are indeed "normal responses to an abnormal situation." They should be made aware that although the process of coping with loss is similar for most families, individuals must find the coping strategies which will prove most effective for them. Family members should also be thoroughly briefed immediately prior to reunion since there will be many apprehensions at that time. Both husbands and wives should be informed that wives and children will probably have changed much more drastically during the prolonged separation than will the POWs.

Wives may be fearful or anxious about their husbands' physical or mental condition upon return. Although they need to be aware of possible residuals of prolonged extreme stress, they also need to be assured from the testimony of former POWs that human beings are able to cope with much more physical and psychological stress than they ever imagined they could prior to their captivity. Wives whose husbands' fate is doubtful should be encouraged to face the realistic possibility that their loved ones might *not* return. In such a case, the therapist should encourage them to retain family rituals and routines, but to begin to engage in activities which are not merely "time-killing," but are also growth-producing.

The reunion period will be particularly stressful, and families need effective support services at that time, perhaps even more so than during the separation. Open family communication can facilitate family reintegration. Communication skills training, as well as family counseling, should be available for reunited families.

These Vietnam POW families worried much about how the men's casualty status would affect their children. Mothers can perhaps be comforted that children are likely to reflect directly the mothers' own reactions to the crisis. If they cope well, the children will cope admirably. Many children of the POW/MIAs believed they had actually benefited from the experience. They felt they had become more mature, responsible young adults than they might have been otherwise. Just as knowledge about what typically happens to families during a captivity or hostage situation can assist them in coping, therapists who respond to these families' needs must also be knowledgeable, as well as empathic and caring. Above all they must be good listeners and be there when they are needed. Time is also a healer, and families must be encouraged to be patient and cope 1 day at a time. The longer the separation, the more time it will take for the family to once again attain a new and comfortable homeostatic balance. For the Vietnam POW families the process took an average of 2 to 3 years after the 5-year or longer separation. Time and the therapist are the families' ally; support for these families when needed may keep the crisis from becoming a lifelong catastrophe.

REFERENCES

Beebe, G. W. Follow-up studies of World War II and Korean war prisoners: II. Mortality, disability, and maladjustments. *American Journal of Epidemiology*, 1975, *101*, 400–422.

Berg, S. W. Medical aspects of captivity and repatriation. In H. McCubbin, B. Dahl, P. Metres, Jr., E. Hunter, & J. Plag (Eds.), *Family separation and reunion: Families of prisoners of war and servicemen missing in action* (Cat. No. D-206.21: 74-70). Washington, D.C.: U.S. Government Printing Office, 1974.

Berg, S. W., & Richlin, M. Injuries and illnesses of Vietnam war POWs: IV. Comparison of captivity effects in North and South Vietnam. *Military Medicine*, 1977, *141*(10), 757–761.

Boss, P. The relationship of psychological father presence, wife's personal qualities and wife/family dysfunction in families of missing fathers. *Journal of Marriage and the Family*, 1980, *42*(3), 541–549.

Ebbert, J. MIA? In F. Kiley & T. Dater (Eds.), *Listen the war*. Colorado Springs, Colo.: U.S. Air Force Academy, June 1973.

Foley, B. *Reflections of an MIA wife*. Paper presented at a meeting of the Task Force on Families of Catastrophe, Purdue University, Family Research Institute, West Lafayette, Ind., February 1980.

Hunter, E. J. *Future shock and the POW*. Paper presented at the DoD Medical Conference on Prisoners of War, Naval Health Research Center, San Diego, Calif., November 1972.

Hunter, E. J. (Ed.). *Prolonged separation: The prisoner of war and his family* (DTIC No. AO51-325). San Diego, Calif.: Center for Prisoner of War Studies, Naval Health Research Center, 1977.

Hunter, E. J. Combat casualties who remain at home. *Military Review*, 1980, *60*(1), 28–36. (a)

Hunter, E. J. *Treating military families*. Paper presented at the Quality of Family Life in the Military Workshop, National Council on Family Relations, Portland, Ore., October 1980. (b)

Hunter, E. J., & Plag, J. A. *An assessment of the needs of POW/MIA wives residing in the San Diego metropolitan area: A proposal for the establishment of family services* (Technical Report No. 73-39). San Diego, Calif.: Center for Prisoner of War Studies, Naval Health Research Center, 1973.

Kushner, F. To live or die. *AMEDD Spectrum* (U.S. Army Medical Department), 1974, *1*(1), 16–21.

McCubbin, H., Hunter, E. J., & Metres, P. J., Jr. Children in limbo. In H. McCubbin, B. Dahl, P. Metres, Jr., E. Hunter, & J. Plag (Eds.), *Family separation and reunion: Families of prisoners of war and servicemen missing in action* (Cat. No. D-206.21: 74–70). Washington, D.C.: U.S. Government Printing Office, 1974.

McEvoy, P. *Navy wives of deployed servicemen: Their awareness of, interest in, and willingness to use support services.* Unpublished doctoral dissertation, United States International University, San Diego, Calif., 1982.

Nice, S. D., McDonald, B., & McMillian, T. The families of U.S. navy prisoners of war five years after reunion. *Journal of Marriage and the Family*, 1981, *43*(2), 431–437.

Orthner, D. (Ed.). *Proceedings of the Quality of Family Life in the Military Workshop.* Portland, Ore.: National Council on Family Relations, October 1980.

Plag, J. A. *Proposal for the long-term follow-up of returned prisoners of war, their families, and the families of servicemen missing in action: A basis for the delivery of health care services.* Paper presented at the POW Research Consultants' Conference, Naval Health Research Center, San Diego, Calif., April 1974.

Plag, J. A. *An overview of POW clinical and research findings since Operation Homecoming: The future of POW research.* Paper presented at the Fourth Annual DoD Joint Medical Meeting Concerning POW/MIA Matters, San Antonio, Tex., November 1976.

Richlin, M. Medical follow-up of returned P.O.W.'s and hostages. *Newsletter, Academy of San Diego Psychologists*, San Diego, Calif., March 1981.

Richlin, M., Rahe, R., Shale, J., & Mitchell, R. Five-year medical follow-up of Vietnam POWs: Preliminary results. *U.S. Navy Medicine*, 1980, *71*(8), 19–26.

Segal, J. *Long-term psychological and physical effects of the POW experience: A review of the literature* (Technical Report No. 74-2). San Diego, Calif.: Center for Prisoner of War Studies, Naval Health Research Center, 1974.

Smith, D. Vietnam POWs rebuild their lives. *Los Angeles Times*, September 8, 1976.

Spaulding, R. C., Murphy, L. E., & Phelan, J. D. *A comparison group for the Navy repatriated prisoners of war from Vietnam: Selection procedures used and the lessons learned* (Technical Report No. 78-22). San Diego, Calif.: Naval Health Research Center, 1978.

Stratton, A. The stress of separation. *U.S. Naval Institute Proceedings*, 1978, *104*(7), 53–58.

9

Treating Military Families Overseas: Focusing on Conjoint and Multiple Impact Therapy

JOHN E. CHURCHILL

This chapter will describe a specific treatment modality that was modified to meet the particular mental health needs of American military families abroad. It focuses primarily on the Family Mental Health Center at the U.S. Air Force in Europe (USAFE) Regional Hospital in Wiesbaden, Germany, from 1974 to 1976. The approach was aimed at treating families as a collective unit, and it is believed that such a program continues to constitute a viable treatment alternative for service families overseas.

Traditional medical resources readily available in most stateside communities are rare and often nonexistent in the military community in Europe. The burden of care for patients often weighs heavily on the various regional military installations. One such supporting unit is the USAFE Hospital in Wiesbaden, Germany. At times, this regional center has provided services for an area population of approximately 150,000 people, including Air Force, Army, Navy, and civilian personnel located throughout Western Europe. In addition to the immediate European vicinity, families have been seen from as far north and south as Finland and Ethiopia, and as far east and west as Russia and the Azores. With very little advance notice, patients requiring care often are sent from these

The opinions or assertions contained herein are the private views of the writer and are not to be construed as official or as reflecting views of the Department of the Air Force or the Department of Defense.

John E. Churchill. Chief of Hypnotherapy, Adult Outpatient Mental Health, Wilford Hall U.S. Air Force Medical Center, Lackland Air Force Base, Texas; and Assistant Practicum Professor, Our Lady of the Lake University, San Antonio, Texas.

various countries by military plane (air evacuation) to this regional facility. They are then returned to their respective bases or sent back to the continental United States (CONUS) for more long-term and intensive care. Due to the limited hospital personnel and heavy patient load, such cases, often of a crisis nature, can only be seen on a diagnostic, emergency, or short-term treatment basis and then given an expedient disposition.

STAFF COMPOSITION AND FAMILY THERAPY AS A DISTINCT ENTITY

Within this arena, the USAFE Family Mental Health Center was challenged to provide services to troubled military families, with particular emphasis given to their children and adolescents. In order to provide optimal services in a realistic manner, several key issues had to be addressed. Of paramount importance was the treatment of those families in the immediate Wiesbaden area and other nearby German communities. Also crucial was the issue of treating those families stationed in the more distant and isolated areas. The amount and type of treatment for patients in both near and remote locales was contingent upon the size, composition, and orientation of the mental health staff. In the mid-1970s, the clinical team was comprised of nine professionals, including the director, a child psychiatrist, three psychologists, four psychiatric social workers, and one speech pathologist. Such a combination is certainly not unusual in many traditional child guidance clinics. However, few clinics of this type are located in foreign countries. This distinctive factor tended to weave the staff into a rather cohesive and close-knit unit with its own familial atmosphere. This added dimension seemed to provide a strong model of identification for those families with whom the staff came into contact. Ironically, and quite by coincidence, the senior psychologist, senior clinical social worker, and myself, also a social worker, each had previous training from and exposure to Alberto Serrano, MD. This noted psychiatrist and his colleagues' original work (MacGregor, Ritchie, Schuster, & Serrano, 1964) had a tremendous impact on our clinical team. Their particular approach will be elaborated on more fully in a subsequent paragraph. Serrano's treatment philosophy and influence were quite apparent in our approach to families, both in the immediate and remote military communities. With few exceptions, all families were seen initially in a conjoint session. Those persons living in Wiesbaden and the surrounding area were seen 1 hour a week by at least two cotherapists, preferably a male and female.

The numerous families living in outlying countries, often in a state of crisis, had to be evaluated and treated on a different and more intensive basis. Prior to the treatment of such families, the referral sources and the patients had to be fully informed that the entire family was to be air evacuated to our center. This was a continuous process due to the transient nature of personnel in jobs overseas. For the most part, persons living in these isolated areas were without the traditional legal and medical resources, such as local, fully staffed hospitals, community mental health centers, legal centers, and child welfare/resource departments. A single physician, a mental health professional, a chaplain, and perhaps a school counselor were the most common sources of referral for families. Due to their heavy work loads, it was all these professionals could do to send a brief consult and evaluation report of the disturbed families and arrange for them to be air evacuated to Wiesbaden. Other than in an extreme emergency, such action was usually preceded by a phone call detailing the case as thoroughly as possible. Families were then flown to the Wiesbaden area where they remained for evaluation and treatment from 7 to 10 days at government expense. The firm request that complete families be air evacuated to our center was often met with resistance by both the referral sources and the clients. A common retort from the referral source was, "The one child was the only problem, so why not just send that child and the mother for the evaluation?" Other common responses included the following: "The father has a critical position and it will be impossible for him to make it," and "This family has so many problems that it will just make matters worse if they all come." The parents in the initial interview often echoed similar sentiments. As an adjunctive clinic of one of the largest regional hospitals in Europe, the Family Mental Health Center used its leverage to insure that entire family units were transported. Bell (1975) was adamant in the position that if the whole family was not available, then he would not see any of them. The center at Wiesbaden held this same view. The family, as a total entity, was to be treated as the patient and not any particular individual.

This modality had its inception in the 1950s when family therapy began to materialize with studies by Bateson (1956), Laing and Esterton (1964), and Lidz (1973). Treating the family as a distinct unit really blossomed in the early 1960s with books by Ackerman (1958), Satir (1964), and MacGregor et al. (1964). Sonne, Jungreis, and Speck (1962) pointed out that the absence of one family member leads to resistance in therapy and prevents healthy development of that family. Serrano (1974) related that he and his staff expended considerable effort in inviting fathers to the family sessions. Kaslow (1981a) also elaborated on the significance of involving peripheral fathers. If fathers were reluctant to come in our particular setting, they were quite often ordered to do so! It should be emphasized that most families were quite responsive and generally found their experience to be a positive one.

After their evaluation and brief crisis-oriented treatment, the family members were then returned to their home stations with recommendations for further follow-up. Many such families could be treated at their respective bases if they possessed sufficient ego strengths and there was a medical or mental health professional available. A great number in this same category were invited back to the Wiesbaden clinic for periodic treatment. However, there were also families with significant and serious psychopathology, who warranted a trip back to CONUS for more comprehensive care. Examples in this latter category included numerous patients with blatant psychoses, others with crippling phobias, and still others with chronic recalcitrant difficulties. Such cases required long-term treatment and often extended hospitalization and residential care. The evaluation and brief intensive therapy given the long-distance family at our clinic was often the decisive factor as to whether they could stay in Europe or had to be returned to the United States.

SPECIFIC TREATMENT APPROACH

A modification of multiple impact therapy (MIT) (MacGregor et al., 1964) was utilized on incoming families from the more distant military outposts. The MIT format was particularly appropriate as it was originally designed in the United States to meet the needs of families in geographically isolated areas. Those families also had been experiencing various crises and had limited access to mental health facilities. This specific therapeutic model incorporated techniques by such noted group and family therapists as Johnson (1953), Ackerman (1958), Whitaker and Napier (1972), and Peck (1953). It was conceived and developed by an orthopsychiatric team at the University of Texas Medical Branch in Galveston, Texas (MacGregor et al., 1964). The multidisciplinary group worked with families of disturbed adolescents over a 4-year (1958–1962) period. It departed from traditional once-a-week therapy sessions and met for 2 to 3 consecutive days. The intakes and therapy sessions included a variety of intense meetings between the professionals and the families. A more thorough understanding of the effectiveness of brief intervention measures in the MIT model was aided by the works of Haley (1963) and Watzlawick, Weakland, and Fisch (1974).

In our project the distressed families were air evacuated to the Wiesbaden area for a period of 7 to 10 days. This allocation of time was necessary because of the crisis nature, the geographical distance, and the time and expense involved in transporting and treating such cases. Often the patients required additional medical attention and care once they were in the area. The Wiesbaden clinic scheduled approximately two families a month. Each one arrived on a different weekend and was evaluated and treated throughout the subsequent week. The family was housed comfortably in a nearby military hotel within walking distance of the hospital facilities. Unless additional diagnostic work-ups were necessary, the group was usually prepared to leave approximately a week after their arrival. The professional staff at the center had set aside 2 to 3 full days that same week to work with the incoming family (MacGregor *et al.*, 1964). Prior to the family's arrival, at least three therapists and a selected consultant made a commitment to work with the incoming family. These same staff members had discussed available information from the referral source before their first meeting with the family. This discussion usually proved helpful in that it prepared the staff for the particular family and many of the psychodynamics that were likely to emerge.

FIRST DAY

The initial meeting consisted of the three clinicians and the family in a conjoint session. This generally took place about 9:00 A.M. on the first morning. Introductions were made, with the usual remarks about the airplane trip and the surprisingly good accommodations for sleeping and eating at the nearby hotel. After these preliminary amenities, a staff member would state that our basic approach was that of viewing the family as a unit. Thus, from the very beginning, the family was made cognizant of our particular orientation. It was further explained that over the next few days they would be seen together at times, and at other times individually or in subsystems with parents in one office and children in another. It was also mentioned that psychological testing might be done in order for the treatment team to obtain a clearer understanding of their special case. The constellation was then informed of our assessment of their particular situation; this was usually followed by asking them for feedback and clarification. Such inquiry was done in a fashion typical of Satir (1964) with each member getting his turn to talk about the problem.

In this first meeting, it was imperative that each individual understand that his or her unique feelings or needs would be heard. Meeting each family member where he or she was, at that place and time, was crucial for any further progress. Family therapists are generally on the lookout for such factors as resistance, guilt, and scapegoating in the initial session, and this was equally true in this setting. For example, it was not uncommon for parents or children to speak up or to act out and completely ignore the inquiry about the family's situation. Parents would divert attention away from their particular problems to discuss the type of plane trip experienced, the conditions of their hotel, or the peculiarities of their home base or country as compared to that of Germany. Several of the fathers, who had been required to temporarily halt or modify their work schedule, chose this particular moment to vent their anger and frustration at having been "ordered to come." Mothers would decide at this juncture to change their babies' diapers. Quite often one of the children would ask to go to the restroom or the child with the presenting problem would act out. Some parents would take this opportunity to express their own guilt regarding their son's or daughter's behavior. Remarks such as "I have been too rough (or too lenient) with my child," and "I am really the problem and not my 6-year-old," were frequently heard. Some parents projected their guilt by blaming each other for the child's difficulty: "If you had not been so demanding, the boy never would have run away in the first place." Scapegoating the "sick" child was probably the most common problem encountered: "I am glad we are finally here to help Mary. She really has difficulty getting along with other children." "Joey reminds us of his uncle who also has feminine traits." "The whole family is fine as long as Jill is out of sight, but when she is around, everything falls apart!" "In 2 years, Linda will be out of the house and we can have peace again." "I don't mean to place all the blame on Bill, but he is so pessimistic about life." Although they were largely unintentional, these tactics were often used by families in an attempt to distract from the real problem.

Whichever staff member was most comfortable in addressing the particular issue at hand would do so. He or she would then skillfully direct the family back to the presenting difficulty and how it was created by a dysfunction within the unit itself. No serious effort was made at this point to confront or involve family members in the treatment process (Serrano, 1974). They were there for the "child's sake" and the clinical team's primary responsibility was to develop significant rapport with the unit and allay any anxiety. The family's strengths were emphasized throughout the treatment process. Each therapist, at different times, would reiterate that the family had numerous strengths and resources, and perhaps some of these could be tapped during their stay in Germany. We indicated it was ultimately up to the family, not the therapists, to work out its problems. This helped to reassure the various members that they were not up against insurmountable odds and that their own health could see them through the storm.

From the beginning, the staff also had to be cognizant of whether they or their colleagues were overly identifying with any of the family members. Such overidentification, if not perceived early, could disrupt the evaluation and treatment process. Since the professionals were also an entity—having labored, traveled, and socialized at length—they were well aware of each other's idiosyncrasies. This reduced the element of over-identification considerably. Likewise, issues of transference were readily known and recognized with surprising clarity and predictability. It was agreed that cotherapists could confront one another on these issues in front of the family. This served several important purposes. It proved to the family that we too were human and had similar tendencies to get ourselves subjectively caught up in our own thought processes. It also conveyed a message that most families desperately need to hear: that it is all right, even healthy, to confront and disagree with someone and still like them.

After the first hour of "warming-up," the staff and family proceeded to the next stage. The family members were told they would be given separate interviews by the various therapists. For example, one professional would meet with one parent, while another would meet with the other parent, and the third would see the child and any siblings. The choice as to which therapist was to see which family member was made in front of the family (MacGregor et al., 1964). Arriving at such a decision meant the staff had to consider the family's movement up to that point. In most cases, the family's faulty communication patterns had begun to emerge, as had the individual personality of each member. Here again, the staff's knowledge of each other proved to be a distinct advantage. The senior psychologist was extremely adept at dealing with angry, overbearing adults, the child psychiatrist was uniquely suited to the adolescent population, two of the social workers were proficient with nonverbal individuals, while the other two were skilled at dealing with the more verbal persons, particularly those possessing martyrish or condescending qualities. The other two psychologists and the speech pathologist were able to adjust to most situations with ease, and their relaxed manner carried over to both family and staff members. After the appropriate pairings between team and family, the different groupings moved quickly to their own sessions. In keeping with the original treatment plan, these separate sessions served to reinforce, rather than fragment, the family unit. Clinicians asked the various subsystems to take personal responsibility for the family's predicament and not blame it on the other members. Parents and children were reminded to focus on "I" or "we," rather than "you" or "they." Bowen (1971) makes this "'I' position" clear and describes how valuable such a technique is in allaying anxiety among family members, while simultaneously improving their relationships. Such an approach enabled us to intervene in existing pathological alliances and prevented certain other disruptive alliances from forming. As the tendency to blame decreased, so did other kinds of controlling behavior.

The second hour usually brought a more relaxed response from the different individuals as they were given an opportunity to present their version of the picture. Parents and children often altered or changed remarks made earlier in the joint session. They were most eager to have the individual clinician understand "what really is happening." Consistent refocusing of attention back to the individual and his or her particular needs and feelings often yielded valuable insights. Numerous mothers took this opportunity to express their feelings of inadequacy and even depression at having to deal with their children's emotional problems. These disturbances ran the gamut of psychopathology. Enuresis, encopresis, school phobia, and autism were not unusual problems seen in the younger children evaluated at our clinic. Running away, depression, failure at school, delinquency, and anorexia nervosa were often seen in the adolescent population. Frequently, the wives would acknowledge that handling the children's problems left them with no time or energy for the husband. Likewise, many husbands complained of going from the "pressure cooker of work to the pressure cooker of home." On occasion, both men and women would take this time to mention somatic complaints. Children took this opportunity to vent feelings of anger toward a particular parent or describe their embarrassment over a special problem. Thus, during the second hour, there were often hints that it was more than just the identified patient who was in emotional pain. This second session was also a time to scrutinize each family member to determine if other methods of evaluation were needed. Often, psychological testing was warranted. Sometimes, a quick consult had to be requested from Internal Medicine, Pediatrics, Neurology, Speech Pathology, Audiology, or the Adult Outpatient Mental Health Clinic. It was imperative that any difficulties be detected early to ensure a thorough and comprehensive evaluation prior to the family's return to their home base. It was not unusual for medical professionals from other departments, who had evaluated the child or parent during this time, to sit in and provide feedback in later family sessions.

MacGregor et al. (1964) mention the value of "overlapping sessions" in which one interviewer might terminate his or her session early and join another who was still in progress with his or her particular family member. The purpose of the interruption is to clarify issues between therapists and patients at an early stage. However, our professionals did not follow this procedure but instead chose to stay the full second hour with their respective parties. The family was then reunited for a joint family–staff feedback session just prior to lunch. Serrano (1974) states how important it is at this point for therapists to be selective in the information they share. This procedure promotes communication among family members while simultaneously reducing resistance and insuring trust with the clinicians.

At the Wiesbaden clinic, individual staff members discussed and gave interpretations regarding the material discussed during separate sessions. Members of the family who had been in different meetings were asked if this information was consistent with their particular views. This hour usually brought together a confluence of ideas and feelings by both team and family members. The feedback often was surprising as families began to detect issues other than those of the identified patient. Some of these "different" agendas would later emerge as full-blown family secrets which had previously helped to perpetuate a pathological system. Other issues revolved around unexpected strengths in certain family members and unexpected weaknesses from others. In a number of cases, the "sick child" was not looking so sick, but another child or parent was! Alliances between certain family members were becoming more evident. Therapists were getting in touch with their own subjective feelings and biases, as well as those of the involved family. It was necessary to start seeking a general direction to go with this plethora of acquired data. Toward the end of this third hour, a sense of anticipation or apprehension could usually be felt by all as they braced for further impact. After a few general statements about the afternoon routine, the family departed with the understanding that the staff would be discussing their case over lunch (MacGregor *et al.*, 1964).

The noon staffing was usually conducted in a quiet, out-of-the-way German *Gasthaus* (hotel–restaurant) away from the hospital setting. It was to this meeting that we invited a previously selected outside consultant, usually a professional from the Adult Outpatient Mental Health Clinic or one of our staff who had set aside mid and late afternoons of that week to be with us. For the sake of consistency, it was necessary for the same consultant to be involved throughout the duration of the existent case. The function of this outside clinician was twofold. First, he or she could offer objective input into an otherwise subjective experience. This person, more than anyone else on the staff, could point out problems with transference and countertransference. Second, a more viable direction of treatment could be pointed out. Since the staff was analogous to a family unit, we often were at odds as to which approach would best suit our needs as well as those of the family. Satir, Stachowiak, and Taschman (1975) discuss supportive measures for building trust within the family system, while Minuchin (1974) utilizes techniques aimed at offsetting the old dysfunctional system and allowing more functional patterns to emerge. The consultant was most helpful in our decision as to which strategy or combination to employ. The noon luncheon also provided the clinical team and family with a come-down time from the experience that morning. Different therapists would take this opportunity to express their personal frustrations or observations regarding the family's interactions. They also found this time helpful for airing their views toward other staff members. Plans for staff–family pairings in the afternoon sessions and decisions regarding psychological tests for children or parents were also addressed. While the staff convened over lunch, the families, who frequently were from out of the country, used this time out to go sightseeing, shopping, or eating. Like the clinicians, they too were in need of a change of pace after the morning's activities. The lunch hour, similar to that used in the original MIT format, was an extended one and generally lasted about 2 hours (MacGregor *et al.*, 1964). This gave both parties ample time to regroup before the afternoon sessions.

The staff and family reconvened around 2:00 P.M. After briefly discussing what transpired during the lunch hour, the various staff members left with their assigned family members. That therapist who had met with one parent in the morning interviewed the other one in the early afternoon session. With the focus still being placed on the "I," parents were given more of an opportunity to ventilate the pressures they were feeling. The interviewer was given an opportunity to compare this parent's views with those of the parent seen in the morning. Inconsistencies in rearing, disciplining, and educating the children often became visible. Mothers and fathers acknowledged that the family system was either too controlling or not controlling enough, and they were at a loss as to how to draw the balance. They revealed that as a crisis situation heightened, the unit either became more rigid or entirely lost control, depending on the family's particular structure. Both patterns of family interaction led to a stunting of healthy growth and communication. In addition, a pathological form of symbiosis nearly always characterized such families. For example, those fathers who were so strict that their children always had to go through the mother, created unhealthy alliances within their respective settings. There were mothers who always had to be the referee between the adolescent sons and their fathers. Such behavior prevented fathers and sons from taking responsibility for resolving their differences, and chaos generally prevailed. As the early afternoon sessions progressed, more of these issues around dependency and control emerged in such statements as these: "I always have to ask my husband for every little thing"; or "I cannot make a move without my wife asking why." Problems with marriage and depression became more clearly defined and staff members saw these as integral to the overall disruptive behavior of the children.

While the parents were being interviewed by two members of the clinical team, the identified patient was being administered a battery of psychological tests by a third clinician. If deemed important, the psychologist also gave tests to the siblings as well. It was necessary to have this diagnostic tool applied and scored early in the evaluation process because the data derived helped in formulating a more comprehensive treatment plan. It was also useful to have such data readily available when making recommendations to the referral source. If testing was not warranted, the third clinician would spend the hour interviewing the index patient and the siblings in conjoint and separate sessions. If children needed other medical intervention, this also was arranged at this time. By the early afternoon session the children were more trusting and willing to share their feelings. It had become apparent to them that this therapist cared for their particular views and would treat them in a fair and impartial manner. This was a vulnerable time for the professional who was subjected to a variety of subtle and manipulative tactics by the children. Verbal ploys were sometimes used: "I will tell you a secret if you promise not to tell my parents"; "I have never been able to talk to an adult like you"; "Could you please explain my side to my parents?" Nonverbal ploys were just as devastating as children and adolescents gave messages, via their body language, that they were extremely hurt and misunderstood. These devices for the most part were quite unconscious and unintentional. Despite this rationale, such ploys were still a means of sabotaging open and healthy communication within the family constellation. The skillful therapist recognized this and negotiated the session in such a way as to assure the children that their opinions and experiences were important and became more so when discussed openly in front of the family.

The final staff–family meeting of the first day took place at 3:00 P.M. and generally ran for 1½ hours. By this time there was an abundance of subjective and objective information known to both family members and clinicians. Except on rare occasions, such knowledge was discussed with the entire family. Serrano (1974) and Whitaker and Napier (1972) indicate this is a more honest approach and facilitates healthy family interaction. It also tended to keep the staff members more objective in their observations and interpretations. The fallacy of such an approach occurs when there is a dearth of staff cohesiveness, unity, competence, or experience. This was not the case with the Wiesbaden staff and the method worked extremely well. The therapists diplomatically shared their perceptions of the feelings and needs expressed by various family members. The children and parents were encouraged to share also and correct any misunderstanding the clinicians might have. Therapists typically served as advocates for various subsystems of the family, being careful not to allow parents to exploit each other or their children regarding what was said. Crucial areas of family dysfunctioning, which were hinted at in other sessions, tended to flow freely in this late afternoon conference. Children perceptively expressed their concern over their parents' marital problem. Husbands and wives confronted one another with their pent-up feelings of anger and frustration. Control issues, such as scapegoating and passive and/or aggressive dominance, also were openly discussed. Parents from a chaotic milieu often expressed the need for more structure while parents from a strict setting expressed the need to be more tolerant. Staff members held firmly to a supportive role at this time, as family members were quite vulnerable, allowing their guilt and blame to run rampant. The most significant message that evolved from this profuse interaction was that the family, and not just the disturbed child, was in trouble. Thus, the cardinal principle behind family therapy was deeply experienced by the family itself.

After a brief wrap-up of the final session, the family was dismissed for the evening to process their seemingly countless number of feelings and emotions. The professional team again retreated to a nearby German *Gasthaus* for the purposes of having a snack, meeting with the consultant, and venting the various pressures of the day. This brief gathering usually provided the staff with a healthy balance between business and pleasure before we ventured home to our own families. Again, the consultant was helpful in keeping us objective and in mapping out the strategy for the next day. Supportive techniques had largely been the order of the first day. The second day generally brought about more confrontation as the evaluation and treatment phases began to merge.

SECOND DAY

With few exceptions, the second day followed the same format as the first. If there were variations, these revolved around the different pairings between those therapists and family members who had not experienced separate sessions together on the previous day. The family's night in the hotel was typically a strained one. The temporary plight of living in a new and strange country forces members to rely on one another. This factor, plus the impact of the first day's proceedings, often convinced them of their inability to communicate effectively. By the morning of the second day, they were somewhat apprehensive, but nearly always willing to look further at themselves. As might be expected, there were more frequent confrontations between staff and staff, staff and family, and family and family. These interactions brought about an even more intense expression of feelings. This atmosphere often provided the impetus for family secrets to be revealed. These secrets probably would not have surfaced for months had these same families been seen by clinicians in orthodox meetings of 1 hour a week. If such information were divulged in the morning session, then it could be dealt with in the afternoon. If these skeletons in the closet surfaced in the afternoon, then more time was made available to deal with them. Although most families initially appeared devastated by such disclosures, they soon experienced a strong sense of relief. Now that the "terrible truth" was known, the family members and clinical personnel could get down to the necessary business of correcting the existing pathology. The secret itself might be the source of the problem, as was often discovered in cases of incest. More often than not, it was a contributing stimulus as in the case of an angry and belligerent teenager who discovered what he had always intuitively sensed —that he was an adopted child. Whether it be the root of or a contributing factor to the problem, such secrets contaminate families and often lead to a loss of functioning.

Case 1

One family with three sons was being seen because the oldest boy, age 11, was acting out at school and the middle boy, age 9, was quite reclusive. The third child, age 6, had been burned in a freak accident several years earlier and was quite disfigured around the face and hands. Surprisingly, the third child was the best adjusted of the three. The parents explained that the youngest child, when approximately 3 years of age, somehow had lit a match and placed it in a gas stove that had been turned on for some time. The stove exploded and seriously burned the child. The child had no conscious recollection of the incident.

During the second day of this family's treatment, the oldest child divulged it was he who had turned on the stove and given his youngest brother the lit match. The middle child had been aware of this and both boys had been keeping this terrible secret and suffering the accompanying guilt for 3 years! In this case, the parents were quite strong and supportive, and the youngest child, with his healthy attitude, was able to forgive the two older brothers. Such revelations and experiences were not uncommon in the second day.

Case 2

A 16-year-old girl and her parents were referred to our clinic because of the daughter's increasing feeding disturbance. As is the case with many anorexia nervosa patients, she was a bright adolescent who presented as a model student at school and a loving child at home. Both parents and the presenting patient were at a loss as to why the girl continued to have an aversion to food and was adamant about losing weight. The girl weighed approximately 80 pounds and there was definitely a reason for concern.

The second day brought forth several secrets from this family. The mother divulged she had been depressed for the past 2 years and this daughter, the younger of two girls, felt she had to assume her mother's role in the family. When asked about the older daughter, age 20, the family stated she had recently gone to live with relatives. Upon further inquiry it was learned that the older daughter had also experienced serious emotional problems and was probably psychotic. The family admitted they had denied the severity of the older daughter's psychopathology. Thus the younger daughter was left with the burden of being the model female for this family. Like other members of her family she had internalized much of her anger and was an expert at denying strong emotions. With the understanding that she was not expected to be "Cinderella," and that her expression of anger was healthy, she and the other family members were soon on their way to recovery.

The final staff–family conference of the second afternoon found most family members willing to admit and face up to their own particular problems.

Case 3

After adamantly refusing to acknowledge any past history of a learning disability, one father broke down on the second afternoon and admitted he had overcome this difficulty in early adult life through tireless work and study. This brought tremendous relief to his young son who was then experiencing similar problems and had felt dad was unable to understand.

Numerous parents acknowledged that their depression might be causing acting-out behavior in their children. Many families came to have a better understanding of their psychotic children who had gravitated into deviant behavior in an attempt to divert attention away from the problems of other family members. Couples began to understand that their marital problems did not stop in the privacy of their bedroom, but spilled over into their children's lives. Still other adults were relieved to discover their personal influences had really not been a factor in their children's difficulties when neurological and pediatric reports indicated an organic problem.

The second day, which frequently began with so many unresolved emotional issues, usually ended with a rather calm understanding of how the family developed its negative patterns. For most reasonably healthy families, this now meant channeling their energies in a more constructive direction. The clinical team also relaxed at this point and our relaxed state was even more evident in our brief meeting with the consultant later in the evening when plans for the final staff–family session were made for the third day.

THIRD DAY

The morning of the third day usually provided the time that was needed to finalize treatment plans and recommendations. In addition to the therapy team, other professionals who had some involvement in the case were invited to attend. It was not unusual to have representatives present from Pediatrics, Neurology, and Audiology. All of the clinicians again met with the whole family to deal with issues left hanging from the day before, answer any further questions, and make recommendations regarding further treatment. This joint session began around 10:00 A.M. and generally ended around noon. Those families that had responded well to treatment and had sufficient resources were lauded by our staff and asked to continue their treatment with the clinical authority or professional who had referred them. In some instances, we invited families back at 3-month intervals for continued treatment in our clinic. In other cases, we had to confront the parents with the news that their family was in need of more specialized help and resources than were available in the overseas area. These families were told they would have to return to CONUS. They were also informed that specific arrangements would be made for them to be sent to a base where, ideally, both the family's mental health needs and the father's career field could be accommodated. No matter what the outcome of the 3-day period, all families were assured that we would immediately call their referral sources regarding our particular findings and recommendations. In addition, we mentioned that a summary of our evaluation and treatment, as well as any other diagnostic information, would be forwarded within the week. Since the family and staff had been involved in an intensive 3-day encounter, it was necessary to devote some brief, but valuable time to termination. This was particularly relevant in light of the fact that many of the troubled families overseas had experienced serious problems with separation and loss.

PARTICULAR STRESSES OF THE
OVERSEAS ENVIRONMENT

As has been described, the modified MIT model was well suited for treating military families in the overseas environment. However, this chapter would be remiss if it did not mention that each member of the child guidance team had a thorough understanding of the overseas setting and its particular implications for disturbed families. Attention to such implications had to be incorporated into the aforementioned treatment plan. While there are certain studies that indicate a significant correlation between geographical mobility and emotional problems of military children (Werkman, 1972; Gabower, 1960; Bower, 1967), there are others who contend that there is no significant relationship between the two (Pedersen & Sullivan, 1964; Shaw & Pangman, 1975). Despite these conflicting views, there is general agreement that the living and working conditions in foreign countries do pose rather unique psychological stresses for the military family.

Living overseas, with its different culture, language, life-style, and loss of familiar ties and surroundings, is an obvious strain on every family's homeostasis. Although most active duty personnel and their dependents live on or near the base or post assigned to them, they must contend daily with the larger and more predominant culture around them. Many families experience "culture shock." To what degree this influences the equilibrium of families is still unknown. Certainly, being uprooted from one culture and transplanted into another creates stress on parents and children alike. If families do not acquire a basic knowledge of the language and customs of their host country, such essentials as shopping or traveling in that country are and remain difficult. It was my opinion that faulty communication with the larger extended populace often contributed to faulty communication within the immediate family as well. For example, in several families, adolescents complained that their parents experienced a great deal of turmoil and confusion because of the demands of their new environment and these feelings eventually filtered down to the other members.

Living in a different culture is likely to mean a life-style markedly different from that experienced in the United States. In Germany, many active duty personnel and their dependents live in quarters known as stairwells. This base or post housing consists of six to eight families living in separate, but close, quarters and sharing a common stairway. Such living arrangements are necessitated by the limited land space in Europe.

Nonetheless, the fact remains that if one family is experiencing problems within a stairwell unit, it is likely and highly probable that repercussions will also be felt by the other families living there. The pace of life is also much different in the European countries in that it is much slower than in our own. In most instances, families consider this a positive stress, but certainly one that requires an adjustment. Recreational and job opportunities for children and adolescents are often limited. Conversely, opportunities to travel and meet new people and see a variety of sights are often unlimited. For those families who can afford frequent travel, such adventure often has the effect of bringing families together in an even more cohesive fashion. However, those who cannot pay for regular journeys or who are afraid to venture out from the security of their immediate vicinity may find the experience extremely stifling. Such families definitely feel the negative effects of an overseas milieu.

Latency age children will often express their fears in the form of enuresis, encopresis, and sleep distrubances. Adolescents are daily subjected to moral and ethical codes markedly different from the ones they and their parents are attempting to incorporate. The fathers' jobs are often more demanding than those they had in the United States. In addition, they are frequently absent from the home. This leaves the mothers to shoulder most of the burdens of the family in a strange world. Furthermore, the woman has to handle all of this without her usual support system of extended family and friends. Terrorist groups are also a threat with their proclivity to kidnap family members of high-ranking government officials. For literally thousands of families adequate mental health facilities and other medical resources are scarce and traditionally reached only at great distance and sacrifice.

CONCLUSION

There is no doubt that the move overseas causes temporary disruption and challenges the adaptive capacity of the military family collectively, as well as each of its members individually. It was my perception that those families possessing sound inner strengths and reasonable communication skills were inclined to grow healthier while those families with existing pathology and poor communication systems were likely to become worse. It was also my observation that parental attitudes, more than any other single ingredient, accounted for family stability or instability. If parents were negative and angry about their new location, these feelings often pervaded the family unit and rendered it vulnerable in the event of a crisis.

If parents were positive and optimistic about their new setting, such feelings carried over to other family members and frequently helped them through troubled times. Shaw and Pangman (1975) tend to corroborate these impressions in their study of military children referred to a child guidance clinic in Germany. Kaslow (1981b) also emphasizes the significance of optimism in healthy families. Those parents who have a tendency to balance out their lives physically, emotionally, and spiritually tend to view their foreign home as a challenge and look forward to the opportunities in store for them. Such a balance usually transcends any temporary disruption caused by the move to a new and distant land.

The MIT treatment model, as it was modified in Europe, was felt to be a potent tool for assisting numerous disturbed families to cope and function more effectively. Many patients learned their unique difficulties could only be resolved through cooperative efforts with other family members rather than unhealthy partisan alliances or "doing it alone." Such knowledge was imparted by a group of professionals who rigorously adhered to the standards of conjoint family practice and were also well aware of their own biases and limitations. The efficacy of the Family Mental Health Center, as it existed in Wiesbaden, was due to the staff's cohesion and orientation, to the ideal location within the regional hospital structure, to the motivation of the patients, and most certainly to the office of the USAFE Surgeon General for allowing such flexibility in order to best meet the treatment needs of its personnel in Europe. The clinic is now located in an area near Ramstein and Kaiserslautern, Germany, and its name has been changed to The Family Guidance Service. Although the size and composition of the staff is essentially the same, there is no longer an orientation toward treating families as a total unit. The fact that the clinic is now geographically separated from the regional hospital in Wiesbaden also means less access to air evacuation capabilities and adequate lodging facilities. It is my conviction, that if given a similar staff milieu and regional hospital location, the plan mentioned could again become a strong and viable treatment force to military families in European and other territories abroad.

REFERENCES

Ackerman, N. W. The psychodynamics of family life. In *Diagnosis and treatment of family relationships*. New York: Basic Books, 1958.
Bateson, G. Toward a theory of schizophrenia. *Behavioral Science*, 1956, *1*, 251–264.

Bell, J. E. *Family group therapy* (Public Health Monograph No. 64, Public Health Service Publication No. 826). Washington, D.C.: Government Printing Office, 1961.

Bell, J. E. *Family therapy*. New York: Aronson, 1975.

Bowen, M. Family therapy and family group therapy. In H. I. Kaplan & B. J. Sadock (Eds.), *Comprehensive group psychotherapy*. Baltimore: Williams & Wilkins, 1971.

Bower, E. M. American children and families in overseas communities. *American Journal of Orthopsychiatry*, 1967, *37*, 787–796.

Gabower, G. Behavior problems of children in navy officers' families. *Social Casework*, 1960, *41*, 177–184.

Haley, J. *Strategies of psychotherapy*. New York: Grune & Stratton, 1963.

Johnson, A. M. Collaborative psychotherapy: Team setting. In M. Heiman (Ed.), *Psychoanalysis and social work*. New York: International Universities Press, 1953.

Kaslow, F. W. Involving the peripheral father in family therapy. In A. Gurman (Ed.), *Questions and answers in family therapy*. New York: Brunner/Mazel, 1981. (a)

Kaslow, F. W. Profile of the healthy family. *Interaction*, Spring/Summer 1981, *4*(1), 1–15. (b)

Laing, R. D., & Esterson, A. *Sanity, madness and the family: Families of schizophrenics*. Baltimore: Penguin Books, 1964.

Lidz, T. *The origin and treatment of schizophrenic disorders*. New York: Basic Books, 1973.

MacGregor, R., Ritchie, A. M., Schuster, F. P., & Serrano, A. C. *Multiple impact therapy with families*. New York: McGraw-Hill, 1964.

Minuchin, S. *Families and family therapy*. Cambridge: Harvard University Press, 1974.

Peck, H. B. An application of group therapy to the intake process. *American Journal of Orthopsychiatry*, 1953, *23*, 338–349.

Pedersen, F. A., & Sullivan, E. J. Relationship among geographic mobility, parental attitudes and emotional disturbances in children. *American Journal of Orthopsychiatry*, 1964, *34*, 575–580.

Satir, V. W. *Conjoint family therapy: A guide to theory and technique*. Palo Alto, Calif.: Science & Behavior Books, 1964.

Satir, V. W., Stachowiak, J., & Taschman, H. A. *Helping families to change*. New York: Aronson, 1975.

Serrano, A. Multiple impact therapy with families—Current practical applications. In R. E. Hardy & J. G. Cull (Eds.), *Techniques and approaches in marital and family counseling*. Springfield, Ill.: Thomas, 1974.

Shaw, J., & Pangman, J. Geographic mobility and the military child. *Military Medicine*, 1975, *140*(6), 413–416.

Sonne, J. C., Jungreis, J. E., & Speck, R. V. The absent member maneuver as a resistance in family therapy of schizophrenia. *Family Process*, 1962, *1*, 44–62.

Watzlawick, P., Weakland, J. H., & Fisch, R. *Change: Principles of problem formation and problem resolution*. New York: Norton, 1974.

Werkman, S. L. Hazards of rearing children in foreign countries. *American Journal of Psychiatry*, 1972, *12*(8), 992–997.

Whitaker, C., & Napier, A. A conversation about cotherapy. In A. Ferber, M. Mendelsohn, & A. Napier (Eds.), *The book of family therapy*. New York: Science House, 1972.

10

Retirement from the Service: The Individual and His Family

ROBERT E. STRANGE

For civilians, retirement is a much anticipated event occurring when someone is usually between the ages of 60 and 70. Some people look forward to leaving a lifetime of labor and enjoying later years of leisure and security. Unfortunately, the sometimes bitter reality of retirement often does not match the pleasant fantasies of anticipation, and it can be a painful and difficult experience for both the individual and the family. Leaving the work force and then feeling unproductive, becoming socially isolated, questioning one's self-worth, and struggling with minimum financial support can precipitate a variety of emotional difficulties (Butler, 1975). Clinicians are generally aware of and sensitive to the problems suffered by many elderly civilian retirees. The problems of military retirement, however, are less well understood and frequently unrecognized.

UNIQUE FEATURES OF MILITARY RETIREMENT

Military retirement varies significantly from its civilian counterpart and therefore differs in its effects on the individual and the family. These differences can be grouped into two basic categories: (1) differing age of retirement and therefore its impact on the individual's and the family's developmental stages, and (2) variations between civilian and military life-style and identity.

Military retirement occurs at a much earlier age than the usual civilian retirement. Combat requires the physical and emotional charac-

Robert E. Strange. Captain, Medical Corps, U.S. Navy, Retired, and Director, Northern Virginia Mental Health Institute, Falls Church, Virginia.

teristics of youth, and throughout history wars have been fought primarily by young men. Because of the limited value of and need for military personnel during and after midlife, armed forces have traditionally separated most of the middle-aged from active service. In the United States, the formal military retirement system with pensions which was set up in Civil War days has continued, with some modifications, to the present. This system is based on length of active duty, so that military personnel become eligible for retirement after 20 years of service, with an immediate pension of approximately half of their active duty base pay. Retirement may be postponed until the accumulation of 30 years of service, with a corresponding increase in pension income.

If a young man enters the military in his late teens or 20s, he becomes eligible for retirement between his late 30s and 50 years of age. Most officers retire in their 40s after a 20- to 30-year career in the service, and many enlisted personnel retire a few years earlier, frequently before age 40. This is far different from civilian retirement at age 65. Termination of one's military service occurs in middle adulthood at a time when most people are at their highest levels of status, productivity, and complex family interaction. Therefore, the military retiree and spouse must work out their emotional adaptation to retirement as part of their overall midlife adjustment, their children must integrate this major transition into their own development, and family relationships must readjust accordingly.

Not only does military retirement occur at an earlier age than civilian retirement, but it also requires a much more drastic change of life-style. Military life, compared to civilian life, tends to be a self-contained system which influences all aspects of individual and family life. For the individual, it emphasizes group identity and goals; a clearly delineated hierarchal system; geographic mobility; and a high level of structure and support. For the family, it means being part of an overall support system constituted like an extended family which offers base housing; commissary and exchange purchasing; base schools; close association with other military families under sometimes isolated conditions, such as overseas assignments; identification with military values; and a social network which tends to be separate from civilian society.

When the retiree enters civilian life, he and his family are no longer automatically provided with the support and structure of the service, although some limited entitlements such as commissary and exchange privileges and medical care continue. He is confronted by new expectations, and because of both financial and psychological needs, he must find a new way to make a living. The family has to adapt to the nonmilitary community. Since repeated family separations are a common fact of military life, the newly retired family may now actually have to learn how to live together on a more intense daily basis. For military careerists, both enlisted and officer, and the families, retirement may mark a cataclysmic change in many aspects of living.

IMPACT OF MILITARY RETIREMENT
ON INDIVIDUAL AND FAMILY DEVELOPMENT

Since it usually occurs in the fourth decade of life, military retirement coincides with that stage of an individual's life which has come to be known as the midlife transition when early adulthood ends and middle adulthood begins. Levinson, Darrow, Klein, Levinson, and McKee (1978) have pointed out the developmental changes of this age period and the adaptation to these changes which must occur in order to maintain good emotional and physical health. It is a time of gradual change in biological functioning, with increasing awareness of decline in physical prowess and energy level. All adults must learn to live with these alterations and it may require considerable change of activities, career emphasis, and life focus. Indeed this may contribute to the decision to retire for some military personnel who are in particularly physically demanding duties. Departure from the male-oriented society of the military may reinforce fears of declining masculinity and thereby contribute to the anxiety of this period. It is generally agreed that even emotionally healthy adults experience some degree of emotional crisis at this time of their lives, and military retirement may exacerbate this. Conversely, it may serve a valuable defensive function and help resolve midlife crisis issues by offering the opportunity for a positive change in career and identity. The challenges of new job, new friends, and new situation often promote real psychological growth and the retirement transition becomes a rewarding developmental experience.

This is the generation between developing adolescent children and aging parents, and as early adulthood is terminated and middle adulthood begins, there is new and necessary awareness of generational sequence. As the children become more independent, grandparents are becoming more dependent, and therefore the adult at midlife is faced with new generational roles, responsibilities, and conflicts. Erikson (1959) addresses this as the seventh stage of ego development, the stage of generativity versus stagnation. Generativity means more than simply having offspring. It means the assumption of new responsibilities and new relationships in contrast to stagnation in a life of unfulfilling sameness and emotional isolation. The military retiree must realign his relationships with both the older and the younger generations, avoiding emotional stagnation at a time when he is being thrust into a new environment and has lost his familiar service role and identity. This may further compound an already difficult period of adjustment. It may, however, also offer new ways of resolving these problems and help prevent stagnation by opening new possibilities in civilian life at a time when there is new parental freedom. The retiree and spouse now have the chance to develop new interests and activities and to accomplish things which were delayed by the child-rearing years.

For most adults the period of midlife transition is a significant period of career evolution, and this is especially true for the military retiree. It is a time when productivity and goal achievement are reviewed, realistic possibilities and limitations are considered, and future objectives are planned with the understanding that life is finite. This time of review, reconsideration, and planning is frequently centered around some culminating event that results in a change of career direction. For military careerists this event is retirement, which is both an end and a beginning. Obviously, this may be either a negative or a positive event, based upon the career change that is involved; but regardless of whether it is resolved healthily or unhealthily, it requires searching self-examination and goal changes which impact heavily on one's image and self-esteem.

Just as the individual must perform certain developmental tasks during the stage of life in which military retirement occurs, so must the family. As the parent/spouse is passing through the midlife transition, the family is in the phases of developing teenagers and/or launching young adults. Duvall (1971) has described the major developmental tasks of families in these stages as providing expanded resources and facilities, realigning responsibilities, working out marriage relationships, maintaining communications, integrating widening experiences, and reconciling differing loyalties. Military retirement occurs at a time of multiplying and differing resource needs in the family group. Relocation, home-buying, college, and other expenses all place considerable pressure on the retiree for immediate and financially rewarding employment as soon as possible, and make decisions about location and other details of the permanent home especially complex. At a time when the retiree is struggling with his own emotional issues involving dependency and responsibility, he must also confront the inescapable family conflicts caused by varying ages and levels of independence in his children, who are teenagers or young adults working toward autonomy. At this time a major realignment of responsibilities is required in the family structure.

The retiree's spouse is simultaneously working through her own midlife transition and she must now adjust to a husband who has a new role and identity. Many wives return to school or work during this period, and stress may be caused by their new autonomy with careers which are ascending while their retired husbands view their own as declining.

As previously noted, this may be the first opportunity for husband and wife to live together over a prolonged period of time because of the periodic separations inherent in military service, and this new intimacy requires much restructuring of the marital relationship. This is a period of family communication gaps which must be bridged, along with shifting loyalties and different philosophies as family members grow and change. The retiree and his family may be ill-prepared to accomplish these tasks after 20 or 30 years of military life. Finally, in this stage of development, the family must integrate a much wider range of family experiences, and certainly the experience of leaving military society and entering the civilian world can be a new and strange adventure which may severely tax the adaptive capacity of the family group.

CLINICAL ISSUES

The retirement issues discussed above can create formidable stresses for the individual and the family at the time of departure from military service. The situational dilemmas causing these stresses are summarized by Bellino (1969) as (1) the need for employment and finances; (2) the loss of military role and position; (3) the need to adapt to the new civilian way of life; (4) the need to integrate into a permanent community; and (5) the need to adjust to new and more intense family interaction. Most retirees and their families resolve these problems and make the transition successfully. Many, however, are not so fortunate and suffer significant emotional distress and family conflict before, during, and/or after retirement.

The complex of emotional symptoms acompanying military retirement has been well described by McNeil and Giffen (1967) in their discussion of "the retirement syndrome." These authors identify three major stages in this process as the preretirement, transitional, and stabilization periods. The preretirement period may begin as long as 2 or 3 years before actual retirement, and is frequently marked by anxiety, depression, and somatic complaints associated with the apprehension and uncertainty of the preretiree. This looming uncertainty also has obvious impact upon the family and may precipitate symptoms in other family members and/or exacerbate problems in family relationships. Immediately following retirement, a transitional period occurs, marked by role confusion as the retiree struggles with his new and unfamiliar situation. Such role confusion is inevitable during this period and even emotionally healthy retirees report some degree of anxiety at this time. For most, the transitional period lasts for about 1 year and is then followed by stabilization in either a state of adjustment or maladjustment. Many retiring couples plan well, and for them the transition can be gratifying and exciting. Even for those with healthy adjustment, however, it appears to take approximately 3 years for the new civilian identity to become well solidified (Watson, 1963).

A major factor influencing the adjustment or maladjustment of these retirees and families is that of postretirement employment. In our society, one's occupational role is a major factor in one's sense of identity, self-esteem, and self-worth; and work has psychological value far beyond its financial rewards. Preretirement anxiety usually focuses on seeking employment, which may be easy for some but quite difficult for others. Those retirees with professional and other special vocational skills, knowledge, and/or connections which are in civilian demand are sought after and make highly successful career changes. Others, however, may find that their military skills do not always transfer easily into the civilian work force and that a civilian job which is equal to one's military status may be hard to find. The military retiree, although he is comparatively young, may be too old to be in demand by civilian work organizations, especially in positions of rank and status equivalent to his positions in the military.

McNeil (1976) described how preretirees start their job search with initial optimism, experience increasing anxiety when faced by the frustrations which are inevitable in that search, then become despondent, plagued with self-doubts, and often increasingly ineffective in their employment-seeking efforts. Most are able to become more realistic and eventually obtain employment which is a satisfactory compromise between what they initially anticipated and what they later feared. It is not uncommon for job changes to occur as part of the role confusion in the transitional year following retirement as the retiree gains understanding of the civilian world and himself and finds his initial job choice to be inappropriate. In a study of second careers, Platte (1976) found that perceived direction of social mobility was a predictor of psychological and marital adjustment for military retirees and their families. Not surprisingly, maladjustment usually accompanies movement to what is perceived as lower social status. Since status is so intimately associated with employment, employment is therefore of crucial importance in the adjustment of both retirees and their families.

It is important for the clinician to remember that some mild anxiety and depression are a natural part of the military retirement process, and minor emotional discomfort must be expected as the individual and the family experience this major life change. Reassurance and counseling should be available, but mild symptoms should not be given exaggerated importance, since they are part of a normal adjustment process.

Frequently, however, the therapist will be confronted with individuals and families in whom these symptoms have become dysfunctional and/or serious psychopathology has been precipitated by retirement. When such problems have their onset during the preretirement or transitional periods, they are more responsive to treatment than if allowed to stabilize into prolonged maladjustment. In my experience, such maladjustment is most often expressed in depressive syndromes, marital conflict, substance abuse, and acting-out behavior. Military retirement occurs in an age group that is at high risk for depression; and, as previously discussed, the retirement transition involves significant losses, both real and symbolic, and serious potential problems in status and self-esteem, all of which provide fertile ground for the growth of depressive illness. The role confusion, restructured relationships, and general anxiety of the retirement period often precipitate marital conflict or exacerbate that which has already existed. This is also true for substance abuse, with alcoholism in the retiree and/or spouse, and abuse of other drugs in the younger generation. Some aspects of military life may reinforce patterns of alcohol abuse and predispose the retiree to this problem. Drinking to relax, socialize, escape, or preserve a macho image while in the service may easily progress to pathological drinking after retirement. Often the maladjustment of the retiree and/or spouse is expressed behaviorally as they act in an impulsive and self-destructive manner, and the children become increasingly rebellious. The therapist frequently finds these symptoms and maladjustment patterns to coexist with depression, marital conflict, impulsive behavior, and alcoholism of the retiree and/or spouse, and drug abuse and open rebellion of the children.

The treatment of these retirement-related disorders is no different from the treatment of other emotional problems in that it must be individualized and follow the basic principles of good psychotherapy. Several factors, however, should be emphasized:

1. Be aware of retirement issues. The psychological effects of retirement on military retirees and their families must be considered by the therapist, even if the presenting emotional problems seem to have no immediate relationship to retirement. It is especially easy to overlook the importance of retirement issues as the years pass following retirement; and as maladjustment becomes fixed with the passage of time, the psychological significance of retirement may seem insignificant. It is important that the clinician maintain a high level of awareness concerning the crucial impact military retirement has on the emotional life of the retiree and his family.

2. Treat as soon as possible. Emotional problems and family conflicts involving retirement are most easily resolved during the periods of natural psychological change that are occurring in the preretirement and immediate postretirement transitional periods. This principle of crisis intervention (Caplan, 1964) is vital, for if maladjustment patterns in the individual and the family become fixed beyond those periods, therapeutic change becomes much more difficult.

3. Involve the family. Although the retiree or another individual family member may present with symptoms, it must be remembered that military retirement is a family event and requires a major readjustment for all family members. Consequently, if maximal results are to be achieved in treatment of disorders which are closely associated with military retirement, the family should be involved in the treatment process as much and as soon as possible.

4. Do not overtreat. Mild anxiety and depressive symptoms are an inherent part of the retirement transition. They respond to reassurance and supportive therapy and should not be maximized, overly medicated, or reinforced in a way that might encourage unnecessary therapeutic dependence.

Military retirement can serve a valuable and unique function in providing a vehicle for helping resolve the midlife transition of individual retirees and their families. Like most stressful experiences, it offers not only the risk of maladjustment but also the opportunity for positive emotional growth.

REFERENCES

Bellino, R. Psychosomatic problems of military retirement. *Psychosomatics*, 1969, *10*, 318–321.

Butler, R. N. *Why survive? Being old in America*. New York: Harper & Row, 1975.

Caplan, G. *Principles of preventive psychiatry*. New York: Basic Books, 1964.

Duvall, E. M. *Family development* (4th ed.). Philadelphia: Lippincott, 1971.

Erikson, E. H. Identity and the life cycle. *Psychological Issues*, 1959, *1*, 1–171.

Levinson, D. J., Darrow, E. B., Klein, E. B., Levinson, M. H., & McKee, B. *The seasons of a man's life*. New York: Knopf, 1978.

McNeil, J. S. Individual and family problems related to retirement from the military service. In H. McCubbin, B. Dahl, & E. Hunter (Eds.), *Families in the military system*. Beverly Hills, Calif.: Sage, 1976.

McNeil, J. S., & Giffen, M. B. Military retirement: The retirement syndrome. *American Journal of Psychiatry*, 1967, *123*, 849–853.

Platte, R. J. The second career: Perceived social mobility and adjustment among recent army retirees and wives of army retirees. In H. McCubbin, B. Dahl, & E. Hunter (Eds.), *Families in the military system*. Beverly Hills, Calif.: Sage, 1976.

Watson, J. H. *A study of social and occupational adjustment in relation to civilian and military identification of United States Air Force officers*. Unpublished doctoral dissertation, Mississippi State University, 1963.

11

Veterans: Their Families

JOHN ELDERKIN BELL

Hospitals are among the most dynamic institutions in our society. If not the leaders in dramatic changes, they are at least forced into rapid shifts in medical and administrative concepts and technologies by changing resources, public demands, political dynamisms, and personnel. To capture the essence of hospitals at any point in time does injustice to their past, and inadequately represents what they are in the process of becoming.

Among the most rapidly changing hospitals, in spite of a public image of entrenchment, are those of the Veterans Administration (VA). The political base from which they secure their support requires a unique sensitivity to the changing fortunes and demands of the country as a whole. Although forced by political direction most changes would be considered progressive by medical personnel.

The VA services are potentially available to slightly over 30 million veterans, a figure standing at an all-time high in the 1980s (Veterans Administration, 1981). The average age of eligible veterans is 50 years. Major peaks of population occurred in relation to the various wars. Personnel of World War I now average 84.9 years, and all are at least 75 years of age; of World War II, 60.6 years; of the Korean conflict, 48.8 years; and of the Vietnam era, 32.6 years. In addition, VA services are potentially available to 24.2 million spouses, 23.3 million dependent children under 8 years of age, and 10.3 million other family members.

The opinions or assertions contained herein are the private views of the writer and are not to be construed as official or as reflecting the views of the Veterans Administration.

John Elderkin Bell. Associate Professor Emeritus, Department of Psychiatry and Behavioral Sciences, Stanford University; Lecturer, Department of Psychiatry, School of Medicine, University of California, San Francisco; Adjunct Professor, Reader, San Francisco Theological Seminary; and formerly, Psychologist, Veterans Administration Hospital, Palo Alto, California.

More male veterans (84.8%) than nonveteran males (80.9%) worked during 1979. In addition, 89% have other than VA health insurance.

To serve these populations, the VA received an appropriation of over $20 billion for the fiscal year ending September 30, 1980. Within the VA Department of Medicine and Surgery, treatment services were provided to 1.25 million hospital inpatients, 12,750 nursing home patients, 15,180 domiciliary patients, and 18 million outpatients. A full range of medical, surgical, psychiatric, and rehabilitation services is available in 172 medical centers, 226 outpatient clinics, 92 nursing homes, and 16 domiciliaries. In addition, 91 community-based Veterans Centers have been founded to assist Vietnam-era veterans.

Any discussion of the place of the family within this massive program must be sketchy at best. Thus, one of the largest and most diverse of the service facilities, the Palo Alto VA Hospital, has been chosen to illustrate the range of available family services. The Palo Alto VA Hospital is composed of two hospitals under a single administration—the Palo Alto and the Menlo Park Divisions, about 8 miles apart.

The Palo Alto Division, with 694 average operative beds, is a teaching hospital associated with Stanford University and various other training centers. The Training Program provides formal and/or clinical training for medicine and surgery, psychiatry, psychology, social work, rehabilitation medicine, dentistry, nursing, occupational therapy, podiatry, and pharmacy. This Division houses one of two Regional Comprehensive Rehabilitation Centers, one of 18 Spinal Cord Injury Centers, and one of four Blind Rehabilitation Centers. In addition, it hosts one of eight Geriatric Research, Education, and Clinical Centers.

The Menlo Park Division, with 583 average operative beds, centers on mental health and rehabilitation, and provides an additional 150 beds in a nursing home care unit. Some clinical teaching programs there increase the total program range. This Division operates under an essentially separate administration, headed by a Chief of Staff who functions under the Director of the total Hospital.

The whole Hospital organization is complicated further by the presence of three 50-bed wards of the Menlo Park Division on the grounds of the Palo Alto Division, namely, part of those in the Extended Care Service, a treatment and rehabilitation program for long-term treatment of patients who usually have multiple physical and/or psychiatric disorders, and whose average age is well over 60 years. The other part of the Service occupies 90 beds in the Menlo Park Division. In addition, some of the programs in the Hospital serve the Western Region of the VA, Region 6, which includes Alaska, Arizona, California, Guam, Hawaii, Idaho, Nevada, New Mexico, Oregon, Washington, West Texas, and the Veterans Memorial Hospital, Manila.

Because of the regional rather than local pool of patients, distance from home becomes a critical deterrent to continuing family relations. This applies also within the average catchment area for the Hospital, which normally involves Northern California and occasionally extends to Nevada. Some patients even transfer into the Hospital from distant states to take advantage of particular services, or to be closer to relatives.

In an unpublished study of the patients in the Extended Care Service, where the average age is well above 60 years, the average distance from home for patients was found to be 52 miles. Inevitably such distances create hardships for spouses and others who themselves may be advanced in years.

Within the Hospital, the first 10 most common diagnoses in the period from October 1979 through March 1980 were as follows, in order of frequency: alcoholic addiction; habitual excessive drinking; schizophrenia; emphysema; schizophrenia, chronic undifferentiated type; chronic ischemic heart disease, without hypertensive disease; essential benign hypertension; diabetes mellitus—no acidosis, coma, or other complications; fracture and dislocation, any vertebrae, late effect, spinal cord lesion; other and unspecified diseases of the bladder.

FAMILY PROGRAMS

The following attempts to describe the family activities and relations throughout many services in the two units of the Hospital.

THE WESTERN BLIND REHABILITATION CENTER

The earliest of existing family programs is found in the Western Blind Rehabilitation Center, which opened in 1966 (Glass, 1980/1981). At that time families who lived nearby were encouraged to come in, but no arrangements were available for assistance to those from a distance. The Military Order of the Purple Heart began to help financially by arranging "Sleighride," a Christmas program for Northern California, to give the veteran a chance to spend the holiday at home. Later the Order assisted families to come to the Hospital to participate actively in the training program, since it had been found that patients who had developed new skills at the Hospital would deteriorate on return home because families would continue to care for them as they had done before rehabilitation.

Soon the Disabled Veterans of America picked up the costs for room and board for family members for 1 week, at a time when it would be most productive, usually about midway or nearer to the end of a patient's stay. After this orientation the families tended to accept better the capabilities of the patient. Later, the Order of the Purple Heart joined in the funding of the program. Ultimately, the VA provided the funds for relatives' transport, living accommodations, and meals. Now plans have been developed to add a new wing to the Blind Center, wherein a four-bed apartment will be constructed to house a visiting family.

A significant family member in the veteran's life, usually the one with whom he will live, comes to the Hospital. Nonrelatives cannot be accommodated, even though they may have a deeper relation with the patient. It is hoped that this might change in the future. When at the Hospital, the family learns what changes have taken place, the new capabilities of the patient, and the residual limitations. The relatives are helped to adapt to the patient's new developments, and are instructed how to assist, as for instance in guiding.

While the patient is in the program, he or she learns personal management techniques; new methods of personal hygiene; how to function in a kitchen, pay bills, write checks, and keep records. Many objections are raised by family members, who may be threatened by the veteran learning functions that he has not performed before. Staff usually resolve this by statements that they are not trying to change the ways in which the family has lived, but are trying to provide an alternative in case there is illness or other crises in the family.

It is recognized that some relatives have adjustment crises, also, and have to learn tasks that the patient formerly attended to. Staff try to help them in their learning. Usually there is more to worry the family. Sometimes a patient's wife gains more control and influence, and assumes responsibility because of the patient's disabilities. Staff try to anticipate where conflicts may arise and cause persons to deteriorate. Staff also help family members to mediate with other relatives, neighbors, and friends who may attempt to deprive the patient of learned competences. The patients learn that they must take their time about demonstrating their abilities until an occasion when a task is inconvenient for the family.

The general philosophy of the Center program is to remove as many restrictions as possible for the patient. Disability becomes handicapping when a person lacks a needed skill or is restricted to only one way to do things. For example, when a person learns to travel with a cane and with a dog, to take public transport, and to call a taxi, he has options. Acquiring these options constitutes freedom.

REGIONAL SPINAL CORD INJURY SERVICE

A similar program functions within VA Region 6 Spinal Cord Injury Service. Depending on the level of a patient's injury, the family is frequently involved in preparation for the patient's return home. Patients with injury of the upper extremities usually become completely independent and may choose to live elsewhere than in their own homes. Those with more severe injuries who cannot become fully independent may depend on the family for assistance, at least temporarily, although sometimes they hire supporting services.

Decisions about whom to involve in preparation for community rehabilitation are coordinated within a psychosocial team that includes the patient. Sometimes a choice is made for the veteran to return home for a temporary period. If a nonfamily member is to be involved, he or she may be included on the planning team.

Commonly, the family preparation begins on the Monday prior to the patient's discharge on the succeeding Friday. Transportation is provided for the families who live a considerable distance from the Hospital. The aim of the preparation is to help ease the transition from the hospital to the home. Even though the patients know the principles and procedures for their own care, the family may complicate the rehabilitation at the time of the first move home. If, for example, the patient is almost independent, a family may need to learn how to avoid doing things for him. If the family member is at the Hospital and around the patient full time for several days, he or she is eased into the new situation faced with the patient, and becomes a partner with him in achieving the maximum possible independence.

If families live within easy access of the Hospital, their training and preparation is accomplished more gradually. If the patient so wishes, a family member may be invited to attend the predischarge staff–patient conference.

THE FAMILY PROGRAM

Another early formal family program at the Hospital began in 1969 within the Inpatient Psychiatric Service. The program was founded by Dr. Sheldon Starr, a psychologist staff member who had received training in family therapy at the Mental Research Institute (Starr, 1981). With the assistance of three other professionals he began a seminar in family therapy for psychology interns, psychiatry residents, and some staff. A cadre of workers formed and the program developed into the Family Study Unit, a research and training program within the Psychology Service. It is probable that the early successes were contingent on the separation of the Unit from direct service operations, since semiautonomous status allowed much freedom in experimentation and limited expectations for production.

Many years later, after family-oriented activities proliferated throughout many of the Hospital's programs, separate status for the Unit became less strategic. Thus it has been incorporated into the Outpatient Psychiatric Clinic, and renamed the Family Program, so as to engage more easily the growing number of families referred by medicine and surgery. Five professionals continue to provide therapy and training.

The caseload in the clinical program consists of three groups of families:

- those referred for the treatment of medical problems (about 25% of the caseload);
- inpatient psychiatric referrals (about 25% of the caseload);
- outpatient referrals.

The referrals include families who, it is assumed, can be treated by family therapy in lieu of hospitalization: families where a son or daughter of a veteran is troubled; where sexual dysfunction is disturbing a couple; where prospective divorce, or mediation to prevent it, is sought; couples who are living together and contemplating marriage; same-gender couples; and an occasional transsexual couple. The total caseload averages 70 to 80 couples per week.

Family therapy and family-oriented programs are no longer exclusive to the Clinic, and other units use staff of the Family Program as consultants.

Four doctoral research projects have been conducted within the Program over the years, and staff themselves have used the services as a base for research.

INPATIENT PROGRAMS

THE EXTENDED CARE SERVICE

The next major family development came as an outgrowth of my experiences during 12 years as program director for the National Institute of Mental Health in the most western region of the country. During the course of this work throughout the nine states and territories I learned thoroughly the consultant role. During 3 of the years I conceived and carried out an extensive study of family participation in about 150 hospitals and clinics in Africa and Asia where the family cared for the patients (Bell, 1970).

It was not difficult for me to adopt a nearly full-time consultant role in the Palo Alto VA Hospital when appointed to the staff in 1973. My commission was to develop roles and functions for the family within the whole institution, beginning with the Extended Care Service, wherein patients with multiple physical and mental disorders were hospitalized for long periods.

Prior to my joining the staff, a limited involvement of patients' families was in process within the Extended Care Service. Staff had prepared a pamphlet addressed to patients' relatives in 1971. It described the composition of the staff, some of the patients' daily schedules, matters of personal hygiene, dining facilities, religious services, mail, handling of patients' funds and valuables, treatment, visiting hours, smoking, recreation, and discussion group meetings.

In 1972, staff and students from Stanford University made a sociological analysis of the Service over several months. Many revisions to improve the organization and interpersonal relations in the unit were proposed. Staff involvement was intensive, and the readiness for change was thought to have been well prepared. Regrettably, new proposals were shelved by top administration, leaving bitterness and pessimism among many staff, and a feeling that any efforts to involve the family would have to move very slowly.

I tread softly to gradually build relations with the few staff members who continued ready to increase family involvement. They consisted primarily of a social worker and a nurse whose tasks at that time involved community placement and follow-up of patients, that is, functioning in a staff rather than line role. The readiness of line staff to facilitate family participation was problematic; after the Stanford debacle, any move in the same direction might be suspect.

Six months after my appointment I was invited to attend a meeting of the chief nurses from each of four wards in the Palo Alto component of the Service. Wives of two patients had become what some staff, particularly the two staff physicians, regarded as unduly obnoxious. My presence was sought for some suggestions to handle this matter.

The approach to the meeting was careful and slow. While gathering information, a plan was developed to establish a committee with nursing representation from each ward, using other personnel such as the medical doctors as consultants. The committee operations were initiated by collecting staff ideas to define its central functions. The clinical coordinator, a nurse, became the first consultee. A report of the conference with her, stressing her positive support and her suggestions, was circulated to key staff.

The committee then met in turn with the head nurse on each of the four wards. We asked for information about the ways in which the nursing staff related to families, and for illustrations of their positive features. We knew the negative would be expressed anyway. Each session was fully transcribed. Copies were made available to each of the top staff in the service.

Little did we realize that it would be 18 months before a Family Committee would be formally organized. During all this time the ad hoc planning committee, expanded to include one of the chaplains, met nearly every week and, though initiating some positive actions, mostly waited.

Once the Family Committee had official standing, many delayed activities began to fall into place. For example, there were monthly family meetings on one of the wards; throughout the Service, a relaxation of stringent visiting hours; family participation on holidays and special occasions; inclusion of patients' family members on patient outings; major increases in staff consultation for families about caring for their patients; family involvement in treatment and rehabilitation planning sessions; training of staff for family participation; encouragement of relatives to assume practical and helpful duties for the patients, such as feeding them and taking care of their clothing; reexamination of the role of family members in hospital admissions; a ceremony of appreciation for family members who visited frequently; provision of special parking privileges; attention to the problems created by limited public bus service on Saturdays—and none on Sundays and holidays; securing special bus fares for families of patients; dinners for a fee on Christmas and New Year's days when the Hospital Canteen was closed; arrangements for visits by children; visits by volunteers to patients who had no families; arranging for family viewing at the morgue of the remains of a patient who had died; and so on.

Such practical efforts overcame some of the distress when patients were unable to communicate readily on account of disabilities. Enabling members of families to become acquainted with one another, to take part in group discussions and training sessions, and to plan and conduct various seasonal celebrations also modified the hospital climate toward a family orientation (Bell, 1975, 1978).

It is not unusual for polarization to develop between a family and certain hospital staff. Commonly this arises out of minor issues that are allowed to escalate to the level of open hostility. It is less common for groups of families to develop antipathies, but occasionally this happens, usually to the distress of staff. In the extreme, open warfare breaks out, and after escalation it is common for parties to lodge complaints with higher authorities.

On one occasion such an escalation took place in one ward of the Extended Care Service. I was asked to mediate and help reduce the tension. I requested an opportunity to speak with the family members who were in the habit of meeting monthly, quite often to complain about staff, as they were now doing. My approach perhaps took them off guard. I set up a lecturer's easel with a large pad, and asked them to tell me what they found good about the hospital—with the understanding that I would tell the ward staff. They reeled off a list of positives that I wrote on the pad—"patients are kept very clean"; "they take care of accidents right away"; "they answer every question—even if I don't like the answers"; and so on. Positive emphases unleashed some unexpected complaints and led to some suggestions. I did not agree to transmit these complaints and suggestions, and wrote them in small script on a separate sheet of paper.

A week later I attended a regular meeting of staff on the ward to tell them what the families had said. Staff were tense to start, but soon relaxed as compliment after compliment was recounted. Staff in turn were asked to tell what they found "good" about the relatives, and these items were similarly passed on to the relatives. A noticeable change took place in ward–relative relations, reducing the level of staff–family tensions.

The Family Committee within the Service continues to function, and now meets once a month to deal with ongoing family issues. Earlier stresses in relations between staff and family members have largely disappeared, and families are well accepted as part of the total treatment team.

Meanwhile, changes both in amount and form of family participation throughout the Hospital were beginning to take place. Today families are involved widely in both Divisions of the Hospital. According to the chief of the Nursing Service for the whole Hospital, including both Divisions, nurses have come gradually but firmly to the realization that the family is as much a part of the health team as medical staffs and the patients. The implementation of consequent programs is accelerating, and covers all services in the Hospital in at least some ways.

These programs take many different forms, related to variable factors —the nature of the illnesses and disabilities, the length of treatments, the extent of problems created by lack of family participation—which is closely related to the nature of persisting disabilities among patients. Further potent influences include the training and investment of staff, the extent of residual competence among patients, the community alternatives to the Hospital, the distances between the Hospital and homes, patient and family finances, entrenchment of certain treatment methods and service traditions, availability or lack of personnel and program resources, conservatism of some personnel, and political factors that determine the budget and patterns of organization and functions of the VA.

Even though the philosophy of family care has spread, in certain units of the Hospital this emphasis has not become translated into action. Where hospital stays are brief and pressures on staff are especially heavy, as in acute treatment, it is evident that staff find it difficult to deal with the family needs. Family visiting may be controlled within carefully defined limits. Consultations with staff may become aggravated and disruptive in the face of crises. Even so, some staff make themselves available to assist families. So also do the Hospital chaplains, whose crisis assistance for relatives is given top priority, and whose range of help shifts all the way from defined religious services to the most mundane but necessary help— as when they appear with a sandwich brought for a family member who waits near the ward, find a cot so the relative can catch a few moments rest, provide transportation to a local motel, and perhaps even, on occasion, cover the living costs out of volunteered funds.

One of the most dramatic developments in Hospital programming in recent years had been the creation of a wide range of family programs in the inpatient medical and surgical units of the Hospital. According to the Chief of Social Work, the psychiatric population has become more chronically ill and less responsive to social work efforts. In contrast, the medical staffs have been helped to become more sensitive to the social needs of their patients, and social work has shifted its focus to the developing of support systems for these patients.

Some further examples are as follows:

The Ear, Nose, and Throat Service

Support groups for family members are provided jointly by ward and Psychology Service staffs within the Ear, Nose, and Throat Service. The primary diagnosis on this unit is cancer. The social worker on the Service interviews a new patient to learn about the history of the illness, the family, and their living situations. When family members have problems around the illness and disfiguring consequences of the treatments, they are referred to the staff psychologist who serves on the ward. He reports his findings to the biweekly staff meeting, attended by the social worker, public health nurse, residents, nursing staff, dietitian, and others as available. Following a very free discussion, the person who has the closest relation with the family is assigned to follow them and deal with their problems.

Prior to surgery, the nurses try to teach the patient some of the things to be expected, such as the anticipated problems with eating, moving around, perhaps talking and respiration, and the discomfort of procedures of care and treatment. An effort is made to reassure each patient at that time, so as not to induce undue anxiety. Family members may also be instructed about what to expect, and this helps them to support the patient.

Once-a-week a group meeting for patients and families provides a forum where they may speak about their feelings, concerns, relations with staff, and reactions to the treatment, ward, and Hospital. In the free environment new participants soon open up and talk.

Later, a multidisciplinary group meets with the family for planning and follow-up. Most patients and families turn to a different style of living which brings its own problems, but also its rewards. For example, a former patient who has since died had the entire side of his face removed. In spite of this, the woman with whom he lived would take him out of the Hospital on pass and was very supportive throughout the whole period until his death. Staff regarded this as a considerable achievement on her part, as well as their own, for he had been known as a wastrel who gave her many sorrows by running around with other women and neglecting her badly. She learned from staff to provide much nursing care, changing the dressings, supervising the medications, helping to feed him, and caring for him until his death.

Artificial Kidney Center

Around 30 patients are in the Center at any one time. About 15 are supported by home dialysis, for which staff provide follow-up. Five or six patients are on continuous ambulatory peritoneal dialysis. In the Center, family involvement began 7 years ago. The head nurse has promoted a strong family role, within which other staff are allowed to participate as they choose.

Before dialysis begins, if the patient allows it, family are invited to attend an orienting education series. The patient and family, usually together, are seen by the social worker, dietitian, and nurse. When dialysis starts, training for home treatment is begun with the wife, other family members, or home help. Nursing staff encourage as many as possible to get involved, and especially those in the home support system.

Almost all of the inpatient nurses become involved with the family. After the return home, nursing staff, a social worker, and home nurses continue contact as needed.

The Family-Oriented Biofeedback Clinic

The clinic functions within the Health Psychology Program, under the direction of a psychologist. The Program links intrapsychic systems with those in the patients' environments, and particularly to relations with family members. During the period while a patient is on a waiting list for biofeedback, a group didactic stress management course has been developed for patients and their spouses. During this course basic relaxation skills are taught.

It has been found necessary, especially with spouses, to deemphasize the psychological and psychosocial aspects of biofeedback during the training, in order to avoid the impression that the major purpose is psychotherapy. The biofeedback lowers the tension level of couples, and appears to bond their relations by providing new ways for them to be together.

Oncology Service

The family program in the Oncology Service varies immensely from day to day, and is contingent upon the patients who are presently hospitalized, the availability of relatives, and the extent of problems and issues that concern them. An average of four out of ten families receives help, particularly from the head nurse.

A major component of the support and counseling relates to the prospects that the illness will be terminal. Discussions may be initiated by the patient alone, by relatives, or with both together. Counseling is highly personalized, although problems between the doctor and the patient, and those associated with patient stress management, are common.

The doctors tend to keep the patient and his family at arm's length. The nurse helps to break down the distance and solve problems between the doctors, the patient, and his family. She sums up her role as "providing support wherever she learns that it is deficient"—a functional and inventive role.

Further, patients are now being helped and encouraged to die at home. Social workers are organizing emotional supports and helping to work out nursing care at the bedside.

Inpatient Psychiatry Service

One of the wards in the Menlo Park Division has been designated as the "family" inpatient psychiatric ward. A clinical specialist nurse takes primary responsibility for implementing the treatment program. She is a trained family therapist who started on the ward with the concept that the family of each patient would become involved. This proved unrealistic. Many patients are hospitalized involuntarily. This is the only VA Hospital in Northern California that admits such patients. Inevitably distance from homes prevents easy access for many families. Further, families are frequently burned out by efforts to assist their patients, and thus unprepared to engage in further efforts.

When a patient first comes to the ward, a staff assessment group determines if relatives live in easy reach of the Hospital, and where and with whom the patient has been living. If the relatives are willing to come, an independent assessment is made of their suitability for involvement in family work. If a family collaborates with staff on the treatment, family therapy is not necessarily the first choice for treatment. This partly relates to staff availability. Only the specialist nurse is a trained family therapist. Other nursing staff do not seem eager to learn this treatment modality at this time.

Another clinical specialist nurse with family therapy training is needed, but the recession has limited hiring potential. If a coworker for family therapy can be recruited, a new approach will be taken. The ward staff are currently divided into teams to maintain care and treatment of a group of patients. These teams will be joined by the family therapists who will teach and demonstrate that the families are not necessarily the basis of the patients' problems, nor uninvolved, nor unresponsive to efforts of staff to assist the patient and them.

That attitudes to families can be changed has been shown through a monthly "Family Night" on the ward. Each family receives a special invitation, often with appended personal notes. The session is for family members alone. The kinds of treatments are explained, questions are dealt with, entertainment is provided, and food prepared by the patients is served, with due note of the patients' part in the preparation.

Vietnam Veterans Program

Two wards have been opened at the Menlo Park Division to house 90 alienated young Vietnam veterans, "burned up with society." Staff assisted by social workers design groups and build interpersonal responsibility so that new social roles may be practiced. The men serve as volunteers doing the hard labor at Little House, a senior center; assist in the VA Nursing Home; provide an emergency squad to evacuate Hospital buildings in a crisis; and take on other social responsibilities. The veterans then become givers rather than receivers.

In a similar way they and social work staff volunteer to assist some families, for example, those in the hospice program, and serve in concrete ways—sharing rides with those who need transportation, providing child care, finding and passing on recipes to assist a person on a diet. They gain a network of families with whom they remain connected through death and grieving. Encountering, sharing, and resolving the problems of others makes their activities meaningful and strengthens the families.

Nursing Home Care

Also in the Menlo Park Division of the Hospital, a new 150-bed building was opened 2 years ago for Nursing Home Care. At that time the duration of stays in the old Nursing Home for the 100 patients was from 12 years to 53 years. New admissions were contingent, essentially, on beds becoming available through patient deaths. Eighty-seven of the 100 patients no longer held a community place of residence, and fewer than 15% received visits.

When the new facility was opened, many additional staff were employed. A major shift in philosophy of care, emphasizing rehabilitation, family involvement, and short-term care, was initiated. The level of severity of illness among those admitted was not reduced, but the length of stay is gradually being lessened by staff education, new policies, and new patient programs.

In the first major training efforts led by family-oriented psychologists each of three identical workshops on "The Family and the Nursing Home" included one third of the staff. Each workshop was strengthened by an interview with a patient and his family, and by discussions. Focus was placed on discovering family's attitudes to provided care. These interviews stimulated many program suggestions, ideas about providing care, and new concepts of treatment. A similar education program on "depression" was held this past year.

In addition to changing some aspects of daily care to accommodate a family orientation, two new family programs have been initiated to reduce hospitalization for home-based veterans, and to emphasize, as far as possible, alternatives to hospitalization. The first, a hospice, was opened gradually, and now provides five beds for this purpose. A clinical specialist nurse and a public health nurse have been added to offer additional support to families. Social work staff assist the family with planning for the patient's death, and especially for practical realities that must be attended to.

One of the chaplains, along with other staff and a volunteer community group, has assumed major responsibility for assisting families in this program, the nursing home, and the community.

A support group for wives whose husbands have died has emerged. The group helps the wives through the emotional consequences of bereavement, and helps them to experience and deal with guilt, depression, isolation, and similar problems. So also the group assists with the practical matters that have to be taken care of around the time of death, during the mourning, and thereafter.

Dr. Mark P. Graeber, Chief of Staff of the Menlo Park Division, recounts many human stories in the minutes of the hospice. It becomes easily apparent that the process of dying is not an absolute. Many aspects of the involved relations create vast differences. The family and the patient make a "unique patient." Every death has its own character. For example, one patient who had been living with a woman decided to marry her—and he died within an hour of the wedding. Another, a salesman, with an alcoholic second wife and kids who were out of control, spent every minute up to his death trying to sell as much as he could so they would have an economic cushion. As varied also are the families' reactions to a patient's pain—for example, one family welcomes openly the use of morphine, and the next takes the attitude "You're going to get addicted if you take that!"

The second new program, for *family respite*, gives rest to burdened family members taking care of severely handicapped persons. Hospitalization for periods of various lengths is arranged to allow families to recuperate from intense pressures, and to attend to personal business, social needs, and recreation. The hospitalization functions under strictly observed time limits so as to prevent building up an expectation of prolonged hospital care, and to allow maximal use of the five beds devoted to respite care.

Originally there was considerable resistance to seeking the advantages of this program. Gradually, however, the idea has gained enthusiastic support, and the demand has now increased to the point where there is a need to expand the program. Associated with this program is a newly developed respite life support group for assisting the spouses. A mutual support network has emerged. Staff are also considering a day respite program for seriously disabled veterans with extensive nursing needs. There is a general recognition of the humane aspects of these programs, and of economic and social benefits in the collaboration between families and Nursing Home staffs.

Two public health nurses visit patients in their homes or community institutions to provide rehabilitation and maintenance in the community. The functions of these staff are supported by the Menlo Park Elder Veteran Day Center that operates 5 full days per week. Many family activities and special celebrations are offered there during the year, and the psychologist and social worker in charge are very attuned to family issues and concerns. On occasion they are called on for family counseling and backup services.

The hospice and respite programs are really dependent on the communications of the nurse and social worker. According to Dr. Graeber, the oncologists and the bedside aides are invaluable for managing many of the day-to-day tasks, but they are insufficient to handle the communications, the emotions, the relationships, and the setting. Here is where the social worker and the nurses come into their optimal relations.

This also suggests another aspect of appropriate care, the provision of space for the patient *and the family.* Unfortunately, hospitals as they exist have been designed for the past, and it has been the unfortunate policy that if there is new technology requiring space, the space is taken from what is available for the patient and family. The hospice and respite programs are demonstrating the need to rethink priorities, and to acknowledge how indispensable the families are to patient welfare. For example, when the new Nursing Home building was planned, a large recreation room was specified and built. Recently the room was subdivided into four areas: a library, a game room, a television room, and a *family room.* The last offers privacy, and thus removes interference from staff and disturbed psychiatric patients.

Dr. Graeber cited a still further demonstration of the importance of families: In spite of the intensity of hard physical labor and the seeming lack of communication with many Nursing Home patients, the turnover rate of staff is very low. This he attributes to the ongoing presence of family members.

A problem he identified concerns the Hospital's adaptability to family time. For example, with so many women working now, the daytime visiting hours are only seldom available to them, or to those who must transport them. Clearly, visiting hours must change.

The Nursing Home program still advances. Plans have recently been developed to provide an academic home study program for nurses. If the negotiations with the academic center are successful, the course will center on social and family interrelations.

OUTPATIENT PROGRAMS

The family also plays a critical role in the wide diversity of outpatient programs. Some of the family efforts take place at the Hospital, while many are carried on at home. In some of these programs, family activities are minimal. Relatives often do no more than serve as an escort when a patient comes to a clinic to meet with some of the support staff. Other services depend heavily on families, and deliberately program for their involvement.

REHABILITATION OF ALCOHOLICS

In the Menlo Park Division, group sessions with wives and other family members, or for close associates of patients, help with the rehabilitation of alcoholics, even though the patients themselves do not like their wives and girl friends to become involved with staff. Formerly, it was easy for patients to manipulate their families or friends who become distraught over the circumstances leading to hospitalization. With staff help, resistance to manipulation has been developed among patients' associates. They have learned, as well, how to deal with their own feelings about the patients' problems, and thus have moved toward becoming supporters of the rehabilitation program.

THE BRAIN INJURY CLINIC

In an article describing the outpatient program of the Brain Injury Clinic in the Menlo Park Division, Mauss-Clum and Ryan (1981) note that approximately half of the patients are young men from 20 to 35 years of age who are being treated for the residual effects of traumatic injury. The remaining patients are older men (50 to 65 years of age) who have suffered brain injury from stroke or cardiac disease. Most are not referred to the Clinic until after the acute early phases of the disorder have passed, that is, for most, after 6 months.

When a veteran is first referred to the Clinic, an effort is made to provide conferences with the family. First the patient's condition, prognosis, and future capabilities are discussed. Financial counseling is offered, since it may be critical to future family welfare. As the treatment of the patient progresses family reaction to the changes is evaluated, and counseling is offered in regard to decision making or postponement, rest and recuperation, housing, and other major decisions.

The head nurse and psychology technician lead the Family Support Group for relatives of patients who are being treated. About 10 relatives meet twice a month in the late afternoon, and together they cope with problems that individuals have not been able to solve on their own. The stresses upon these family members are intense, since the patients are living at home or in the community, and attending the Clinic through the day to receive treatment, undergo relearning, and begin to master new skills to compensate for those that have been lost or enfeebled.

ELDER DAY CARE CENTER

Within the Elder Day Care Center, established in late 1978, the primary program focus is on older veterans who come during the day to participate in varied activities. There is little direct association with the relatives of the participants, except on occasional open-house visits. Occasionally, family crises draw in staff of the Center. For example, in one case a high-functioning engineer suddenly became disoriented with Alzheimer's disease, and had to be placed in a board and care home in a black neighborhood. He was a regular participant in the Day Care Center which became his principal means of social and psychological support. His daughter, objecting to the neighborhood where he was placed, arranged a transfer to a small village about 100 miles away where he knew no one. His drastic deterioration was rapid, and he became so disoriented that he had to be brought back and placed in the VA Nursing Home. The daughter gave up all relations with him, in spite of efforts by staff to involve her further.

In contrast, one of the few World War I veterans within the Day Care Center brought to Hospital attention a buddy, 92 years old, who was living alone in the nearby community and had recently suffered an acute organic brain syndrome. The Hospital admitted him until his major symptoms cleared, and then, with assistance from the Center staff, helped the family to plan resources of caretakers and other services to enable the man to return to his home.

The Day Care Center, begun in 1978 as a VA pilot program, functions through the week within a family orientation, even though most services are for individuals. Thus staff become acquainted with family members, invite them to special programs, provide consultation to them, and include them in planning for future services. For example, staff are now planning to extend services by forming a support group for spouses of participants.

THE FAMILY FOLLOW-UP PROGRAM

This service in the Outpatient Psychiatry Clinic in the Palo Alto Division began in 1976 as a research project under Dr. David Spiegel of Stanford University. The aim was to study the effects of providing 6-week follow-up for patients discharged to their homes. A visit to a home by staff each week was contemplated, but in practice occurred less frequently. Prior to leaving the Hospital, the patient, and family members if possible, met with a member of the staff to make preliminary arrangements for the visit. The staff and consultants followed these arrangements with a full-scale review of the patient's hospitalization and of what was known about the family and their needs. What could be accomplished in 6 weeks required critical thought, for which the initial planning sharpened perceptions and limited the scope of aims. For instance, in one case a patient was being seen by 11 different professionals in the Hospital, and virtually none of them planned in relation to the others. The follow-up planning session brought to light the conflicts and contradictions among the work that had been done by these staff, and developed a coordinated plan for additional services.

After the first home visit, staff returned to report—sometimes with surprise, commonly with dismay, and seldom with as much hope as might have been predicted at the patient's discharge. Planning took on a sharper edge and more realistic goals were set. An immense variety of interventions were conceived and undertaken—from an intensive effort to secure family therapy to pragmatic efforts to arrange transportation, find a job, help the wife to get occasional relief, bring in a community resource to continue the assistance, or reach some exotic or parochial goal that could never have been anticipated, but now seemed indicated.

After the data collection period was completed, staff met with great success in working with medically ill veterans and their families. The majority of the patients are over 65 years of age, and quite a few are in their eighth and ninth decades. For the most part these have been relatively successful persons who must now accept help. They can no longer afford fees for service; their supports in the family have shrunk, and they are now often removed from former friends and associates in the community who previously had helped them through emergencies.

These patients do not necessarily fit into any specific unit in the Hospital, since many have multiple disorders, including medical, psychiatric, and practical problems. Community Services staff are called to advise on possible resources for assistance.

Staff have found that if there are good family ties, the family can normally be helped through a crisis with increasing ease—it is like calling on a bank for resources—even if the outcome is the death of the patient. Staff have recently gained permission to continue helping a family even after a patient's death. In a sense staff, with administration backing, regard themselves as part of the veteran's legacy to the family members. Staff are not finished with advancing their program, and are now setting forth further ideas to employ.

VIETNAM VETERANS CENTERS

Nationally, and for many years since the termination of the Vietnam War there was a strong reluctance among a majority of Vietnam veterans to become involved with official government agencies, including the VA. Regarding their circumstances and problems as beyond those of other veterans, they and other concerned citizens lobbied for a separate program to "address the emotional wounds of the war." It is estimated that 35% of Vietnam combat veterans have severe emotional difficulties. Five hundred thousand may be experiencing combat distress reactions and are expected to need professional help up to the middle 1980s (Wilson, 1977; Goodwin, 1980).

Accordingly, Public Law 96-22, 1979, mandated a readjustment counseling program for Vietnam veterans. To implement the program, the law specified responsibility of the VA, and charged it to offer priority access for service-connected illnesses and disorders. A basic mission to provide counseling for crises and life-adjustment difficulties to veterans who did not require service for complex psychiatric and medical problems led to the establishing of store-front centers close to where concentrations of veterans were living.

The centers are part of a network of 91 centers nationally, which served 27,850 veterans during 1979–1980, and recorded 15,377 visits from family members. The majority of veterans suffer from the disorder now called "posttraumatic stress disorder." This follows a course of development from (1) trauma in a climate of violence; (2) repression of the trauma which it had not been possible for them to work through in Vietnam, nor upon their return to the United States; (3) recurrences of intrusive thoughts, nightmares, flashbacks, and other trauma; and (4) psychic numbing, leading to difficulties in relating to others, social distancing, restlessness, and a lack of meaning to life. Most of their disordered behavior is internalized and self-destructive, with records of heavy use of alcohol and drugs, multiple employments, marital problems, separations and divorces, and legal problems. Anxiety and depression are common; interpersonal problems frequent; and even with opportunities for employment, work problems typical (Goodwin, 1980).

Ninety-nine percent of the mission of the established centers is to provide individual, group, and family counseling, normally offered to veterans on a weekly basis for a mutually determined time. The core of the work is the excavation of impacted grief or guilt.

In the case of the Palo Alto VA, two centers were developed in the city of San Jose, about 20 miles from the Hospital. One center is headed by a young social worker who functioned in Vietnam as a cross-cultural social worker. He leads a four-man team. Each month 40 to 60 new clients are seen. Over 200 separate contacts with clients are made each month, mostly with individuals. Each counselor also meets with three groups of eight veterans each week for 3-hour sessions. Occasionally, groups of wives are also formed to deal with problems of abuse by husbands.

Many referrals are made by family members. By staff preference, counseling involves couples and occasionally, families with children. The veteran's wife comes to know better what her husband experienced in Vietnam, how to help her spouse, and how better to protect herself and gain her own time and cathartic benefits.

It is common for the veterans to flirt with personal issues in the counseling and then withdraw, almost as though waiting to hit bottom. The irony is that they have a deep longing to achieve relations but an immense fear of exposing themselves. It must be remembered that the majority of the recruits were in the late adolescent years (average age, 19.7 years) when they entered the service. They were in a sense forced into maturity, but without the necessary development of emotional maturity— children charged with the tasks of men.

In the other center, where a psychologist is in charge, there is a total staff of four, including two technicians and a secretary. They meet about 50 new cases each month, and conduct about 100 separate patient contacts.

This center was colocated with the American GI Forum, a center under the U.S. Department of Labor, primarily for the Chicano population, to meet the needs for job counseling and finding, GI upgrades, and to deal with problems associated with disabilities. The Forum program centered on job placement. It tended to avoid persons with emotional disturbance, psychoses and illnesses. The collaboration did not work out.

At the end of 1980, the center moved to a nearby separate location. Some new personnel were hired to bring the staff up to full complement. The caseload escalated, and they are now negotiating for larger space.

Snapshots taken in Vietnam showing themselves in uniform were requested of those coming to the center. The pictures were enlarged and put on the walls. This signals an attempt to integrate the Vietnam life with what took place before the service, and what will now follow.

Staff are also involved in a Vietnam Veterans Club to provide an informal setting for them to meet, so they can start from the commonalities of the Vietnam experience to come back into the mainstream. Before Christmas, 981 members of the Club arranged to sell 1000 trees, providing jobs for 8 to 10 unemployed veterans. This marked a first step toward a nonprofit employment service for the more diffident of veterans. This program may ultimately eventuate into organized chapters of the Vietnam Veterans of America.

Couples are seen individually, or on Thursday evenings there is a couples' group, mostly discussing marital problems. For combat veterans, group meetings are held on Monday and Wednesday evenings. The veterans commit themselves to 10 sessions. The group is open for the first 2 weeks and then those who will continue make a commitment; 12 to 15 start, and it is typical for 6 to 8 to stay through to the end.

Those persons coming to the center who need intensive treatment are referred to the VA Hospital. Because there is great reluctance on their part, staff personally bring the prospective patients to visit. A special Young Vets Program with 90 inpatient beds has been developed at the Menlo Park Division. About 60 to 70 of these beds go to Vietnam veterans. After the initial contact, even though they are wary of the VA and the government, most enter the program. Staff preparation for the hassle of the bureaucracy seems to give the veterans enough confidence to go through the whole intake process and a lockup for a couple of days prior to entering the full program.

In sum, we have identified the following program elements within the Palo Alto VA Hospital:

1. promoting public recognition of the importance of families in the hospital;
2. increasing family access and participation during admission of a patient and throughout treatment;
3. building informal social relations between families and staff through joint events, seasonal activities, public recognition;
4. planning and problem solving, jointly between families and staff;
5. educating, training, and counseling families by courses, workshops, lectures, and consultations;
6. changing hospital protocol, procedures, and attitudes toward family aims, as well as those of the patient and staff;
7. assisting families by emotional support and catharsis, tension reduction, financial assistance, improved communications;
8. providing space for families in the hospital;
9. individuating staff activities with and for patients;
10. job finding and placement;
11. offering family respite from the stresses of intensive care for a disabled and difficult family member;
12. planning and assisting posthospital follow-up through planning resources in the community for the patient and the family;
13. supporting the family through a patient's dying, death, and postdeath follow-up.

AN OVERVIEW

The effect on the family of illness of a veteran is as varied as that found in response to males in other hospitals. The proportions of patients of low and lower-middle socioeconomic status tend to parallel those for males in the largest public hospitals. The family patterns range all the way from rejection of the patient to intensive family presence and involvement.

Earlier, relatives tended to be regarded by staff as inevitable responsibilities, to be put up with but expected to conform to staff's expectations. Exceptions were more commonly made for those who were deferent, unobtrusive, uncomplaining, undemanding, and generous to staff. Those who made demands, sought many special privileges, complained to social workers, chiefs in a service, the hospital director, or wrote to their congressional representatives, were of necessity tolerated, but often became "enemies" to staff.

Thus, for the families a central part of handling the illness of their patient became a political issue, confounded by the dependency of the patient and the family on public resources.

Many complexities in patient–hospital relations are introduced by the welter of regulations that govern the hospital. Many of these regulations, and the greater part of the funding are generated in Washington and transmitted throughout the total VA system. Other regulations are developed and enforced by the local hospital. This makes it possible for staff to cite a regulation for almost any problem created by relatives—and if there is not one, for one to be developed.

An issue of importance for the family arises as well from the entitlement that controls the availability of VA care for the veteran and his family. Eligibility for treatment is rated according to percentage of involvement of military service in the development of the illness or disability. Ratings are determined for many on a periodic basis, and affect the patient and his family as well. Thus a patient whose illness is rated as due entirely to military service will have top priority for admission, and the family will receive maximum government support while the patient is hospitalized. Inevitably this promotes extension of hospital stays, and induces some families to encourage illness and prolong their own benefits thereby.

Some family members become adroit in managing the complicated system for their patient's and their own welfare. At the other extreme are some with little clout who are pushed hither and yon, and may not even receive benefits to which they are entitled.

Thus, perhaps more than in most large hospitals, the patient and the family become aware of and constrained by hospital management. In spite of the above, however, there has been a progressive improvement in family–hospital relations. Most of the working staffs on the wards are involved in their work and dedicated to patient welfare—often extending themselves far beyond hospital expectations.

The roots of the move to include families in the hospital extends back into the 1930s, for instance, to Adolf Meyer (1948). Families had been participants in hospitals during the early 1800s. Then a long gap followed, essentially until the end of World War II. Thereafter, a major cultural shift accompanied the resumption of family participation in the hospital. The nation poured resources into the training and placement of veterans, and an upgrading of work and family ensued. Even the most lowly jobs assumed titles of respect and dignity. The GI Bill supported education from short-term training all the way to the PhD. An air of optimism prevailed, and out of that climate came the "baby boom."

During this period, medicine began widely to emphasize the family. In 1948, a major national conference to discuss the place of the family in medicine was held in Berkeley, California (Richardson, 1948). Journal articles on medical care began to stress the importance of the family, especially in the care of children (Levy, 1945; Prugh, Staub, Sands, Kirschbaum, & Lenihan, 1953; Senn, 1945; Spence, 1946). The family moved into prominence as a unit in public health. Family therapy was initiated by psychiatrists and psychologists, and, somewhat later, by social workers. Bowlby (1949, 1952) and others (Peplau, 1952; Robertson, 1958) proposed professional moves to counter separation of families by institutions, especially hospitals. The family rather than the individual as a unit of service began to be strongly endorsed, and strangely enough was accentuated by the Vietnam War, against which family protest emerged, even though the war itself disrupted family living, and added the problems of protest among youth and their supporters.

Psychiatry, assuming stature in medical circles, began to spread its impact beyond the treatment of mental disorders to command significant attention to the emotional factors in all manner of diseases and health. This became represented in increased attention to emotional factors in outpatient medical treatment, and ultimately within the hospital. It was not until the 1970s, however, that a growing family orientation began to have a major impact throughout wide segments of the hospital.

In support of these shifts, models of family treatment and sociological and psychological theories to support institutional changes were developed. But it has taken interpreters and developers of these models to mobilize widespread movements to include families in hospitals. Assisting in these changes have been key staff persons who have supported family and other social transactions in the hospitals. Such change agents sometimes occupy prestige positions in the hospital; others move from less prominent bases to induce change—sometimes slowly, but perhaps therefrom allowing assimilation of change to take place organically and with greater impact.

The VA was duly affected by these many cultural shifts. Now, with its capacity to generate change on a national level, we find it at the center—if not in the forefront—of hospitals and clinics that are adopting a family-oriented model of treatment and care for disabled persons. Perhaps no more telling sign of these changes has been the unpublished results of a survey of VA mental health programs in 1978. The survey showed that there were more hospitals (145) offering family therapy than any other of 41 treatment programs. Nor is it surprising that nearly 100 new positions for family specialists were created within the VA in 1977–1978, and that they have been dispersed throughout most of the VA hospitals and clinics.

REFERENCES

Bell, J. E. *The family in the hospital: Lessons from developing countries.* Washington, D.C.: U.S. Government Printing Office, 1970.

Bell, J. E. *Family therapy.* New York: Aronson, 1975.

Bell, J. E. Family context therapy: A model for family change. *Journal of Marriage and Family Counseling,* 1978, *4*(1), 111–126.

Bowlby, J. The study and reduction of group tensions in the family. *Human Relations,* 1949, *2,* 123–128.

Bowlby, J. *Maternal care and mental health* (WHO Monograph No. 2, 2nd ed.). Geneva, Switzerland: World Health Organization, 1952.

Glass, E. J. Problem drinking among the blind and visually impaired. *Alcohol World.* 1980/1981, *5*(2), 20–25.

Goodwin, J. *The etiology of combat-related post-traumatic stress disorder of the Vietnam veteran.* New York: Basic Books, 1980.

Levy, D. M. Psychic trauma of operations in children and a note on combat neurosis. *American Journal of Diseases of Children,* 1945, *69,* 7–25.

Mauss-Clum, N., & Ryan, M. Brain injury and the family. *Journal of Neurological Nursing,* 1981, *13,* 165–169.

Meyer, A. *The common sense psychiatry of Adolf Meyer* (edited and with biographical narrative by Alfred Lief). New York: McGraw-Hill, 1948.

Peplau, H. E. *Interpersonal relations in nursing.* New York: Putnam's, 1952.

Prugh, D. S., Staub, E. M., Sands, H. H., Kirschbaum, R. M., & Lenihan, E. A. A study of the emotional reactions of children and families to hospitalization and illness. *American Journal of Orthopsychiatry,* 1953, *23,* 70–106.

Richardson, H. B. *Patients have families.* New York: Commonwealth Fund, 1948.

Robertson, J. *Young children in hospitals.* New York: Basic Books, 1958.

Senn, M. J. E. Emotional aspects of convalescence. *The Child,* 1945, *10,* 24–28.

Spence, J. C. *The purpose of the family: A guide to the care of children.* London: Epworth, 1946.

Starr, S. The Palo Alto VA Center Family Program. *The Family Therapist*, 1981, *2*(2), 7–12.

Veterans Administration. *1980 annual report*. Washington, D.C.: U.S. Government Printing Office, 1981.

Wilson, J. P. *Identity, ideology and crisis: The Vietnam veteran in transition*. Testimony given before the U.S. Senate Subcommittee on Veterans Affairs, Senator Alan Cranston, Chairman, Washington, D.C., June 22, 1977.

12

Military Family Service Centers

RUTH ANN O'KEEFE

MELANIE C. EYRE

DAVID L. SMITH

The composition, outlook, and priorities of military families have changed dramatically in recent years (Orthner, 1980b; Orthner & Chandler, 1980). While the reasons for these changes are many and varied and will be briefly sketched below, the net result has been an across-the-board, broadly based appeal for more organized, institutionalized services for military families. In the past few years, these services have begun to appear.

Only recently has the phrase "military families" been seen on lists of defense priorities. Several reasons exist for the conspicuous, earlier absence of this term.

First, there are many more military families now than ever before (Parry, 1981; Sarkesian, 1975; Simon & Zald, 1964). Global and strategic priorities since World War II have required the United States to maintain a formidable, standing peacetime military for the first time in our history. The recent emphasis on nuclear parity and discussions revolving around nuclear confrontation tend to obscure the fact that our requirements for conventional warfare are also massive. Since the end of the draft in 1973, the United States has attempted to maintain over 2 million volunteers in uniform (Moskos, 1978). The Army has thousands of servicemembers stationed overseas to fulfill our NATO commitments. Due to tensions in

The opinions or assertions contained herein are the private views of the writers and are not to be construed as official or as reflecting the views of the Department of the Navy or the Department of Defense.

Ruth Ann O'Keefe, Director and founder, Navy Family Support Program, Washington, D.C.

Melanie C. Eyre, Budget Specialist, Navy Family Support Program, Washington, D.C.

David L. Smith, Deputy Director, Navy Family Support Program, Washington, D.C.

the Middle East and the increasing importance of foreign oil, the Navy's manpower, mobilization, and support requirements have seen a corresponding rise.

As of March 1981, 2,062,050 military members were on active duty. Over 1,090,000 were married. In September 1980, *dependents alone* numbered more than 2,826,560 (Parry, 1981). Military families now comprise 2 or 3% of all U.S. households (Orthner & Chandler, 1980).

Where did all these members and dependents come from? More importantly, what is the military doing for them?

BACKGROUND

A SINGLE MILITARY

Prior to World War II, the military services were the bastion of single men (Bowen, 1981). The level of education of enlisted personnel was not as high as today (Train, 1978), and the gap between them and the officer corps was pronounced. Officers, many of whom were Academy graduates, constituted a small, elite, and homogeneous group coming from similar backgrounds and generally ascribing to similar viewpoints on their role specifically and the military profession in general. Integration of these officers and enlisted personnel into the civilian community was limited, military duties and civilian occupations being vastly different.

MILITARY EXPANSION

World War II changed a great deal of that. First, mobilization demanded a huge influx of uninitiated civilian personnel into both the officer and enlisted communities (Simon & Zald, 1964). Many enlisted personnel ventured into the commissioned ranks through Officer Candidate School. These officers brought with them experiences, backgrounds, and educations previously unknown in the officer corps and succeeded in greatly "democratizing" that body.

Through the Reserve Officer Training Corps (ROTC) program, graduates of civilian universities were introduced into the services in large numbers, also for the first time. For many, joining ROTC was a desirable way to avoid the draft, serve one's country in time of war, and achieve the prestige of the commissioned officer. ROTC entrants brought with them an essentially civilian outlook. Most had no plans to continue in a full-time military career (Simon & Zald, 1964).

FAMILY GROWTH AND SERVICES

As military end-strength increased, so too did the number of dependents. Increased numbers were accompanied by a new, official concern over family problems, especially those of the enlisted community since most troubles developed there. Programs were begun to ease the transition of these "citizen soldiers" into the military life-style. Families were given assistance in the areas of housing, financial management, schooling, medical services, and personal/family adjustment (Sarkesian, 1975). While these programs were designed for enlisted families, officers and their dependents also felt the impact of this new "taking care of our own" philosophy.

This attitude extended into the period of massive demobilization following World War II. Efforts made to help veterans were indeed impressive and consisted of mustering-out pay, educational benefits, guaranteed loans, homestead preference, vocational rehabilitation, hospital care, readjustment allowance, civil service preference, and much more (Glines & Land, 1956). The same benefits were extended to veterans of the Korean conflict. Military families, no longer in the forefront, were encouraged to pursue a course of "self-help," and, indeed, this attitude did take hold and is still with us in some fashion today. What does this mean?

THE ROLE OF THE WIFE

The military wife really came into her own, for better or for worse, in the period between 1945 and 1965. She was encouraged to be adaptable, uncomplaining, compliant, flexible, supportive, and competent in any situation. As Admiral Robert B. Carney, Chief of Naval Operations in 1956, said:

> Much has been said and written about the hardships in a serviceman's life, but there has not been a great deal of sympathy lavished on the "little woman" who must be able to set up and run a household any place in the world on the tightest of budgets; who must look forward always to packing up and moving again, sometimes on a moment's notice; and who must try to bring continuity and a sense of security into the lives of her children and

serve at the same time as a social assist to her husband. (Glines & Land, 1956, p. ix)

Understandably, military wives organized informally into clubs and networks for the purpose of sharing ideas, resources, and support.

EARLY AVAILABLE RESOURCES

In the same year, 1956, the official agencies offering support to the military wife included the dispensary, aid societies, the Red Cross, and the Veterans Administration. Various officers assigned to a base might have collateral duties such as legal officer, personnel officer, transportation officer, insurance and benefits representative, and disbursing officer (Glines & Land, 1956), but the use of these different service providers depended on an enterprising wife's knowledge of their existence and location.

MAJOR DYNAMICS OF CHANGES

Several powerful factors have recently conspired both to challenge the military family and to provide support for easing its burden. As a result, our military has changed a great deal in both outlook and composition.

THE ROLE OF WOMEN

The recent massive influx of women into a peacetime military is unprecedented in our history. Between 1964 and 1977, the percentage of women in the Army's enlisted ranks grew from .9 to 6.7%. In 1977, women accounted for 8.2% of all enlisted accessions (Moskos, 1978), and until the recent "pause," the Army envisioned a final percentage end-strength of 10%. Whatever the result of the Army's current reassessment, the participation of women in the military is a fait accompli (Landrum, 1978; Moskos, 1978).

The reasons for this growth are basic. First, the pool of available manpower from the traditional source, males aged 17–21, is dwindling (Snyder, 1978). In 1977, roughly 2.14 million males reached the age of 18, the usual "target" recruitment age. By 1990, projections indicate this figure will drop to 1.7 million (Moskos, 1978).

The women's movement, legitimizing aspirations outside the home, has undoubtedly had a considerable impact on numbers and use of women in the Armed Forces. Recognizing this and responding to immediate manpower needs, the military has pursued a course of integration into all fields except those directly related to combat (McCubbin, Marsden, Durning, & Hunter, 1978). In 1967, President Johnson signed PL90-130, which removed the limits on the total number of women the services were allowed. Following that, each service has taken steps to increase the utilization and career opportunities of qualified women (Sarkesian, 1975).

"CIVILIANIZATION"

Military duties and civilian occupations are more similar than they used to be. Military and civilian personnel work closely together; some 97% of military executives in a recent study reported daily contact with civilian executives of comparable stature. Civil service personnel in 1981 constituted almost one third of all Department of Defense's (DoD's) manpower (Broedling, Lau, & Newman, 1981). The reasons for this are many. The requirements of advanced technology and weaponry naturally lead to utilization of civilian expertise in electronics, computer technology, and communications. In recent years, many in DoD have viewed the "civilianization" of many military functions to be cost-effective. Civilians are present in nearly every military enterprise; sometimes "technical representatives" are even assigned aboard Navy combat vessels.

As the officer's role has changed from one of strictly leadership to one including technical management, his job and that of a civilian are often almost indistinguishable (Biderman, 1964). The same is true for our highly qualified and trained enlisted personnel, who, with their military technical training, frequently transit effortlessly into a civilian job doing basically the same thing they were doing in the service.

Moskos (1978) calls this phenomenon one manifestation of the shift into an occupational mode of military services, as opposed to the earlier institutional mode. Basically, his distinction posits that, like their counterparts in the civilian world, military members look upon their military service as a job. He points out that the defense leadership has unwittingly encouraged this attitude by an econometric approach to personnel issues. For example, he points out leadership's acceptance of the Gates Commission Report, which advised a shift toward reliance on monetary inducements based on marketplace values to man the all volunteer force. This dependence on pay and compensation alone served to obscure the traditional military values of duty, sacrifice, patriotism, and honor and instead encouraged a military member to look upon himself and his skills as valuable, marketable commodities up for sale to the highest bidder. Unfortunately for the services, many members did just that and left after acquiring the desired training. Now that this attitude is firmly entrenched, military leaders are often faced with the necessity of buying personnel back and keeping them in the Armed Forces.

MARRIAGE

By far the most dramatic shift is in the area of marital trends. More junior enlisted personnel are entering the service married or they are marrying during their first tour of duty. In 1978, 20% of new accessions were married, and this percentage doubled by the end of the first 4 years of service (Snyder, 1978). Marriage figures have risen for the general military population also. Using the Army's figures, which are representative, between 1953 and 1974 the percentage of married servicemembers rose from 35 to 54%. In all services, the percentages of married *careerists* is much higher; for example, a full 80% of Navy careerists are married (Orthner, 1980a).

A basic reason for this formidable increase is money. Between 1964 and 1976, recruit pay rose 193% in constant dollars, compared to 10% for average unskilled laborers (Orthner, 1980a). More young people entering the military felt they could afford to marry, and financial and other inducements such as dependents' allowances and permission to live off-base were available for doing so.

These changes and others have given us our military of today, a force in transition. Where do we go from here?

THE MILITARY RESPONSE

Military service providers of today generally agree that efforts are best directed toward support for the healthy, functioning family (Orthner & Chandler, 1980). Healthy families are by far the majority, and since military combat readiness must be our primary concern, these are the families we want to retain.

Clearly, when addressing retention, one must address *families*, not just the servicemember. As General E. C. Meyer (1980), Chief of Staff, U.S. Army, has so succinctly stated, "We recruit soldiers, but we retain families!" In a recent (1980) study of Air Force families, the researchers found a high correlation between family support and career commitment. Fully 70% of men queried who plan on an Air Force career have wives who support that choice, while only 14% of those who do not plan a career are married to women who wish they would remain (Orthner, 1980b). In a 1980 study of Navy personnel, the spouse's desire for the member to remain or leave was the single largest direct determinant of retention intent (Szoc, 1982). As intrafamily roles become more egalitarian, such a shift is to be expected.

The military response to changing times and family circumstances also recognizes the particular stresses that accompany military family life. The stresses most common to military families include frequent relocation, separation from family of origin, deployment, separation from immediate family, and increased risk of injury or death (Parry, 1981). Thus, as will be seen, the military has focused support efforts primarily on these areas (Montalvo, 1976).

What, then, is the military doing specifically to support its "military family"?

MODERN MILITARY FAMILY SUPPORT PROGRAMS

RESPONSIBILITY OF THE COMMAND

Commanding officers have always been charged with responsibility for providing assistance to servicemembers and their families. For years all the military services have provided or sponsored chaplains, medical services, alcohol and other substance abuse programs, relocation assistance, wives' organizations, some degree of child care, housing, preparation for moving overseas or intercultural relations, and information to help people adapt to and enjoy military life.

However, as a direct result of the factors discussed earlier and the recognition that military families have changed significantly in recent years, all military services have taken new steps to intensify their efforts on behalf of servicemembers and their families. For example, the Army, which began its family support efforts in 1965, revised its Army Community Service Program in 1978 and again in 1983 (Army Community

Service Program, 1983); the Navy established its Family Support Program in 1979 and began funding a network of Family Service Centers in 1981 (Navy Family Support Program, 1981, 1983); the Marine Corps issued a White Letter 9-79 in 1980 announcing Marine Corps plans, and by early 1982 had a full complement of 17 Family Service Centers on-base and operational; the Air Force began establishing new Family Support Centers in 1981; and the Coast Guard[1] established a headquarters staff to focus on family issues in 1982.

IDENTIFICATION OF NEEDS

To a large extent each of these intensified efforts was an attempt to meet needs that were being identified within each military service. For example, the Navy held a Family Awareness Conference in November 1978. Over 750 people representing active duty personnel, retirees, Naval Reservists, family members, and civilian service providers took part in the conference and together worked to identify needs, problems, and possible solutions and to discuss ways of improving coordination of existing resources as well as establishing new programs on behalf of families. In 1980, the Army and the Air Force held separate, similar conferences to discuss family issues and plan new approaches to addressing family concerns; and in 1981, the Marine Corps held a directors' conference to plan future efforts. In all cases, the highest levels of military leadership were present; moreover, they were active participants in the meetings, clearly projecting their commitment to addressing family considerations.

FAMILY SUPPORT SERVICES

In fact, by 1980, modern organized family support efforts[2] were becoming galvanized, and by 1981 the surge of development of family service centers was well underway. Military family support was no longer con-

---

1. The Coast Guard is normally part of the Department of Transportation but, in time of war, moves to the Department of Defense. With regard to planning for family support services, the Coast Guard has a close, but informal, liaison with the Armed Services.

2. The Navy and Marine Corps use the term "Family Service Centers"; similar organizations in the Air Force are called Family Support Centers and, in the Army, Army Community Service Centers. The Army has 162 centers; the Marine Corps has 19; the Air Force has 32 and plans a total of 124 by 1990; and the Navy has 62.

sidered a one-time benefits package offered in time of national emergency or demobilization but was (and is) an institutionalized service provided as a right of military personnel and families in recognition of their special stresses, challenges, and ongoing needs. While each military service had its own plan for programs to be offered, there were many similarities. For example, the stated overall mission of the Navy's program, "to improve the Navy's awareness of, and access to, reliable and useful information, resources and services that support and enrich the lives of Navy families and single servicemembers" (O'Keefe, 1981), could well apply in large part to the other military services. The Navy's five major objectives for its overall Family Support Program are applied in some measure to the overall efforts of the other military branches. Those objectives are as follows:

- to establish a network of Family Service Centers;
- to provide training, technical assistance, positive support and guidance to commands desiring to develop or improve their own family support programs;
- to develop awareness programs emphasizing the importance of families to the Navy's mission;
- to increase effective coordination and use of existing military and civilian resources; and
- to conduct research and studies which document and guide future Navy family efforts and policy.

All the Family Service Centers are intended to serve as a focal point to bring about closer coordination of a full range of military and civilian resources on behalf of servicemembers and their families, and all centers offer information and referral services for a wide array of personal and family matters. Other support services that are, for the most part, seen as crucial for most centers to provide are personal counseling; financial counseling or education; assistance to new arrivals; assistance during relocation; assistance during crises; employment assistance for spouses; family development education; assistance related to deployment (i.e., when the servicemember is separated from the family due to duty); assistance to families with special needs (such as handicapped children); and programs related to domestic violence and child abuse and neglect.

With regard to personal or family counseling, the centers are geared primarily for short-term assistance rather than to meeting long-term psychotherapeutic needs. The Navy guidance, for example, explicitly indicates that counseling provided at Navy Family Service Centers should be complementary to existing Navy and civilian resources (not duplicative) and is specifically intended to:

- help the client (Navy servicemember or family member) assess the problem/distress/reason that brought him or her to the FSC;
- inform the client about appropriate and available resources in the civilian and/or military communities;
- link the client effectively with another resource if longer-term counseling is needed;
- provide interim support to the client while he or she awaits the services to which he or she is referred; and
- assist clients, when feasible, on a short-term basis, normally one to eight visits (O'Keefe, 1983).

Sometimes child care services and youth recreational programs are handled through the Family Service Center; and a myriad of other programs may be developed to meet particular local needs. As examples, there may be programs geared to non-English-speaking wives; income tax assistance; programs welcoming new babies; programs promoting intercultural relations; homemaking classes; or informal support groups—whatever is needed and does not duplicate an already existing and accessible resource.

The tradition of self-help remains significant. Army Community Services rely heavily on volunteer staffing and support, as does the Navy in its Ombudsman and Sponsor Programs. The various support programs not only rely to some extent on volunteers to assist, but many, such as the Family Service Centers, also try to help these informal support networks by providing office and meeting space, training, or other appropriate assistance. In fact, some centers have a mandate to support local, command-sponsored grass-roots efforts.

In sum, the Family Service Centers can be viewed as offering three general modes of support: (1) direct help or intervention such as short-term counseling or assistance during a crisis; (2) proactive efforts such as workshops or classes on topics of interest and concern to commands, servicemembers, and families; and (3) routine maintenance–support such as the extensive information and referral services provided by most centers. The centers were designed primarily to be supportive to healthy, functioning servicemembers and families, and to avert or alleviate questions or problems before they become major ones.

In all cases, the Family Service Centers have been established not only to assist servicemembers and their families but also to be responsive to the base commanding officer. Within the Navy, for example, the director of the Family Service Center is normally a department head of the base commanding officer's staff. In fact, one of the many challenges of Family Service Centers is to balance appropriately responsibilities to clients *and* to the military since the principal goals of the family support efforts are to increase retention and on-the-job productivity of valuable servicemembers and improve the nation's combat readiness. Obviously, issues of confidentiality and security are vital and must be considered at all times.

CHALLENGES OF SUPPORTING FAMILY SERVICE EFFORTS

For the most part, providing adequate facilities for Family Service Centers is a problem. Ideally each Family Service Center would be centrally located, easily accessible to parking and public transportation, and large enough to house related services under the same roof. For example, the Navy Family Services Center building in Norfolk also contains a large Navy Relief office and an office to serve retired personnel. The Navy Family Service Center in Washington, D.C., is in the same building with Navy Chaplains, Navy Relief, and an alcohol counseling and assistance program. Unfortunately, the extent of colocation of resources is rarely as great as desired, but all the services plan to improve their facilities to bring about more effective and coordinated services to families.

Staffing at Family Service Centers is usually a combination of military, paid civilian, and volunteer. In principle the Navy, Marine Corps, and Army have called for the director of each center to be a military person; the Air Force has planned for a civilian (civil service) director supported by both military and civilian staff. In all cases, the intent is for the Family Service Center to be responsive to military, servicemember, and family member needs and to reflect a "caringness" on the part of the military command. In 1981 and 1982 the Navy, to emphasize its high level of commitment to its fledgling program, provided 12 senior captains and commanders to direct 12 of its new and large centers.

Staff orientation and training are key factors in maintaining effective staff. The Army runs an 8-day intensive training program at Fort Benjamin

Harrison in Indiana. A number of personnel from the other military branches have also received training there. In addition, the Navy and Air Force provide training programs and materials for their staff. The Navy's *Guide for Planning and Operating Navy Family Service Centers* (1980) and the Army's Regulation 608-1 on the Army Community Service Program (1983) are probably the most detailed and comprehensive documents ever written on military family service centers.

Generally, the military Family Service Centers are well received by commands, servicemembers, and family members alike; and evidence is growing that they do have a positive effect on retention of valuable service members and on their productivity. For example, during the spring of 1982, the Navy sponsored an evaluation of four Family Service Center locations representing a cross-section of naval communities engaged in submarine, surface, and air operations and support services overseas and in the continental United States (Bishop, Peters, & Woolley, 1982). The purpose of the study was to begin to determine the actual and perceived benefits to the Navy of the Family Service Centers. The centers were perceived by almost everyone interviewed (commanding officers, executive officers, command master chiefs, and clients) as having a highly positive impact on quality of life, attitudes toward the Navy, job performance, and morale. They were viewed as contributing to personnel retention and fleet combat readiness. Navy commands cited reduced work loads, improved productivity, and reduction in emergency leaves during deployment. The evaluation concluded that Family Service Centers were filling a definite need and filling it well, that they had been well received, were generally highly regarded, and stood as a major symbol of the Navy's commitment and support for Navy members and their families.

In another more informal attempt to develop specific cost-savings information resulting from Navy Family Service Centers, 39 servicemembers were identified who indicated that assistance rendered by a Navy Family Service Center was a major factor in their decision to remain in the Navy. For just these 39 personnel alone, the replacement cost would have been approximately $7 million.

In addition to emerging evidence on the centers' impact on retention, productivity, and cost savings, ample evidence exists among all the services that the centers are being heavily used by a wide range of personnel—officer, enlisted, married, single, and people living off-base as well as on-base. For example, the routine quarterly Navy Family Service Center statistical report covering January–March 1982 showed an average of 630 clients *per center* obtaining assistance or information in person, plus an additional 430 per center receiving assistance via telephone or letter (O'Keefe, 1982). About 50% of the clients were male, 60% were married, 60% lived in private housing (off the base), and 66% were in the petty officer–chief petty officer range of experienced, trained individuals.

In addition to services and assistance to individuals, of course, all centers offer other kinds of support, such as briefings, classes, newcomer orientations, and "Welcome" information. In fact, the military Family Service Centers are directly and indirectly reaching a broad cross-section of thousands of people each month.

What, then, does the future hold for the expanding military family support programs?

FUTURE DIRECTIONS

Clearly, once all centers are established, the continuing concerns will be to maintain a competent, high-quality staff; to continue to improve coordinated use of existing services; to inform servicemembers and their families about the centers; and to create a widespread awareness of the centers and what they do. Currently the most frequently held misconceptions about the centers are that they are just for problem (inadequate) people, just for enlisted servicemembers and families, just for married people, and just for crisis situations.

The branches of the military service will undoubtedly continue to coordinate their efforts, sharing information, learning from each other's experiences, and dovetailng their efforts whenever possible. The Air Force has contracted Dr. Dennis Orthner to conduct a comprehensive, long-term evaluation of Air Force Family Support Centers. This study will eventually yield comparative data on bases with and without centers. Because of the similarities among programs, the results of the Air Force study should have considerable value for the other military services.

The military services have, without doubt, actively acknowledged the changing times and the direct importance of the military family to the military mission. The future should bring a combination of efforts, with those efforts becoming ever more finely tuned to address constantly changing circumstances and needs.

ACKNOWLEDGMENTS

The authors wish to acknowledge the contributions of Betty K. Hart, former Director, Family Liaison Office, Department of the Army; Major John Gimber, USMC, Head, Human Development Section, Human Resources Branch, Headquarters Marine Corps; Lieutenant Colonel James N. Lanier, GS, USA, Director, Community Support Program, Department of the Army; Rear Admiral Paul J. Mulloy, USN, former Director, Human Resource Management and Personal Affairs Department, Department of the Navy; and Ms. Suzanne Nash, Military Family Resource Center.

REFERENCES[3]

Army Community Service Program. Army Regulation 608-1, June 1983.*

Biderman, A. D. Sequels to a military career: The retired military professional. In M. Janowitz (Ed.), *The new military*. New York: Russell Sage Foundation, 1964.

Bishop, S., Peters, M., & Woolley, S. *Impact evaluation of the Navy Family Service Centers* (USN Contract No. 00600-79-D-0845). Washington, D.C.: Naval Military Personnel Command, 1982.*

Bowen, G. L. *Family patterns of U.S. military personnel*. Paper presented in conjunction with the Seventh National Association of Social Workers Professional Symposium, Philadelphia, November 1981.*

Broedling, L. A., Lau, A. W., & Newman, A. The relationship between senior Navy civilian and military executives. *Naval War College Review*, November–December 1981.

Glines, C. V., Jr., & Land, E. *The complete guide for the serviceman's wife*. Boston: Houghton Mifflin, 1956.

Guide for planning and operating Navy Family Service Centers. Department of the Navy, OP-156, Washington, D.C., 1980.*

Landrum, C. S. Role of women in today's military. In J. B. Keeley (Ed.), *The all-volunteer force and American society*. Charlottesville: University Press of Virginia, 1978.

McCubbin, H. I., Marsden, M. A., Durning, K. P., & Hunter, E. J. Family policy in the armed forces. *Air University Review,* 1978, *29*(6).*

Meyer, E. C. Remarks to first Army Family Symposium sponsored by the Army Officers' Wives' Club of the Greater Washington Area and the Association of the U.S. Army, Washington, D.C., October 1980.

Montalvo, F. F. Family separation in the Army: A study of the problems encountered and the caretaking resources used by career Army families undergoing military separation. In H. I. McCubbin, B. B. Dahl, & E. J. Hunter (Eds.), *Families in the military system*. Beverly Hills, Calif./London: Sage, 1976.*

Moskos, C. C., Jr. The enlisted ranks in the all-volunteer Army. In J. B. Keeley (Ed.), *The all-volunteer force and American society*. Charlottesville: University Press of Virginia, 1978.

Navy Family Support Program. OPNAVINST 1754.1A, 1981, 1983.*

3. Items marked with an asterisk (*) are available through the Military Family Resource Center, 6501 Loisdale Court, Suite 900, Springfield, Virginia 22150; (703) 922-7671 or (800) 336-4592.

O'Keefe, R. A. *Backgrounder*. Washington, D.C.: Navy Family Support Program, 1981.*

O'Keefe, R. A. *Navy Family Service Center operations: Status report*. Washington, D.C.: Navy Family Support Program, 1983.*

Orthner, D. K. *A demograpic profile of U.S. navy personnel and families* (USN Contract No. N0071-79-M-8577). Washington, D.C.: Navy Family Support Program, 1980. (a)*

Orthner, D. K. *Families in blue* (USAF Contract No. F33600-79-C-0423). Washington, D.C.: Office of the Chief of Chaplains, USAF, Bolling Air Force Base, 1980. (b)*

Orthner, D. K., & Chandler, B. A. Quality of family life in the military. *Proceedings of National Council on Family Relations Pre-Conference Workshop*, Portland, Ore., October 1980.*

Parry, J. S. *Conditions of military life*. Paper presented in conjunction with the Seventh National Association of Social Workers Professional Symposium, Philadelphia, November 1981.*

Sarkesian, S. C. *The professional Army officer in a changing society*. Chicago: Nelson-Hall, 1975.

Simon, W., & Zald, M. N. Career opportunities and commitments among officers. In M. Janowitz (Ed.), *The new military*. New York: Russell Sage Foundation, 1964.

Snyder, W. P. Military personnel procurement policies: Assumptions—trends—context. In J. B. Keeley (Ed.), *The all-volunteer force and American society*. Charlottesville: University Press of Virginia, 1978.

Szoc, R. *Family factors critical to the retention of naval personnel* (USN Contract No. N000123-80-C-1444). San Diego, Calif.: Navy Personnel Research and Development Center, 1982.*

Train, H. D., II. *Address by Commander in Chief, Atlantic*. Paper presented at the Navy-wide Family Awareness Conference, Norfolk, Va., November 1978.*

13

Training and Supervision of Mental Health Professionals to Understand and Treat Military Families

FLORENCE W. KASLOW

How does one attempt to describe, depict, or portray the topic of training and supervision when it is such a complex and mammoth one? Given the inherent space limitations of a single chapter, condensing all that is relevant into a short, succinct, and meaningful entity dictates parsimonious selectivity.

Thus the initial section of this chapter will cite extant pertinent literature sources so that the reader particularly interested in this arena can pursue the topic in greater depth and breadth. Portions of the five books cited herein will also be alluded to later in this chapter when they illuminate a specific aspect of the material being covered.

In 1970 when I was first asked to teach a graduate course in supervision and consultation, I found a paucity of current resource material. Lacking suitable text material, I edited and served as a contributing author to *Issues in Human Services: A Sourcebook for Supervision and Staff Development* (Kaslow & Associates, 1972). Since the issues which arise in supervision as well as the viable techniques and the settings utilizing supervisors continued to change and expand, a complementary sequel appeared 5 years later entitled *Supervision, Consultation and Staff Training in the Helping Professions* (Kaslow & Associates, 1977). Berger's (1970) *Videotape Techniques in Psychiatric Training and Treatment* pro-

Florence W. Kaslow. Private practice, West Palm Beach, Florida; Director, Florida Couples and Family Institute, West Palm Beach, Florida; and Adjunct Professor of Medical Psychology, Department of Psychiatry, Duke University, Durham, North Carolina.

vides an in-depth perusal of the utilization and efficacy of videotape as a tool to enhance teaching–learning. *Psychotherapy Supervision: Theory, Research and Practice* (Hess, 1980a) is an excellent and inclusive volume. The most recent arrival is *Applied Supervision in Psychotherapy* (Blumenfield, 1982) which addresses many of the focal concerns covered in the Hess and Kaslow volumes. In addition, there is a new journal, *The Clinical Supervisor*, being published by Haworth Press. All of this seems indicative of the importance currently being attached to supervision, training, and consultation in all of the mental health disciplines.

Much of the literature deals with tutelage of beginning trainees— graduate students in social work, psychology, or marital and family therapy, or psychiatric residents—during their clinical internships. Some articles deal almost exclusively with the paraprofessional receiving on-the-job training (Richan 1972, 1977). Less material analyzes the nature and process of supervision and training of intermediate- and advanced-level clinicians who may want to learn a new specialty like marital and family therapy or expand their depth and breadth of clinical acumen after a period of practice in individual and/or group therapy. There is a developing body of material on peer supervision—a viable alternative arrangement to hierarchical supervision in certain situations.

This chapter will offer an overview of the following aspects of supervision, training, and consultation as they are specifically applicable to understanding and treating the military family: definitions and accountability; history; kinds of training programs and approaches, process, content, and techniques; goals and evaluation; and supervisor–supervisee match. The intent is that it will be valuable for civilian as well as military mental health practitioners. In order for this to occur, training must be conceived of with a broad multicultural perspective rather than a provincial, ethnocentric one since the Armed Forces are comprised of a heterogeneous racial, religious, and ethnic population. Although the special competencies of each discipline, such as that of psychiatrists in psychopharmacology and psychologists in psychodiagnostic testing, need be delineated and fostered, the verbal psychotherapeutic methods should be taught and supervised utilizing a multidisciplinary perspective applicable to professionals from the various specialties.

Given the rapidity with which new orders may be received for someone to ship out, clinicians will need to be adept in doing crisis intervention and brief therapy with families beset by the panoply of issues like substance abuse, incest, and relocation–separation–reunion, described in earlier chapters. They will need guidance regarding confidentiality given that it is often military policy that the commanding officer can have access to military records regarding personnel under his command and that information acquired from such records might be used to block a career move, offsetting the benefit of "free" treatment. Military personnel can go to civilian agencies and invoke patient "privilege," but here services will be more financially costly. Therapists in both the civilian and military sectors learn the routes for collaboration, laws which regulate their practice, and the essential dicta of both bodies of law regarding families who entrust themselves to the therapists' ministrations. Part of their learning should include not only the Uniform Code of Military Justice but also a respect for the ethos, history, traditions, values, benefits, and mission of the military establishment.

DEFINITIONS AND ACCOUNTABILITY

According to the *Random House Dictionary* (Steen, 1980), supervision entails the overseeing of work or workers during execution or performance (of a task). Implicit is the fact that the supervisor carries some responsibility for the quality of the work—in this clinical instance, the practice of the supervisee—and therefore is in a position of authority and power. Inherent is the supervisor's accountability to the agency director, board, community, and clientele for the type and quality of service rendered (Kaslow & Associates, 1972). Since the late 1960s, with the advent of Peer Standards Review Organizations and Committees (PSROs and PSPCs), and the increasing numbers of inquiries from third-party insurance payers about the nature of the therapeutic services rendered, supervisors have had to scrutinize carefully their supervisees' practice, to make certain their records accurately reflect their practice and that the quality is substantial enough to pass a review committee's standards and/or to warrant reimbursement. Where supervisors have to sign or co-sign reports and insurance forms, their responsibility becomes much more obvious.

In the past decade, mental health professionals have become increasingly cognizant of their vulnerability to malpractice suits. Generally, they have been less attuned to liability issues. Slovenko's (1980) discussion of "Legal Aspects of Psychotherapy Supervision" does a superb job of raising a reader's conscious awareness about the supervisor's responsibility for the practice of his or her supervisee. He states, "One may be held legally responsible not only for one's own faulty conduct but also for that of others." Under the doctrine of "vicarious liability" or "imputed negligence," an employer could be held liable for the tortious conduct of a supervisee committed in his or her work role, by virtue of the employer–employee relationship between them. Modern legal theory makes a "metaphysical identification of the employer and employee as a single 'persona' jointly liable for the injury. The employer is made to carry the risk as his enterprise benefits economically . . . by the acts of employees" (Slovenko, 1980, p. 453). Since major responsibility for overseeing a clinician's practice is delegated to the supervisor, the supervisor not only has authority but a weighty responsibility and legal accountability. Given the fact that a spate of recent legislation has mandated disclosure of well thought out treatment plans prior to undertaking therapy, a supervisor would be expected to approve or disapprove of the direction and techniques about to be pursued and to leave little that will likely influence a person's emotional and psychological well-being to impetuosity or chance.

The psychotherapy supervisor bears clinical responsibility tantamount to that borne were the patient under his or her care. If this were not the case, there would be little ethical justification for assigning troubled individuals to the care of partially trained students, who are likely to make errors based on inexperience and a lack of knowledge and clinical wisdom. The supervisor must insist, for example, that trainees keep adequate records that support and document the treatment plan; maintain confidentiality; make feasible and appropriate arrangements for coverage if they are to be unavailable; inform patients accurately of their trainee status; and understand that they (and their records) can be subpoenaed to testify in court. In this event, the supervisor is obligated to give as much preparation assistance and back-up support as necessary. Slovenko (1980, pp. 468–469) concludes on an ominous note that litigation involving supervisors may be considered the "suit of the future" and that the supervisor must, like the accountant, be a "watchdog" and perhaps even a "bloodhound." With these warnings in mind, perusal of this topic becomes a serious and compelling matter.

BRIEF HISTORIC OVERVIEW

During the 1960s and 1970s there was a burgeoning of the specialty of family therapy in private practice, mental health and child guidance clinics, family service agencies, special school settings, psychiatric outpatient clinics, and hospital inpatient units. Since the late 1940s the field has evolved from its infancy, when only a handful of courageous pioneers experimented with it and are even reputed to have practiced it covertly; to its infrequent use as an intervention strategy when all else seemed to have failed; to the present, when family therapy has been catapulted into the therapeutic limelight as a major philosophic system of thought and treatment modality:

> an entity unto itself with a magnetic appeal for fledgling and experienced therapists alike. The awakening of the psychiatric–psychological–social work establishment to the centrality of the family system and its impact and hold on all family members has led to an increasing demand for professionals trained in family therapy who can function as an integral part of the staff of many kinds of human service agencies. In many localities, treatment-oriented agencies are considered deficient or not fully staffed, if they do not have a family therapist. The mounting interest in and conviction of the efficiency and efficacy of family therapy has alerted professionals—practitioners and administrators, as well as educators—to the need for programs to train competent therapists. The response has been the establishment of a vast array of educational, supervisory, and training programs to meet the demand. (Kaslow, 1977, pp. 199–200)

In this section, a concise history of the intertwined fields of marital and family therapy will be painted, as a canvas against which to discuss the types of supervision and training which have evolved. (For an in-depth historical overview, see Guerin, 1976; Kaslow, 1980a.) Various kinds of programs in existence will be mentioned, and different supervisory models will be described and analyzed in terms of learning objectives, techniques, and treatment goals. While the extant literature is cited illustratively, it is not expected that this chapter will provide an exhaustive review. Rather, a creative synthesis derived from clinical experience and observations gleaned from teaching, training, and consultation has been attempted.

MARITAL COUNSELING

To fathom where the marital therapy field is today it is essential to trace its quick growth since its beginnings. The aftermath of World War I (1920s and 1930s) was a time of social unrest, the weakening of family ties in the wake of accelerating job mobility, and a decrease in the authority of parents. Divorce laws were slowly liberalized and divorce was accompanied by less stigma. Thus increasing numbers of Americans found themselves able to terminate their marriages physically, psychologically, and legally.

Leading clergy, physicians, and attorneys tried to counsel clients who were distressed by family dissolution and intrapsychic conflicts. Initially, treatment took place in the one-to-one model, even though the focus was often on interpersonal family dynamics and problems. Thoughtful practitioners became cognizant of the influence of the patients' changing views and behaviors on their significant others, especially on their spouses. Thus sensitive clinicians gradually switched from treating one person alone to conjoint marital counseling. Seeing patients in tandem enabled their conflicts to be enacted in the therapists' presence. This caused counselors to recognize their own need for additional understanding of interpersonal transactions and dyadic interviewing. The couples' sexual dysfunctions became more apparent and were deemed a valid target of therapeutic intervention. Clearly, new treatment approaches were necessary; this realization stimulated both probing discussions between colleagues and clinical experimentation.

The upward spiraling divorce statistics caused alarm and generated awareness that immediate action was imperative. As a result, in 1932 three marriage counseling centers were founded—in Los Angeles, New York, and Philadelphia (Everett, 1980)—by farsighted clinicians. Their new therapeutic ventures marked a departure from traditional analytic theory and practice and were met with some degree of antagonism and censorship by their more orthodox colleagues. Although individual therapy remained the most utilized modality during the early 1940s, the more innovative practitioners in the mental health disciplines began treating couples as a unit. They came to believe that this approach constituted a new specialty and that *additional*, unique, and specific training beyond that essential to function as an individual psychotherapist was essential. Also, they felt a need for a separate professional organization through which to share their endeavors and discuss their observations, to disseminate accurate and timely data, and also in order to provide an opportunity for aspiring marriage counselors to come for training. In 1942 the American Association of Marriage Counselors (AAMC) was organized and for over the past 40 years has carried out these original purposes. It runs clinical conferences and professional meetings, accredits degree- and non-degree-granting training programs, attempts to influence legislation dealing with family life, and has promulgated a code of ethics. A major goal since the early 1960s has been to achieve legal certification and/or licensing for practice.

The name of the organization was changed to AAMFC in the early 1970s, because by then many of the members had become family therapists. In the late 1970s it was again modified to the current title, AAMFT, reflecting the family emphasis and the deeper level of treatment signified by the word "therapy."

Since supervision was deemed an essential part of clinical training and not all therapists could avail themselves of formal academic programs, the category of "approved supervisor" was created during the 1970s. Clinical members and fellows of AAMFC with sufficient supervisory background could be so designated after application to and evaluation by the Committee on Supervision (AAMFT, 1978). With the reported incidence of family dysfunction and divorce continuing to mount, existing programs could not meet the demand for competent marital counselors. This innovative route for receiving training has apparently worked reasonably well, and as of 1983 the Committee on Accreditation was transformed to a more prestigious Commission with expanded impact on the larger marital and family therapy scene.

FAMILY THERAPY

The initial cadre of family therapists who came to the fore in the early 1950s were self-trained. Seemingly concurrently, in different regions and not well known to each other, several groups of therapists of varying professional origins began to experiment with seeing members of the same family simultaneously. Like the first marriage counselors, they were disenchanted with the slowness of results of individual therapy and the undermining of progress by the patient's relatives. They sought to find more powerful and rapid methods of enabling people to cope and function better. They were also dismayed by the escalating number of disintegrating families and gloomy forecasts about the death of the family in America.

Among the more notable early endeavors were clusters on the East and West Coasts. The Palo Alto group included John Weakland, Don Jackson, Gregory Bateson, and Jay Haley, who were soon joined by Virginia Satir. They drew their theoretical formulations from systems and communication theory and focused on the "here and now." In New York, Nathan Ackerman at Jewish Family Service was an acknowledged leader. He established the New York Family Institute which was renamed the Ackerman Institute after his death. His book. *Exploring the Base for*

Family Therapy, coedited with Frances Beatman and Sanford Sherman in 1961, was one of the initial major works to give shape and substance to the emerging profession. He followed this by authoring numerous other books and articles and by his instrumental role in launching the journal *Family Process* in 1961. In Philadelphia, Ivan Boszormenyi-Nagy, James Framo, Geraldine Spark, David Rubinstein, and Gerald Zuk comprised part of the group at Eastern Pennsylvania Psychiatric Institute. Nearby, at Philadelphia Psychiatric Center, another group, which included Geraldine Lincoln (Grossman), Al Friedman, and Oscar Weiner, was experimenting with the family system as a client unit growing out of their involvement with schizophrenogenic families. These two groups joined, along with others like Ross Speck, to form the Family Institute of Philadelphia, which has continued to expand (Kaslow, 1977).

Parallel developments occurred in Boston, Washington, Atlanta, Chicago, and Madison. Charismatic, innovative, energetic therapists seemed to move into the limelight in each metropolitan area. The names of the first generation of family therapists are well known. In addition to those already mentioned, they include Donald Bloch, Murray Bowen, Fred Duhl, David Kantor, Chuck Kramer, John Warkentin, Carl Whitaker, and Lyman Wynne. They heard about one another's work and established contact in a loose network. Occasionally they came together to discuss and view each other's evolving treatment approaches and to collaborate in writing books. In the edited collections of the 1960s, the names of the select "in-group" of therapist–authors reappear quite consistently (Kaslow, 1980a).

As other clinicians read their works and heard their presentations at conferences, they apparently felt and perceived the compelling nature of this approach despite the fact that family therapy was viewed as highly controversial, since, like marriage counseling, it transgressed orthodox beliefs and methods. As clinicians tried to do what they were reading and hearing about, many found their therapy became more stimulating and fruitful. They clamored to observe the leading first-generation therapists conducting live interviews through one-way mirrors, they borrowed videotapes of their sessions, and they went to study with them directly—in an apprentice—master type model of guild training. Some of the masters became venerated and imitated. These vibrant, active, dynamic interventionists, who were willing to be watched while doing therapy, were quite a different breed from their analytic counterparts, who often engaged in nondirective, attentive listening, preferred low visibility, saw the therapy room as a private sanctuary, and believed confidentiality was violated when others observed treatment.

As the groundswell for their tutelage and (symbolic) "laying on of hands" flourished, and standard academic graduate and medical school programs were reluctant to expand their curricula to encompass this new content, family institutes were established to provide training and offer treatment. Here, if accepted as a trainee, one could study with one's favorite leader. Out of this ferment 10 major theoretical schools have emerged which are listed below. (See Kaslow, 1981, for a lengthy discussion of these schools—their major premises, similarities, and differences.)

1. Psychoanalytic–psychodynamic
2. Bowenian
3. Contextual–relational
4. Experiential
5. Strategic
6. Structural
7. Communications–interpersonal
8. Problem solving
9. Behavioral
10. Integrative, diaclectic, and multimodal

Each of the first nine has its main theoretician ("guru") and loyal adherents and there is much competition over which possesses "the truth," and for supremacy as the really "right way" to think and practice. (Number 10 is discussed separately below.) At this time, I believe the 1980s will see each school being pressed to conduct process and outcome research in order to further validate its underlying assumptions and to have a more substantial data base from which to refine treatment interventions.

In addition, others like Duhl and Duhl (1979), Kaslow (1981), and Lazarus (1981) are seeking to integrate selectively and use various approaches judiciously to enable them to intervene most appropriately in terms of the nature of the problem and patients. They call their approaches respectively: integrative, diaclectic, and multimodal.

The 1970s and early 1980s have seen a proliferation of books and journals, an expansion at the leadership and practitioner level to include many second-, third-, and now fourth-generation therapists and a continuous enormous interest in practice, training, and education. This is reflected in such facts as the following: (1) the change in name, in the last half of the 1970s, from AAMFC to AAMFT—in response to a mammoth increase in membership to over 10,000, many of whom identified as therapists and not counselors; (2) the formation of the American Family Therapy Association—now numbering around 700 members, and established as a scientific society or academy by many of the field's most respected leaders; (3) the burgeoning of family therapy in many countries around the world; accompanied by (4) the advent of numerous international family therapy conferences; and (5) a proliferation of journals and books published on this subject.

With this brief historical overview as a backdrop against which to understand the kind of education, supervision, and training that have evolved, we return our attention more specifically to supervision and training.

TRAINING AND SUPERVISION: CONTENT AND PROCESS

In 1963, Satir reported the results of a 3-year training program at the Mental Research Institute. She listed three program goals. In addition to expecting trainees to acquire practice skills, this project sought (1) to have them become proficient in consultation and in-service training; so that they could (2) return to their respective agencies and in turn teach what they had learned; and (3) be provided with the necessary tools for conducting research in family process, diagnosis, and treatment. To Satir's list, I would add, at a minimum, that any training program should (4) "turn out" professionals who possess a sound theoretical knowledge base and (5) a familiarity with and commitment to the ethical precepts of their profession.

The field is still experiencing some adolescent "growing pains" and there is a lack of unanimity as to the "identity" of the marital, family, sex, and divorce therapist, and what he or she needs to know and be able to do in order to be designated as such. Some believe this to be a separate mental health discipline; others posit that a family system perspective is a way of conceptualizing the patients' world—and transcends intervention strategies. Still others in the helping disciplines do not recognize this as a specialty and claim that no extra or special training and practicum are needed.

Professional rivalries and territoriality issues are exemplified in such statements as that by Malone (1974) that "there is no established clear-cut theoretical model" for training child psychiatrists in family therapy and that consequently "professional identity and professional role lack clarity, and the staff and trainees . . . experience a considerable amount of strain" (p. 454). When this paper, "Observations on the Role of Family Therapy in Child Psychiatry Training" (1974), was written, Malone was director of child psychiatry training at the Philadelphia Child Guidance Clinic, a facility geared to family therapy practice. Yet Malone attributed the problems in training partially to the conflict and polarization that existed between analytically oriented child psychiatrists and family therapists. He recognized that along with the numerous advantages of family therapy, there is also the danger that its overutilization can lead to a distorted view of the nature of the difficulties and the treatment of choice, just as total reliance on individual psychotherapy can. He posited that one "danger of family therapy involves the temptation for inexperienced therapists to escape the rigors, growing pains, and vicissitudes of understanding and working with intrapsychic conflict and pain"; even though it makes possible "direct exploration of intrapsychic derivatives at the level of interpersonal process" (Malone, 1974, pp. 456–457), one can avoid dealing with intrapsychic problems by depending solely on environmental manipulation to achieve desired ends. The teacher–trainer who permits this does not help the trainees learn about "psychic development and unconscious dynamics" (p. 457). I believe his statement is still cogent and accurate, and that those advocating and teaching family therapy to those treating military personnel should bear these pitfalls in mind.

This ideological and political battle between the professions is all the more lamentable, considering that in the Group for the Advancement of Psychiatry (GAP) report on *The Field of Family Therapy* released over a decade ago (GAP, 1970) the well-respected authors stated that "family therapy combines two bodies of knowledge: personality dynamics and multiperson system dynamics" and heralded the need for integration of these "two systems levels into a comprehensive theory" (pp. 565–566). They recommended that the *focus on the transactional multiperson level of functioning should be considered an addition to, not a replacement for, the individual system level of understanding and treating behavior dynamics* (pp. 565–566). Obviously their eschewing of polarization has not permeated the field; many psychiatrists, psychologists, and social workers still complete their formal professional training without course work or clinical experience in multiperson system dynamics and intervention strategies.

As of now, four major kinds of training programs exist. First, there are graduate school degree-granting programs like the ones at the University of Southern California (Los Angeles) in the Department of Sociology which offers a PhD and at Loma Linda University in California which grants an MS in Marital and Family Counseling. An excellent program in existence at Hahnemann Medical University in Philadelphia since 1976 awards an MFT degree. The establishment and survival of such combined theoretical-clinical programs is probably the strongest evidence that there is a specific teachable body of knowledge, that there are agencies willing to offer internships in the specialty field of marriage and family therapy, and that there are jobs for graduates with this still atypical degree. Second, there are agency-based training centers such as those at Family Service of Milwaukee and Marriage Council of Philadelphia which usually offer certificates. AAMFT has been accrediting programs in these two categories for quite a while and was designated as the official accrediting agency for marriage and family therapy programs by the Department of Health and Human Services in 1978. This development, coupled with the establishment of the Commission on Accreditation for which members were wisely drawn from the leadership of the larger field and not just organization membership, heralded the importance of credentialing as a way of establishing core content and basic standards.

I understand that since then various freestanding and university-affiliated family institutes (the third category) have also applied for accreditation. The fourth kind of training is that provided under the rubric of continuing education by professional organizations, workshop organizers, agencies, institutes, and universities.

By way of illustration of what is now expected in terms of education and training for one to become a clinical member of AAMFT, I have taken excerpts, shown in Table 13-1, from the 1979 membership brochure. All accredited graduate degree programs conform with the requirements of the course of study.

These requirements are similar to those written into law as essential for licensure in states such as Florida which inaugurated licensing of marital and family therapists in 1982 and are likely to represent the minimum required as more states credential marital-family therapists.

It is recommended here that anyone treating military families be expected to have grappled with and mastered the content delineated above as well as having become familiar with the additional concerns that engulf military families such as frequent and prolonged separations and

TABLE 13-1. AAMFT Clinical Member Requirements

I. ACADEMIC REQUIREMENTS

A. Course of Study Equivalency Provisions

Unitl December 31, 1983, the academic requirement for Clinical Membership is an earned Master's or Doctoral degree in Marital and Family Therapy from an accredited institution; or a Master's or Doctoral degree (from an accredited institution) in an allied mental health profession, which degree is established by the applicant's official transcript to *substantially equivalent* to the Course of Study below. The degree must be from one of the following categories: Master's degree in Social Work; Master's degree in Psychiatric Nursing; Doctoral degree in Clinical or Counseling Psychology; Doctor of Medicine degree; or a Master's or Doctoral degree in a closely allied professional field.

B. Expiration of Course of Study Equivalency Provisions

After December 31, 1983, applicants will be required to have a Master's or Doctoral degree in Marital and Family Therapy from an accredited institution; or a Master's or Doctoral degree in an allied mental health profession, as specified in I-A above, the curriculum of which *fully meets* the Course of Study as listed below.

C. Course of Study (Graduate)

1. Human Development (9 semester hours minimum)
   - Developmental Studies
   - Personality Theory
   - Human Sexuality
   - Behavior Dysfunction/Psychopathology
   - General concepts and principles in the psychotherapies
2. Marital and Family Studies (9 semester hours minimum)
   - Marital and Family Development
   - Marital and Family Interaction
   - Communication Theory and Systems Theory
3. Marital and Family Therapy (9 semester hours minimum)
   - Couple Therapies
   - Structural Family Therapy
   - Transgenerational Family Therapy
4. Professional Studies (3 semester hours minimum)
   - Ethics
   - Professional Organizations
   - Family Law/Legislation
   - Independent practice/Agency practice
5. Supervised Clinical Work (9 semester hours minimum)
   - Individual Therapy
   - Marital Therapy
   - Family Therapy
6. Research Methodology (6 semester hours minimum)
   - Research Design, Methods, and Instruments
   - Statistics
   - Research in Marital and Family Studies
   - Research in Marital and Family Therapy

II. CLINICAL REQUIREMENTS

In addition to the above academic preparation, the applicant for Clinical Membership shall have completed the following:

(*continued*)

TABLE 13-1. (*Continued*)

A. 200 hours of supervision in the practice of marital and family therapy. No more than 100 hours may be accumulated in group supervision. A maximum of 50 individual hours and 50 group hours may be credited while a student is in a Master's degree program prior to graduation.

B. 1500 hours of clinical experience (defined as face-to-face client contact) in the practice of marital and family therapy.
   - 500 of these 1500 hours may have been accumulated while the candidate was a student in a Master's degree program in marital and family therapy.
   - 250 of these 1500 hours may be accumulated from the practice of individual psychotherapy.
   - A minimum of 50 cases in marital and family therapy shall have been treated.

C. Two calendar years of work experience after the awarding of the Master's degree, and while receiving ongoing supervision by an AAMFT Approved Supervisor.

D. Demonstrated readiness for the independent practice of marital and family therapy.

relocations; the more than chance occurrence of incest, sexual abuse, substance abuse, and violence; military law regarding families; what it means to admit to personal problems when in the service, and how this can influence career promotions; and the myriad other issues discussed in preceding chapters.

Realistically, not all mental health trainees or graduate professional staff therapists will have the requisite background when they are employed or assigned and must acquire it while on the job within the institutional setting. By way of an example of how the Navy has incorporated such training, a chronicle of one specific program will be given.

In 1976, I was invited to serve as a family therapy training consultant for the psychiatric residents at the Philadelphia Naval Hospital. This request grew out of the fact that the previous year one of the residents had been on his child psychiatry rotation in the medical school where I taught and had become a cotherapist with a psychology student, whom I was supervising. He accompanied her to supervisory sessions and became increasingly intrigued by family therapy. When he returned to the Naval Hospital, he recommended that they all receive some training in family therapy. The recommendation was accepted and implemented.

By the time the series of 12 weekly sessions were to begin, a receptive group of residents was waiting. These bright, well-trained, mostly analytically oriented naval officers were eager to expand their treatment repertoire. They read avidly from the bibliography and articles provided, struggled with ideas that were strange or seemed in contradiction to what they had already learned, and pushed to start seeing families by the second week. After the first training session, when they decided that it was important for them to begin functioning clinically right away, they realized they would need more backup supervision than the trainer–consultant could offer under the contract. Therefore they persuaded senior psychiatric staff to attend the seminars and demonstrations, share the learning, become committed to the approach, and become prepared to take on some of their supervision. The chief resident slated a family diagnostic intake interview for the second week, to be conjointly led by the resident and the trainer. Since he had no previous family therapy experience, this was a courageous step and one that he handled with much aplomb. Fortunately, the distraught family brought along their young child, and the trainer moved into a nonthreatening maternal role by holding the baby during part of the session. This served to decrease the resident's nervousness and competitive strivings and allowed him to utilize creatively his sensitive and astute therapeutic inclinations.

Consequently, an interesting training model evolved out of the residents' willingness to begin quickly seeing families. Each week a different family was scheduled for intake during the first hour of the session. Two of the trainees served as cotherapists for the diagnostic interview. Next the case was analyzed under the trainer's leadership, and the principles and processes of family therapy were taught from what had occurred during the session. The diagnostic workup team then decided whether both or which one would carry the family if it was deemed suitable for ongoing treatment.

An unexpected by-product of the second session was that the men spontaneously commented that they were impressed with the special qualities a heterosexual cotherapy pair brought into the treatment situation and wondered if, since they did not have any women residents, they should ask a few of the female social workers on staff to join the training group. They agreed unanimously that they should, and, as of the third session, two of the women became steady participants. Since they had rarely collaborated previously, this closer working arrangement changed the dynamics of staff relationships. An internal push arose for the men to examine their own attitudes toward female colleagues and female patients. Ultimately this led to their consideration of their stereotypes about male–female relationships, professional women, Navy wives, and "service" marriages. The staff, as a pseudofamily, went through a wonderful process of getting to know one another better and differently, and several friendships ripened considerably. Within 3 months, almost all were carrying several families and doing so credibly well. This was truly an experiential training model, one with which all seemed quite stimulated and engrossed.

Subsequent 1- and 2-day family therapy training events that I have conducted under the auspices of the Department of Psychiatry Residency Training Programs at Portsmouth and San Diego and of the Alcohol Rehabilitation Service at Long Beach Naval Hospital since 1978 have included didactic seminars presented in sequential order covering the 10 theoretical schools listed earlier, their major premises and intervention approaches, and their differences and similarities regarding such dimensions as role of therapist, importance of past history versus here-and-now problem, intrapsychic and/or interpersonal orientation, and essential therapeutic ingredients which bring about change in families (Watzlawick, Weakland, & Fisch, 1974).

In addition, I usually see one or two families and am observed either live, through a one-way screen or on videotape. Prior to the demonstration interview the primary therapist briefs me for approximately 10–15 minutes. If there is a cotherapist or any other therapist involved, such as an individual or group therapist or nurse on an inpatient unit, his or her input is also solicited. Then I interview the family for 50 minutes to an hour. If children under 13 are to be present, we make certain that age- and interest-appropriate toys, games, and/or art materials are handy and that a play table is provided (Keith & Whitaker, 1981). This diminishes the strangeness of the situation and enables the children possibly to become engaged with the play materials and behave in their more accustomed manner. In becoming absorbed, they are likely to relax and be more responsive to gently probing questions from the therapist. It provides an opportunity to observe their ability to concentrate; kind of activity, or hyperactivity; whether or not parents intervene to set limits or guide activity if need be—and if so, which parent and how; the nature of sibling interaction; etc. An attempt is made to engage the entire family rapidly by asking each, round-robin style, to indicate what the individual sees as the reasons why they requested or agreed to the consultation session, what they hope to derive from it, where they perceive their therapy to be at this time, and what they would like the outcome of therapy to be. After completing my clinical assessment about family structure, rules, dynamics, myths, etc., I give them as much feedback as I think they will be able to tolerate and comprehend in the form of the in-depth portrait of themselves that they have painted as I have translated it by reframing. To this I add recommendations for their future treatment; sometimes at this stage I ask the primary therapist to sit in. Lastly, I query if they have any questions to ask me, and if so, I attempt to answer these.

If I think the family will benefit from hearing the discussion of diagnosis, assessment, process, and recommendations, I invite them to remain. Although trainees, staff and faculty are sometimes initially astonished at this, most families are pleased and report finding this additional input beneficial. They usually are appreciative of the attentive listening and thoughtful comments. Other times the family leaves as soon as the consult is concluded, accompanied briefly by the primary therapist. Upon his or her return I proceed with our family case analysis. It is particularly important that the case be turned back to the primary therapist and that some positive support of the work he or she has done be publicly given (Nielsen & Kaslow, 1980).

This kind of consultation-training format maximizes the freedom of trainees to analyze and critique how other therapists conduct therapy, to have a larger choice of role models, and to expand their observational sensitivity and clinical assessment and intervention repertoire. For the consultant it provides ever new challenges and is a high-risk way to function. Several times, in asking if other therapists are involved with the case (not at Navy installations), I have been confronted with up to eight people signifying yes. In two instances not all were aware of one another's existence and/or involvement. This led to sessions on therapy with the "staff therapist family" to untangle the competitive strivings and assess how they could evolve a more rational, coherent treatment package.

Sometimes one approach I use as a teacher and staff trainer during programs of at least a semester's duration is to have the students bring their spouses in for at least one session. As many worry about what might bubble out in such a session, I mention that my spouse will also be present and therefore I am in a similarly vulnerable position regarding disclosures. We consider such matters as how they can interpret to their mates what family therapy is about, the likely impact of this kind of training and professional life-style on their spouses and children, what apprehensions are present regarding this in their families (Charny, 1982), and what anxieties may have arisen in connection with an evolving fine rapport with a cotherapist of the opposite sex. After the initial shyness and discomfort are overcome, these usually are extremely productive sessions that enhance the kind and depth of communication they can have with their partners about their professional role and world.

A few programs require that trainees be in marital or family therapy as an integral part of their experiential, clinical learning about self in close interpersonal relationships, and what it is like to be the participant in therapy (Guldner, 1978). Others believe this is nonessential and ill-advised. Bowen recommends (perhaps requires) his trainees to make a voyage home and work continuously on their own genogram as a way of understanding intergenerational issues and transmissions. Many others use variations of genograms for teaching–training purposes (Guerin & Fogarty, 1972). Whatever ways are utilized to enable trainees to reexplore and rework their heritage, their conflicts, and their loyalties in their family of origin and family of creation, I believe getting in touch with one's personal roots, animosities, blocks, unmet needs, gratitude, love, and longings is quintessential in becoming a family therapist.

SUPERVISION

Supervision is pivotal to most family therapy training programs and is one of the core processes used to produce skilled therapists. One overall goal of supervision is the transmission of specific relevant data, the "how to" techniques for treatment of a particular family by the novice. On another level, supervision involves the inculcating of a deeper understanding of the principles of family dynamics, relationships, and structure and how to stimulate changes in desirable directions.

The supervisory relationship, at its best, is an alliance that facilitates the trainee's tapping into the vast and worthwhile reservoir of the preceptor's experience. An essential element in the evolving of the family therapist is willingness to relate clinical advances as well as "stuck" places with patient families with another therapist who has traversed similar, often rough and problematic terrain. The growth process, through supervision, should be characterized by mutuality and reciprocity, providing a vehicle for the expansion of the knowledge, competencies, and self of the supervisee and the supervisor and the improvement of the quality of clinical services rendered.

Supervision, in its many facets and forms, moves along a continuum. At one end is the emphasis on content and technique; at the other is a concentration on the deeper process of facilitating personal growth and fashioning the prototypical dyadic helping relationship in the supervisory experience, which is here construed as therapy of the therapy—not of the therapist.[1] Treatment and supervision are considered parallel processes so that it is posited that often trainees emulate in their practice how they are dealt with in supervision (Abroms, 1977). The trainee will initially benefit most from the content–technique orientation as he or she strives to master the material that constitutes the conceptual base for practice and enables him or her to work with families predicated on a more solid knowledge foundation. More advanced trainees and experienced practitioners seeking to add to their treatment armamentarium should be exposed to the more sophisticated and complex interpretations of family history, transactions, structures, loyalties, and intergenerational legacies. They can be encouraged to read, think about, and try not only treatment of one family at a time but also such other intervention variations as couples group therapy, multiple family therapy (Laqueur, 1972), and network therapy (Speck & Attneave, 1972). As clinicians become more proficient, supervision should be on a more "as needed" rather than mandatory weekly basis.

A supervisee with some experience and confidence may gain a great deal from supervision conducted as a process of learning and thinking geared toward achieving greater self-understanding and potency as a person, family member, and therapist. It is with supervision as a technique that varies from "how-to-do-it," in its simplest form, to its most challenging aspect as an existential process of being and becoming that the next section of this chapter is concerned.

Learning Objectives

The mechanics of supervision require an initial determination of the student's fund of knowledge and personal readiness for learning theory and practice as well as a continuous evaluation of the trainee's interpersonal and clinical skills. Such an assessment gives the supervisor and student a launching pad from which the learning process may be set into motion. Unless this happens, the student's learning may be impeded since the pair may be trying to interact on different levels, missing each other in the process. Their objectives, the approximate length of time it should

1. From workshop conducted by the author as Director of Florida Couples and Family Institute. My appreciation to participants Leslie Rothman, PhD, from Gainesville, Florida; and Ruth deBruyn, MSW, and Annette van Rensburg, MSW, from South Africa.

take to achieve each, therapy goals, mutual expectations and responsibilities, and other important details should be clearly articulated and agreed upon by the parties involved, sometimes in writing (Mead, 1982a; 1982b). Once the supervisor becomes familiar with the supervisee's background, experience, strengths, and knowledge gaps, work can be directed along appropriate lines to enable the trainee to meet learning and service delivery aims. Cleghorn and Levin (1973) indicate that defining of clearcut learning objectives as an ongoing facilitative process leads to identifying areas of need and provides both parties with realistic expectations of progress. They state: "Supervision should not become a pernicious game requiring the pursuit of objectives that cannot be defined" (p. 439). Setting objectives channels the student's learning along a definitive, appropriate, and fruitful pathway and lends itself to periodic assessment of progress. Each category of learning objectives carries with it the idea of the essential skill to be learned and concomitantly the best type of supervision. The category of *perceptual skills* pertains to diagnostic ability and the skill "to see" the interactional nature of the family system; supervision of the perceptual skills involves direct observation of the therapy session, either live or taped. The ability of the student to formulate observations into a description of the family system—its rules, roles, and myths—comprises the category of *conceptual skills*. Perhaps the highest level of skills needed are the *executive abilities*, in which the student learns how to enter the family profoundly enough to move its members in the desired direction and to produce pertinent data for treatment. These skills categories are not mutually exclusive, and family therapists at all levels of expertise should achieve these objectives. (See Cleghorn & Levin's excellent discussion for explication of these three aspects.)

Cleghorn and Levin specify sets of learning objectives in terms of the increasing capability of the therapist; the stepwise function represents progressive mastery of each goal as the trainee acquires experience and knowledge. Use of specified goals enables supervisor and student to agree existing strengths and weaknesses so that each knows exactly what must be accomplished. These objectives vary along a continuum that moves the supervisory experience from a content emphasis to a process orientation.

Progress takes time, accumulation of clinical experience, and a preceptor who aids the student in dealing with the acquisition of new and sometimes controversial ideas and in transcending therapeutic limitations and frustrations in *the process* of meeting the learning objectives. In helping the student advance to being able to diagnose and treat more complex problems, the supervisor may specify additional goals to reach and skills to be acquired.

A word about the executive skills to be mastered since these are not often discussed. They include being able (1) to redefine the therapeutic contract periodically; (2) to demonstrate the relationship between transactions and the symptomatic problem; (3) to be a facilitator of change; (4) to develop a style of interviewing consistent with one's personality; (5) to take control of maladaptive transactions; (6) to work out adaptive behaviors and rewards for them; and (7) to relinquish control of the family by terminating when adaptive patterns occur (and become reasonably well solidified).

As trainees become more proficient, the objectives become more subjective. The acquisition of experience is conducive to wanting to achieve some synthesis as the neophyte therapist becomes less enslaved by anxiety about "how to" and becomes qualitatively better able to conduct therapy. The experienced clinician's own deepening and expanding of diagnostic and treatment skills is ultimately most likely to be continued if he or she engages in supervision and, as such, becomes an active participant with the trainee in a continuous probing learning process.

SOME PROBLEMS ENCOUNTERED BY SUPERVISORS

When attempting to become a marital and family therapist, shifting gears creates a huge barrier and a philosophic conflict for some individual-oriented therapists, who must learn to focus on the family system. The energy expenditure required in treating whole families conjointly is much greater than that utilized in individual therapy. Customarily, in family therapy so many data are rapidly elicited that the clinician may feel baffled and overwhelmed. This can pose quite a contrast to the problems experienced in getting a lone reticent or depressed client to express thoughts and feelings. A talented supervisor can help the trainee comprehend the commonalities and uniquenesses in the two different approaches and under what circumstances and with what kinds of problems and people each is likely to constitute the treatment of choice. The "model supervisor" being described here would be flexible, wide ranging, and non-doctrinaire while still holding firm convictions. He or she would subscribe to a stance that each patient constellation has to be viewed on its own terms and that the selection as to the optimal treatment course to pursue flows from this assessment. This is equally applicable whether the decision regards individual, couples, family, or group therapy, or a specific kind of family therapy.

Some of these learning objectives can be tailored around the needs of the psychotherapist-trainee to structure his or her relearning to "see" the hologram of the family system (Duhl & Duhl, 1979). Supervision, then, encompasses content, technique, and sometimes a conversion process oriented to help bridge the gap and facilitate integration.

TECHNIQUES AND METHODS

The *traditional model* of one-to-one supervision has been indirect, consisting of the supervisor meeting with the trainee after a lapse of time following the therapy session(s). The discussion revolves around the interview case report, usually a process record for beginners, and a summary record for the more advanced.

Most often the meeting is held weekly in the supervisor's office. Either or both may determine and control the agenda. Disadvantages may emanate from the indirect nature of the model, the selective aspects of subjective reporting, and the delay between therapy and supervision in time of an emergency. The supervisor learns about the case second-hand. Having no direct observational or experiential contact with the family and its complex system, he or she has no way to ascertain distorted perceptions or nonverbal behaviors.

A second approach, *cotherapy*, has many advantages as a supervisory method. It is particularly effective in situations where past conflicts and anxieties are likely to be reactivated in the therapist; the presence of the supervisor as cotherapist can diminish the adverse effects of countertransference and the number and extent of therapeutic mistakes. One member of the treatment team is likely to be reasonably objective at all times. Many arguments have been advanced for the efficacy of the cotherapist team, particularly a heterosexual pair. Just by being there and working together harmoniously or disagreeing constructively, they serve as good live role models for the patients. They also represent a pair who can function as different kinds of parent surrogates, and as such, do some necessary reparenting and reeducation. Patients of each sex have someone they can identify with; or, if they are more able to relate to members of the opposite sex, this too is offered. A note on this technique: The preceptor who doubles as cotherapist must be careful to reserve time to serve as supervisor; this entails allocating more time and energy to the training of each student than traditional supervision does. Ethically, the cotherapy team should tell patients that their relationship is one of supervisee–supervisor so that they are not deceived and so that seeming power and status differentials are understood in terms of the real nature of the relationship and not permitted to intrude on the patients' concerns about power and control.

When the supervisor is actively present and his or her knowledge of the trainee's diagnostic and treatment skill is predicated on direct observation and shared experience, the selectivity inherently reflected in a process recording does not influence the data presented. That the preceptor is willing to risk sharing patients and opening his or her practice to the trainee to watch and participate, query and comment, makes supervision a livelier and more mutual process and is consonant with the avowed ethos of the field that the leaders are willing to be observed and invite critique and input from viewers. "Such experiences can be exhilarating and highly productive" (Kaslow, 1972, p. 129) for the trainee.

Therapists of equal stature often team up; likewise trainees can be paired together. Working in tandem, therapists can generate a synergic buildup of therapeutic potency for treating highly intense, dysfunctional families. Other advantages of cotherapy are complementarity, support, and a clear communication model. It may also be more stimulating and interesting for the therapist, and this too is important.

Tucker, Hart, and Liddle (1976), in their family therapy training model, also made creative use of *cotherapy* as a supervisory method. In their program, the cotherapists were all trainees. They discussed their reactions and perceptions before the supervisors and other trainees in group sessions; they were expected to describe their feelings about their patient families and each other in order to facilitate the learning and growth experience. Supervisors helped resolve conflicts between cotherapists by seeking resolution of differences. Their underlying rationale for this approach was that they "believed that family therapists need to be aware of and sensitive to their own and their cotherapist's emotional state in order to work with families in a facilitative fashion" (Tucker *et al.*,

1976, p. 270), and "spending time on the cotherapy relationship in the supervisory sessions helps to improve supervisees' level of functioning with the family and with each other" (p. 272).

Cotherapy also has some negative aspects. Trainees may feel overwhelmed by and resentful of the supervisor's advanced competence and ego-syntonic assertiveness, and may perceive that they appear to be what they are, at first, a novice. They may repress their own creativity and sit quietly while the supervisor engages in the major part of the therapeutic action. Ideally, the supervisor will help them express their own individuality, find their own style, trust their intuition, and gradually feel free to intervene more readily, so that ultimately the team will become better balanced. Part of the initiative should also emanate from the trainee.

It is posited that ordinarily, the advantages more than outweigh the disadvantages. Cotherapy experience as part of supervision is an investment that yields high dividends through improved family treatment. Through evoking affective reactions in the trainee cotherapist, the supervisor will acquire greater leverage for promoting growth and learning. When cotherapists take the time needed to discuss their interaction and relationship with each other in conferences, they are not preoccupied with one another inappropriately in the therapy sessions and can be more attentive to the family. They also gain experience in respectfully hearing the other's thinking and negotiating conflicts.

Direct supervision using delayed feedback constitutes a third supervisory method. The advent of one-way mirrors, films, audio- and videotape recorders and playback equipment, and closed circuit video monitors has made direct supervision an important vehicle in training (Berger, 1970). Such equipment enables the supervisor to observe first-hand the actual therapy session, during its occurrence or anytime thereafter. Videotaped or filmed segments can be rerun for analysis and discussion. Such on-the-spot observations or duplications do not permit the omissions or distortions possible in written records and therefore are much more authentic. Therapist and/or client verbal and nonverbal contradictions become clearly visible. Based on personal knowledge of the case, the supervisor can be much more accurate in interpreting dynamics and discussing treatment planning.

The potential difficulties that accompany this method include that watching tapes or live sessions may be considerably more time consuming and inconvenient for the busy supervisor than reading process reports. In addition, the equipment is costly and a technician may be needed to operate and repair it. Some trainees may feel quite apprehensive, knowing that their work will be observed, but this should dissipate in a setting where such a format is customary and as trainees become acclimated to such procedures. Despite these drawbacks, here too the advantages seem to outweigh the disadvantages.

This third approach, which does not afford instantaneous guidance, is criticized by advocates of the fourth approach, *direct supervision with instant feedback* (see Birchler, 1975, for fuller discussion). They find this fourth approach to be a creative way to combine the best aspects of the three models described above and to add a new, dynamic dimension— instant feedback. The supervisor, who observes the live therapy sessions through a one-way mirror or video monitor, is free to interrupt and to intervene directly in the therapy. Explanations for such intrusive external input are given in advance. The type of intervention is based on the supervisor's orientation, the goals of the therapy, and the kind of com- munication system established—for example, a walkie-talkie system be- tween supervisor and trainee, in which both utilize a citizens' band receiver, or a two-telephone hookup with one phone in the observation room and another in the training room. Patient permission is required to have an observer present; it is explained that the viewer may periodically interrupt to call in questions or observations. The supervisor may inter- vene to bail out a therapist who is pushing too hard, or who appears stuck, or to suggest a more fruitful course to pursue. Sometimes the observer–expert is invited in or voluntarily enters the session to make an interpretation or statement designed to jolt the patients into a realign- ment of the system or interactional change. To administer a rapid and painless psychological shock, one may prescribe the symptom, relabel the symptomatic person as the "savior" to whom they should all be grateful, or issue a paradoxical injunction. The unanticipated, unorthodox nature of psychotherapy of the absurd (Whitaker, 1976), combined with its tendency to quickly terminate the previous interaction, may provide the leverage needed to get the patients to alter their transaction pattern and consequently may permit the initiation of more productive ways of relating.

Under the rubric of *instant feedback*, another variation is for the therapist to leave the room and go speak to the supervisor who is observing in an anteroom. To me this seems disruptive to the flow of therapy and potentially undermining of the patients' confidence in the therapist's capacity to competently conduct the therapy. Nonetheless, in the past few years, having an unseen observer team involved has become an approach used with increasing frequency in such places as Milan and the Ackerman Institute. The team often helps formulate the systemic hypothesis and frame a succinct prescription (Selvini-Palazzoli, Boscolo, Cecchin, & Prata, 1980).

Other times the observer makes encouraging comments such as "you are on the right track," or gives instructions for contract negotiation. My own predilection is for trainees to have as much leeway as possible to proceed on their own, needing neither immediate praise nor help with elementary therapeutic tasks such as shaping a contract. Other difficulties seem inherent—battles for control, dependence-independence issues, and feelings of being pawns manipulated on a chessboard. Yet devotees of this method insist that these dangers are outweighed by the benefits of averting therapeutic errors, because the supervisor's superior skill can be pressed into service and the trainee has solid support available immediately (Kaslow, 1977).

A fifth and increasingly utilized approach is *group supervision.* Tucker *et al.* (1976), in discussing group supervision used in an educational setting, state that "a basic assumption of their sequential model is that the supervisory process progresses through a series of phases over the course of a semester and/or full year" (p. 269). Each supervisory session also moves "through an observable, definable, and systematic sequence" (p. 269). Supervision consists of 1- to 1½-hour meetings of 10 students with three supervisors, after group observations of two family sessions. Each student participates both as observer and therapist. Cotherapy teams are composed of trainee–trainee, supervisor–supervisor, or trainee–supervisor.

The first aim of the supervisory sequence is to deal with the cotherapists' reactions to each other and to the session. These responses are discussed in front of the group, in order to minimize distortions and biases. The cotherapy relationship is viewed as an important variable in the therapy; the time utilized in working on these reactions has been deemed to be profitably spent.

The second objective in the sequence is assessing observed family interactions. This stage entails focusing on diagnosis, evaluation, and identification, and on formulating hypotheses about the family as a system.

The third aim is to make valid generalizations about families and family therapy. Students and supervisors (who now shift to the teacher role) discuss family dynamics by exploring basic theoretical concepts. In the next phase, planning for future sessions with families is the focus in which various intervention strategies are considered.

Phases Two and Three of the model proposed by Tucker *et al.* (1976) emphasize the kinds of perceptual and conceptual learning objectives formulated by Cleghorn and Levin (1973, pp. 429–446); their Phase Four parallels the latter authors' executive skills objectives. During the final stage of their developmental model, discussion revolves around feelings evoked by prior supervisory sessions, in which the supervisor functions as a group facilitator as if leading an ongoing sensitivity group. There is an expectation of self-disclosure concerning personal feelings, quality of supervision, and vulnerabilities. Supervision is aimed at both guiding the students and encouraging them to let their individual styles evolve. When cosupervision is utilized, this relationship, like cotherapy, needs to be negotiated; doing so offers growth and learning opportunities to the supervisors.

Group supervision affords a chance for dialogue about conceptual notions and provides the opportunity for trainees to build cohesiveness and trust in working with others. This may be when trainees experience relief in recognizing that others also feel inundated or ignored by their patients (Abels, 1970). Often insights dawn when a member comments about the similarities between the supervision group's processes and those of their patient families. It contributes to reducing anxieties about self-exposure while providing a contemporaneous experience in a small group that in some ways approximates a family and reactivates feelings of sibling competitiveness; partially repressed hostility toward authority figures (the supervisors), who represent parent surrogates; and the desire to have one's dependency needs met. In structuring a milieu in which these emotions can be expressed and dealt with, there is a greater likelihood that unfinished issues from the past will surface and get resolved and not lie dormant to become unconscious interferences in treating families.

If a nonmember attends as a guest or is added as a new member after the group has begun and coalesced, the trainees become aware of their sense of group identity; they are likely to perceive and react to the outsider as if the person were a resented intruder. Experiencing this togetherness heightens their realization of why it is so difficult for a therapist to gain entry into a family that perceives them as a potentially disruptive intruder and whom they then collude to extrude (Kaslow, 1972).

In sum, small-group supervision fosters: eclecticism in encouraging trainees to adapt concepts and techniques from numerous schools of therapy and to be creative within the dictates of the situation; both experimentation and conceptualization to enable the therapist to intuitively determine how and when to join and exit from the family; commitment to flexibility and responsiveness in order to illuminate hidden conflicts; meticulous attention to group dynamics and process; and trainee responsibility for the family's process in treatment with analogous parallel supervisor responsibility for the training group's development.

In group supervision, members participate in the mini-dramas and, when enacting the therapist, can choose other interventions conducive to different outcomes. Similarly, the supervisor may demonstrate family sculpting (Satir, 1972; Duhl, Kantor, & Duhl, 1973), a predominantly *nonverbal technique* useful for both diagnosis and treatment. In brief, any member of the family can be asked to sculpt, that is, to place the family members in a living collage—each in a position the sculptor deems characteristic (and revealing) and in a typical configuration relative to one another. Next the original sculptor may be asked to rearrange the family as he or she would like them to be, thus affording them a chance to convey their needs and wishes and to make some input into the family's thrust toward change. Or, other members may be asked to spatially rearrange the family as they experience it and/or as they would like it to be. In this way, varying perceptions of the family's alliances and moods are choreographed (Papp, 1976) in a way fascinating to all present. When trainees are requested to sculpt their own families, utilizing each other as substitute family members, they not only have an opportunity to experiment with the technique before trying it with patients, but also have a chance to place themselves in their proxy family while emotionally and physically reexperiencing the real family ties and cutoffs.

A sixth method of supervision embodies the use of *role-playing techniques*. Trainees may be asked to depict what took place during therapy by reenacting the parts of various patients so as to enable the therapist to glean a deeper understanding of how it must seem and feel for them. Or a supervisee may replay his or her own role as therapist and then be instructed to intervene differently.

In a delightful article entitled "Bad Therapy—A Way of Learning" (Lang, 1982, pp. 447–460), Moshe Lang discusses a novel training technique. He adroitly describes how the trainee–therapist, practicing on a role-playing family comprised of other trainees, is instructed to do "bad therapy"—that is, to make the family worse by intervening through saying what he or she intuitively feels yet fears is grossly inappropriate to state or interpret as too harsh or stark. Strangely, the actor "patients" and clinician–observers most often regard the so-called "bad therapy" as beneficial, in fact, as better than before. When the more confrontational, honest, straightforward strategies and statements are subsequently utilized with the real families in therapy, they have been found to be conducive to some minor and major breakthroughs moving in the desired direction. Doing bad therapy often entails action in a fashion diametrically opposite to the "straight" therapy they have previously administered and may include the therapist being restricted to making responsible "I" statements (in place of "you" statements) and doing positive relabeling. Lang concludes, in agreement with Whitaker (1976), when next in a "stuck situation," try a seemingly crazy intervention.

No matter what combination of these supervisory methods is used, it is essential to *promote trainee self-awareness and a sense of their own personal roots*, history, and intrapsychic and interpersonal dynamics in relation to their family of origin and, if married, family of creation. Doing this perhaps constitutes a seventh supervisory–training approach. One can urge (or require) trainees to make voyages home (Bowen, 1972) to their families of origin in order to work toward resolution of unfinished relationship conflicts from the past, reconnect to their parents and siblings, and become aware of invisible and not so invisible loyalties (Boszormenyi-Nagy & Spark, 1973), and become more knowledgeable about their own heritage. Having students do detailed schematic family tree genograms of at least three generations is a fascinating way of channeling their quest to know and understand their multiple roots and tap into these as a reservoir of strength and illumination. The trainees can be requested to bring in and respond to family photographs (Kaslow & Friedman, 1977), using these to elicit reminiscences as a personal projective stimulus. As the apprentices explore in depth who they are and how they came to be that way within their family gestalt, they also achieve mastery of techniques they can subsequently translate to use with patients in reconstructing their histories and for healing old narcissistic wounds and family schisms.

When I am supervising a person who is married, part of the training contract is apt to specify that the trainee bring his or her mate along for several "therapy" sessions. In this way, the trainees experience what it is like to be in the role of the person seeking help, how painful it can be to open up repressed conflict areas, and how hard it may be to accept interpretations and confrontations. Just as many graduate and professional programs require that students in the process of becoming therapists become analysands or psychotherapy patients, I think that it is imperative that marriage and family therapists have at least several treatment sessions with their significant others participating (Kaslow, 1977). In the event that their own marriage is fraught with severe strife, the resultant stress and turmoil is apt to exert a negative influence on the trainee's therapeutic objectivity. Therefore, trainees are expected to work through their difficulties and become aware of their resistances and defenses so they do not impede effectiveness in the therapist role.

The supervisor, attuned to the trainee's personality and professional developmental level, sets the tone and pace of the learning experience. In working with mental health personnel in the military, the supervisor must also be mindful of the need to accord respect based on rank and title and to adhere to requirements inherent in the hierarchical structure of the armed services. Trainees may become thwarted by the gaps in their knowledge, seek "cookbook" guidance, express uncertainty about control of the family, and confront the fear that they may act out their personal family dilemmas in the context of the patient's family therapy. Given a supervisor who cares about the intern's learning and is able to convey this, the group process experience will be enhanced by the recognition that they are being guided around and through barriers to their development and are acquiring skill in the art of family therapy.

In sum, supervision can be described as a didactic learning experience that involves the communication of information and provides the essential groundwork for the mastery of theory and clinical treatment of patients. All too often, classroom curricula are slanted toward teaching concepts and developing skill but give inadequate attention to the ethical precepts and value assumptions that undergird clinical interventions. Furthermore, the legal framework within which clinical practice occurs is sometimes ignored or disparaged. In working with military families, it is obligatory that family therapy be taught and supervised within the context of that body of military and civilian law which deals with family affairs.

Some instructors and preceptors operate from a "do as I say," not "do as I do" stance—there are glaring incongruities between what they preach and what they practice. The trainee is much more apt to emulate what the supervisor actually does on the job than to carry out what he or she is told *should* be done but what, in fact, is *not* done. During the training phase and beyond, the therapist should be encouraged to explore his or her own assumptions, hunches, and the creative processes. The supervisor should be profoundly committed to human and humane values and should stimulate learning through opening up vast intellectual and emotional corridors and by engaging in brainstorming-style problem-solving activities with supervisees. A humanistic supervisory process emphasizes the student as a complete organic entity rather than as a recipient of indoctrination.

The supervisory process should enable the learner to examine, critique, reformulate, and validate his or her own framework for meaning and value, as these are the intangibles from which therapeutic intervention unfolds. Although a clinician should not presume that his or her beliefs and attitudes are the most desirable ones nor superimpose them on the patients, the therapist should be fully aware of his or her value base and be able to communicate it for what it is vis-à-vis the therapeutic task. Being cognizant of one's values enables one to decide with which kinds of problems one will probably be ineffective and to refer those presenting such problems to a therapist less likely to be "turned off" by a specific behavior constellation. For example, a therapist who believes homosexuality or divorce is intrinsically sinful should not attempt to treat gay people or divorcees.

Whatever form of supervision is used, periodic verbal and written evaluation should occur to ascertain if the treatment outcomes sought are being brought about and to assess if the learning objectives are being fulfilled. They should be shared with the trainee, who can attach a response, and then with whomever the supervisor is accountable to, before being filed for future reference and utilization.

SUPERVISOR–SUPERVISEE MATCH

It behooves those in charge of supervision and training endeavors to make certain that supervisory assignments and subsequent interventions are appropriately attuned to the supervisees' personal background, substantive knowledge, clinical experience, and level of skill; in the Armed Forces, rank might be another consideration. Certainly, all training efforts should flow from a synthesized theory of how learning occurs and how this may vary depending on whether one is a neophyte or an advanced therapist. In one-on-one teaming up, supervisor–supervisee match is important since some personality incompatibilities do not lend themself to resolution and impede learning. Some resistances can and should be overcome; but at times totally different value systems, life views, or personal antagonisms cannot be resolved and should be circumvented. For some pairings, demographic factors like age, race (Royster, 1972), ethnicity and social class (Kutzik, 1972; Gardner, 1980), and sex (Brodsky, 1977, 1980; Abramowitz & Abramowitz, 1976; Kaslow, 1980b) become salient considerations.

The government has in recent decades made major strides in integrating the Armed Forces in terms of race and sex. Thus, in dealing with military personnel, it is critical that clinicians understand what it means to experience covert or overt discrimination, exclusion, or being bypassed for promotion because one is black, Chicano, or female. These are issues that the supervisor may need to handle with a clinician whose background is provincial and/or whose thinking is ethnocentric. Given the view held herein that supervision and therapy are parallel processes (Abroms, 1977), if supervisor and supervisee are of different racial, ethnic, or socio-economic status, the way any problems emanating from these differences are dealt with between them is likely to be replicated between therapist and patients when similar difficulties arise.

Gender issues are also likely to present an impasse or cause strong transference-countertransference reactions in supervision as they might in therapy. Sexualizing the supervisory relationship is as unethical and unprofessional as sexualizing the treatment relationship (Brodsky, 1977a; Kaslow, 1980b). Power and control issues are also apt to get played out inappropriately if the authority exercised by the supervisor exceeds that inherent in the supervisory role. For example, the male supervisor who is a doctor working with a female trainee who has not yet obtained her doctorate may be quite domineering in his demands or subtly placating— not treating her as a serious young professional. Conversely, a young male supervisee with an older, strong, competent female supervisor may develop a negative transference projecting his unresolved rebellion from mother to supervisor and may be struggling with reworking male-female stereotypical role images. Unless issues like these are confronted and worked through in supervision, they will surface and hamper the trainees' ability to handle analogous issues raised by patients.

In the event that the supervisee is quite experienced and competent, yet supervision is requested or required for personal, agency, or licensure needs, a good match remains an important aspect of the teaching–learning process, perhaps even more so as the supervisee has a better base of comparison and is likely to be more demanding, critically appraising, and appreciative if the quality is top-notch. In a recent workshop on advanced supervision, the following profile for an "ideal supervisor" emerged from the participants. The person should have the following qualities: (1) be able to communicate a vast store of knowledge and stimulate the supervisee to read and pursue new learning; (2) have a clear theoretical position and yet be able to utilize a variety of approaches and be able to accept that the supervisee may also have one and respect it if it is different; (3) have a good sense of humor and of life's absurdity; (4) be challenging and provocative; (5) be courageous; (6) be alive and energetic—not too busy or "burned out"; (7) be authentic; (8) be task oriented and make optimal use of time; (9) retain awareness of accountability; (10) be confident of his or her own skills and position so as not to be threatened by supervisee's knowledge and accomplishments; (11) be up-to-date and at the cutting edge of developments in key areas of his or her practice; (12) be nonauthoritarian yet able to hold out and model high standards of practice; and (13) be reasonably healthy emotionally.

One can only hope there are many paragons like this who are supervising, for to train with them should be an exciting adventure.

In sum, when ignorance, insensitivity, or prejudice exist in the intense dyadic relationship subsumed by the term "supervision" due to any of the aforementioned factors, these mitigate against sound learning and usually cause negative vibrations to course through the larger institutional environment. This is why it is essential for directors of training to require and read not only supervisor's evaluation of supervisees, but also trainees' assessments of their supervisors. Sometimes one supervisor frequently antagonizes supervisees. Thus if similar complaints surface often about a given supervisor, the director of training, or whoever is their higher-up, must confront the problems with a view to eradicating them or, if this is not possible, changing the person's assignment.

The issue of match is less crucial in small-group supervision or training. Here the group process usually defuses strong antipathies. The leader–teacher can rarely engage in a vendetta with one trainee without others coming to the rescue or pooling their strength and seeking recourse with a higher authority (Abels, 1970; Kaslow, 1972). Group supervisors and trainers, like individual supervisors, should be knowledgeable in the subject matter and skills they are to impart and model. They should also be adept in leading role playing, simulations, and critiquing case records and videotapes. It is insufficient for them merely to be facilitators of group discussion!

SUMMARY

As seen in the foregoing, supervision and training may be conducted in a variety of ways flowing from numerous perspectives, including psychodynamic or analytic (Melchiode, 1977; Rioch, 1980), utilizing a one-on-one paradigm based on process or summary recording or a verbal replay of sessions, or a structural–strategic model where there is direct feed in by the supervisor and sometimes even supervision of the supervisor–therapist–family system. Those augmenting their knowledge of and clinical competence in marital and family therapy might be asked to make a voyage home and work with their own genogram, role play and do "bad" therapy, enter marital–family therapy, or sculpt their family. To adapt the more creative approaches for training of mental health personnel to work with military families may take a great deal of advanced planning and skillful interpretation so that it will seem compatible and not "far out" and superimposed. It has been posited that the military therapist should attempt to achieve mastery of the basic recommended curriculum *plus* all the additional facets one needs to know about military families as a "special" group and about the military law that influences their lives. Given that some members of each family are likely to be civilians, where cotrainers are used, a team of a military and a civilian leader is recommended, just as we think it advisable to have a heterosexual team of leaders and therapists whenever feasible.

To supplement the training the Services can provide directly, graduate and medical school courses as well as family institute offerings can be utilized. If sufficient skilled supervision and consultation are not available within the Service's own departments or agencies, these too can be purchased from competent individuals in the civilian sector.

In this chapter, the history of marital and family therapy has been summarized and the evolution of training and supervisory programs and models recapitulated. The techniques and methods extant in the field have been elaborated.

This is a stimulating, challenging, and rewarding field; it invites ingenuity, experimentation, and innovation as well as solid thinking and clear mapping of family dynamics, structure, and treatment plans and goals. For these very reasons, it appeals to the more creative spirits in the therapist community. Therefore, some defining and standardization for quality without stultification or rigidity are essential.

As this volume comes to its end, one final thought: The family is still the most basic institution in our society, and therapists are among those who can help revitalize and enrich family living so that it becomes more satisfying for the members as a group and for each person individually. For our country to continue to flourish, military families, like their civilian counterparts, need to have at their beck and call the best services we can offer them.

REFERENCES

Abels, P. On the nature of supervision: The medium is the group. *Child Welfare*, 1970, *49*(6), 305–307

Abramowitz, S. I., & Abramowitz, C. V. Sex role psychodynamics in psychotherapy supervision. *American Journal of Psychotherapy*, 1976, *30*, 583–592.

Abroms, G. M. Supervision as metatherapy. In F. W. Kaslow & Associates, *Supervision, consultation and staff training in the helping professions.* San Francisco: Jossey-Bass, 1977.

Ackerman, N., Beatman, F., & Sherman, S. (Eds.). *Exploring the base for family therapy.* New York: Family Service Association of America, 1961.

American Association for Marriage and Family Therapy. *The approved supervisor.* Upland, Calif.: AAMFT, 1978.

Berger, M. M. (Ed.). *Videotape techniques in psychiatric training and treatment.* New York: Brunner/Mazel, 1970.

Birchler, G. R. Live supervision and instant feedback in marriage and family therapy. *Journal of Marriage and Family Counseling*, 1975, *1*(4), 331–342.

Blumenfield, M. *Applied supervision in psychotherapy.* New York: Grune & Stratton, 1982.

Boszormenyi-Nagy, I., & Spark. G. *Invisible loyalties.* New York: Harper & Row, 1973.

Bowen, M. *Family therapy in clinical practice.* New York: Aronson, 1978.

Brodsky, A. M. Countertransference issues and the woman therapist. *Clinical Psychologist*, 1977, *30*, 12–14.

Brodsky, A. M. Sex role issues in the supervision of therapy. In A. K. Hess (Ed.), *Psychotherapy supervision: Theory, research and practice.* New York: Wiley, 1980.

Charny, I. W. The personal and family mental health of family therapists. In F. W. Kaslow (Ed.), *The international book of family therapy.* New York: Brunner/Mazel, 1982.

Cleghorn, M. J., & Levin, S. Training family therapists by setting learning objectives. *American Journal of Orthopsychiatry*, 1973, *43*(3), 429–446.

304 / KASLOW

Duhl, F., & Duhl, B. Structured spontaneity: The thoughtful art of integrative family therapy at BFI. *Journal of Marital and Family Therapy*, 1979, *5*(3), 59-76.

Duhl, F., Kantor, D., & Duhl, B. Learning, space and action in family therapy: A primer of sculpture. In D. Bloch (Ed.), *Techniques of family therapy*. New York: Grune & Stratton, 1973.

Everett, C. A. Supervision of marriage and family therapy. In A. K. Hess (Ed.), *Psychotherapy supervision: Theory, research and practice*. New York: Wiley, 1980.

Gardner, L. H. Racial, ethnic and social class considerations in psychotherapy supervision. In A. K. Hess (Ed.), *Psychotherapy supervision: Theory, research and practice*. New York: Wiley, 1980.

Group for the Advancement of Psychiatry. *The field of family therapy* (GAP Report 78). New York: GAP, 1970.

Guerin, P. J. Family therapy: The first twenty-five years. In P. J. Guerin (Ed.), *Family therapy and practice*. New York: Gardner, 1976.

Guerin, P., & Fogarty, T. Study your own family. In A. Ferber, M. Mendelsohn, & A. Napier (Eds.), *The book of family therapy*. New York: Science House, 1972.

Guldner, C. A. Family therapy for the trainee in family therapy. *Journal of Marriage and Family Counseling*, 1978, *4*(1), 127-132.

Hess, A. K. (Ed.). *Psychotherapy supervision: Theory, research and practice*. New York: Wiley, 1980. (a)

Hess, A. K. Training models and the nature of psychotherapy for supervision. In A. K. Hess (Ed.), *Psychotherapy supervision: Theory, research and practice*. Wiley, 1980. (b)

Kaslow, F. W. Group supervision. In F. W. Kaslow & Associates, *Issues in human services: A sourcebook for supervision and staff development*. San Francisco: Jossey-Bass, 1972.

Kaslow, F. W. Training of marital and family therapists. In F. W. Kaslow & Associates, *Supervision, consultation and staff training in the helping professions*. San Francisco: Jossey-Bass, 1977.

Kaslow, F. W. History of family therapy: A kaleidoscopic overview. *Marriage and Family Review*, 1980, *3*(1, 2), 77-111. (a)

Kaslow, F. W. Some emergent forms of non-traditional sexual combinations: A clinical view. *Interaction*, 1980, *3*(1), 1-9. (Also in *Terapia Familiare*, 1977 *2*, 135-148.)

Kaslow, F. W. A diaclectic approach to family therapy and practice: Selectivity and synthesis. *Journal of Marital and Family Therapy*, 1981, *7*(3), 345-351.

Kaslow, F. W., & Associates. *Issues in human services: A sourcebook for supervision and staff development*. San Francisco: Jossey-Bass, 1972.

Kaslow, F. W., & Associates. *Supervision, consultation and staff training in the helping professions*. San Francisco: Jossey-Bass, 1977.

Kaslow, F. W., & Friedman, J. Utilization of family photos and movies in family therapy. *Journal of Marriage and Family Counseling*, 1977, *3*(1), 19-25.

Keith, D. V., & Whitaker, C. A. Play therapy: A paradigm for work with families. *Journal of Marital and Family Therapy*, 1981, *7*(3), 243-254.

Kutzik, A. J. Class and ethnic factors. In F. W. Kaslow & Associates, *Issues in human services: A sourcebook for supervision and staff development*. San Francisco: Jossey-Bass, 1972.

Lang, M. Bad therapy—a way of learning. In F. W. Kaslow (Ed.), *The international book of family therapy*. New York: Brunner/Mazel, 1982.

Laqueur, H. P. Multiple family therapy. In A. Ferber, M. Mendelsohn, & A. Napier (Eds.), *The book of family therapy*. New York: Science House, 1972.

Lazarus, A. *The practice of multi-modal therapy*. New York: McGraw-Hill, 1981.

Malone, C. A. Observations on the role of family therapy in child psychiatry training. *Journal of the American Academy of Child Psychiatry*, 1974, *13*(3), 437-458.

Mead, D. E. *A general procedural model for training and supervision in the helping professions: I. Training.* Unpublished manuscript, Brigham Young University, 1982. (a)

Mead, D. E. *A general procedural model for training and supervision in the helping professions: II. A goal oriented supervision system.* Unpublished manuscript, Brigham Young University, 1982. (b)

Melchiode, G. A. Psychoanalytically oriented individual therapy. In F. W. Kaslow & Associates, *Supervision, consultation and staff training in the helping professions,* San Francisco: Jossey-Bass, 1977.

Nielsen, E., & Kaslow, F. Consultation in family therapy. *American Journal of Family Therapy,* 1980, *8*(4), 35–42.

Papp, P. Family choreography. In P. Guerin (Ed.), *Family therapy: Theory and practice.* New York: Gardner, 1976.

Richan, W. C. Indigenous paraprofessional staff. In F. W. Kaslow & Associates, *Issues in human services: A sourcebook for supervision and staff development.* San Francisco. Jossey-Bass, 1972.

Richan, W. C. Training of lay helpers. In F. W. Kaslow & Associates, *Supervision, consultation and staff training in the helping professions.* San Francisco: Jossey-Bass, 1977.

Rioch, M. J. The dilemmas of supervision in dynamic psychotherapy. In A. K. Hess (Ed.), *Psychotherapy supervision: Theory, research and practice.* New York: Wiley, 1980.

Royster, E. C. Black supervisors: Problems of race and role. In F. W. Kaslow & Associates, *Issues in human services: A sourcebook for supervision and staff development.* San Francisco: Jossey-Bass, 1972.

Satir, V. The quest for survival: A training program for family diagnosis and treatment. *Acta Psychotherapeutica et Psychosomatica,* 1963, *11*, 33–38.

Satir, V. *Peoplemaking.* Palo Alto, Calif.: Science & Behavior Books, 1972.

Selvini-Palazzoli, M., Boscolo, L., Cecchin, G., & Prata, G. Hypothesizing–circularity–neutrality: Three guidelines for the conductor of the session. *Family Process,* 1980, *19*(1), 3–12.

Slovenko. R. Legal issues in psychotherapy supervision. In A. K. Hess, (Ed.), *Psychotherapy supervision: Theory, research and practice.* New York: Wiley, 1980.

Speck, R., & Attneave, C. Social network intervention. In C. Sager & H. S. Kaplan (Eds.), *Progress in group and family therapy.* New York: Brunner/Mazel, 1972.

Steen, J. (Ed.). *Random House dictionary,* New York: Ballantine Books, 1980.

Tucker, B. S., Hart, G., & Liddle, H. A. Supervision in family therapy: A developmental perspective. *Journal of Marriage and Family Counseling,* 1976, *2*(3), 260–276.

Watzlawick, P., Weakland, J., & Fisch, R. *Change: Principles of problem formation and problem resolution.* New York: Norton, 1974.

Whitaker, C. A. Psychotherapy of the absurd: With a special emphasis on the psychotherapy of aggression. *Family Process,* 1976, *14*(1), 1–16.

Author Index

Subject Index